D0295603

Britain's modern
ROYAL AIR FORCE

Patrick Stephens Limited, an imprint of Haynes Publishing, has published authoritative, quality books for enthusiasts for over a quarter of a century. During that time the company has established a reputation as one of the world's leading publishers of books on aviation, maritime, military, model-making, motor cycling, motoring, motor racing, railway and railway modelling subjects. Readers or authors with suggestions for books they would like to see published are invited to write to: The Editorial Director, Patrick Stephens Limited, Sparkford, Nr Yeovil, Somerset BA22 7JJ.

Britain's modern
ROYAL AIR FORCE

Peter F. Guiver

PSL
Patrick Stephens Limited

© Peter F. Guiver

Aircraft Drawings © Colin Paine
Vehicle Drawings © Ken Musgrave

First published in 1994

British Cataloguing-in-Publication Data:
A catalogue record for this book is available
from the British Library

ISBN 1 85260 432 8

Library of Congress catalog card no. 93 81188

Patrick Stephens Limited is a member of
Haynes Publishing, Sparkford,
Nr Yeovil, Somerset, BA22 7JJ

Typeset by G&M, Raunds, Northamptonshire
Printed and bound in Great Britain by
Butler & Tanner Ltd of London and Frome

Contents

Glossary   6
Introduction   7

Chapter One: Strike Command   9
Chapter Two: Personnel and Training Command   60
Chapter Three: Logistics Command   90
                 Aircraft of the RAF   93–100
Chapter Four: The Organization of the RAF   108
Chapter Five: The Royal Air Force Regiment   113
Chapter Six: The Reserve Units of the RAF   124
Chapter Seven: Air Cadets   128
Chapter Eight: Aircraft of the RAF   133
Chapter Nine: Airborne Missiles, Ordnance and Defensive Equipment   199
Chapter Ten: Specialist Vehicles of the RAF   208

                 Index   220

Glossary

A&AEE	Aircraft & Armament Evaluation Establishment	LRMTS	Laser Rangefinder & Marked Target Seeker
AAM	Air-to-Air Missile	MAD	Magnetic Anomaly Detector
AAR	Air-to-Air Refuelling	METS	Multi-Engine Training Squadron
ADV	Air Defence Variant (Tornado)	MoD	Ministry of Defence
AEF	Air Experience Flight	MU	Maintenance Unit
AEOp	Air Electronics Operator	NBC	Nuclear-Biological-Chemical
ALARM	Air-Launched Anti-Radar Missile	NCO	Non-Commissioned Officer
		NVG	Night-Vision Goggles
ASRAAM	Advanced Short-Range Air-to-Air Missile	OASC	Officers and Aircrew Selection Centre
ATC	Air Traffic Control	OCU	Operational Conversion Unit
ATC	Air Training Cadet	OEU	Operational Evaluation Unit
AWACS	Airborne Warning And Control System	PRU	Photographic Reconnaissance Unit
		QFI	Qualified Flying Instructor
CCTV	Closed-Circuit TeleVision	QHI	Qualified Helicopter Instructor
CFS	Central Flying School	QWI	Qualified Weapons Instructor
DRA	Defence Research Agency	(R)	Reserve (Squadron)
DIOT	Department of Initial Officer Training	RWR	Radar Warning Receiver
		SAOEU	Strike/Attack Operational Evaluation Unit
ECM	Electronic CounterMeasures		
ESD	Equipment Supply Depot	SAR	Search And Rescue
ESM	Electronic Surveillance Measures	SARTU	Search And Rescue Training Unit
EW	Electronic Warfare	SKTU	Sea King Training Unit
FLIR	Forward-Looking Infra-Red	SLIR	Sideways-Looking Infra-Red
FTS	Flying Training School	SoTT	School of Technical Training
HAS	Hardened Aircraft Shelter	TIALD	Thermal Imaging Airborne Laser Designator
HDU	Hose Drum Unit		
HUD	Head-Up Display	TWU	Tactical Weapons Unit
IDS	InterDictor Strike (Tornado)	UAS	University Air Squadron
ILS	Instrument Landing System	UK MAMS	United Kingdom Mobile Air Movements Squadron
IR	Infra-Red		
INS	Inertial Navigation System	UKADR	United Kingdom Air Defence Region
IRLS	Infra-Red LineScan	UKAIR	United Kingdom Air Forces
IUKADGE	Improved United Kingdom Air Defence Ground Environment	V/STOL	Vertical/Short Take-Off and Landing
JATE	Joint Air Transport Establishment	VGS	Volunteer Gliding School
LGB	Laser-Guided Bomb	VOR	VHF Omni-directional Receiver

Introduction

THIS BOOK IS, in effect, the third edition of a previous work, the successful *Encyclopaedia of the Modern Royal Air Force*, which was compiled by my colleague and mentor, Terry Gander. The first edition appeared in 1984, to be followed by a revised volume in 1987.

For over 40 years the superpowers of East and West, together with their allies, had participated in the Cold War confrontation. This had resulted in colossal programmes on both sides to produce numerous weapons systems, all designed to be superior to those of the opposing forces. Suddenly, the situation changed. Momentous events in what was the Soviet Union, with the collapse of Communism, an attempted coup, the changes of government in this and other countries of the eastern bloc, and the dissolution of the Warsaw Pact (eastern Europe's counterpart to NATO), are significant milestones in history.

The dismantling of the Berlin Wall and the 'Iron Curtain' across Europe, along with German reunification, also added to the constant stream of major news items that dominated the media outlets as the 1980s gave way to the 1990s. Then came the Gulf War, with dire predictions of possible chemical warfare that thankfully were not realized.

The vast changes in the East-West political situation have resulted in steady reductions in the size and capability of all armed forces. The massive deployments of US forces in the UK and Europe, together with the forces of the former Soviet Union stationed in eastern Europe, are all being steadily withdrawn. Orders for all types of military equipment are being reduced or even cancelled. Although this is obviously very welcome, there is a negative aspect. This is the unemployment that is now facing many who are not now required in the armed forces or in defence-related industries. To make matters worse, these reductions have come at a time of economic recession in many parts of the industrialized world.

There are many who say that the need for significant armed forces has now passed. However, the seemingly endless capability of the human race to create strife continues unabated. The former state of Yugoslavia, remembered by many as a holiday destination, has dissolved into a horrendous, multi-faction civil war. Areas of the former Soviet Union have also erupted into ethnic conflict. In Africa, famine adds to the misery caused by civil war.

The United Nations is attempting to bring peace to many of these areas of conflict, but this can only be achieved with the support of more stable nations and elements of their armed forces. Thus the early 1990s have seen the Royal Air Force heavily committed to supporting United Nations operations in several locations. Indeed, its transport units have been intensively utilized in supporting deployments by combat aircraft of the RAF and units of the British Army.

The programme of the British Government to slim down the UK's armed forces in the face of the reduced threat was entitled 'Options for Change'. Other cuts in defence assets have since been announced, due mainly to the effects of economic recession. The resulting changes in the format of the British Services have been the inspiration for this book, along with its companion volumes covering the British Army and the Royal Navy. Indeed, the changes in the RAF are far-reaching; for example, nine different types of aircraft have been withdrawn from service since 1988. All Tornados, Harrier IIs, Tucanos and Sentries have been delivered, but even these more recent types have seen reductions in the numbers in service. Many RAF stations have been closed or transferred to the Army, and several squadrons have been disbanded. For the future, it does appear that some investment will be made in the modernization of transport assets and support helicopters, to assist in possible United Nations operations. The Eurofighter 2000 project still exists, despite attempted cancellation. Thought is also being given to a Nimrod replacement.

A few words on the layout of this book. The first seven chapters describe the roles of the three commands of the RAF and their constituent units, together with other important elements. Chapter Eight examines the aircraft currently in service with the RAF, while Chapters Nine and 10 deal with weapons, ordnance and some RAF vehicles. Some references are duplicated between various chapters; this is intentional for the sake of completeness within each section. Some units have not been included, as there is a danger that a book such as this could resemble a catalogue. I apologise to those in the RAF who may feel that 'their' unit has been unjustly omitted.

ACKNOWLEDGEMENTS

At the conclusion of a two-year search for data, I can in all honesty say that without the generous supply of information from all the many contacts made over that period, it would be impossible to even contemplate the production of a volume of this type.

Of course, the vast bulk of this information was obtained from serving members of the RAF, together with many civilians who are now connected with the Service. I am deeply grateful to the Station Commanders who kindly granted me permission to visit their stations, and to the various Community Relations and Press Liaison Officers who made the excellent arrangements for the comprehensive tours of the many RAF stations to which I had access. Once on the stations, the helpful co-operation of the many personnel of all ranks with whom I came into contact was very much appreciated. Their patient answering of my endless stream of questions, and the mass of information that they imparted form the main content of this work. To list all these many people would cover several pages, with the added risk that I may omit someone. Thus I hope that a collective but no less sincere thank you to all concerned will be acceptable.

There are many other individuals to whom I extend my grateful thanks for their contributions and help: Michael Hill, Chief Public Relations Officer, Strike Command; Dale Donovan, Strike Command Public Relations; Chris Shepherd, Chief Public Relations Officer, Support Command; Robin Killick, for his kind help and hard work with the photo-processing; Terry Gander, for his invaluable guidance and advice; Colin Paine, for his drawings of aircraft of the RAF; Ken Musgrave, for his excellent vehicle drawings; Richard Cossey; Graham Pike; Denis Calvert; Dave Cossey and Alan Cowdray.

Unless otherwise credited, all photographs are by the author.

Peter F. Guiver

CHAPTER ONE

Strike Command

ALTHOUGH THE HISTORY of the Royal Air Force covers more than 75 years, its main operational element, Strike Command, has only been in existence for about one-third of that period, being formed on 30 April 1968. This multi-role command was created by merging both Fighter and Bomber Commands, with Air Support Command (formerly Transport Command), Signals Command and Coastal Command being added later. With the alterations to RAF assets in Germany, following the 'Options for Change' policy, Strike Command now controls all front-line aircraft units on a worldwide basis from its headquarters at RAF High Wycombe in Buckinghamshire.

It must be remembered that most of the Armed Forces of the United Kingdom are assigned to the North Atlantic Treaty Organization (NATO), and RAF Strike Command is a major element of this system. Part of the NATO structure is Allied Command Europe (ACE), which is (currently) divided into four elements, defined as Major Subordinate Commands (MSCs). One of the MSCs is designated as United Kingdom Air Forces (UKAIR), and the Air Officer Commander-in-Chief Strike Command (AOCinCSTC) is also appointed as Commander-in-Chief UKAIR.

However, there are plans to change this arrangement from mid-1994 when two of the MSCs, Allied Forces Northern Europe (AFNORTH) and UKAIR, will be merged to form Allied Forces Northwest Europe (AFNORTHWEST), with its HQ at High Wycombe. UKAIR will form part of Allied Air Forces Northwest Europe, a subordinate command within AFNORTHWEST. Units currently assigned to a further major NATO command, Allied Command Channel (ACCHAN), will also be incorporated into AFNORTHWEST, and ACCHAN will duly be eliminated.

The peacetime operations of Strike Command on a day-to-day basis are the responsibility of the AOCinCSTC, who is also accountable to the Supreme Allied Commander Europe (SACEUR) for the defence of the UK Air Defence Region (UKADR). The deployment and availability of suitable air assets for the use and support of other MSCs in the NATO sphere of operations is a further task assigned to the AOCinCSTC.

The majority of Strike Command's units are assigned for the use of ACE, but certain elements, mainly those that operate in maritime roles, are provided for the use of the Supreme Allied Commander Atlantic. In order to meet these various commitments, Strike Command controls about 700 aircraft, 46,500 Service personnel and 5,000 civilians, operating from some 200 units, most of which are situated in the UK.

Strike Command is divided into a number of groups, each covering a specific role or roles, or an area of operations. In addition, a number of specialized units report directly to the Command HQ at High Wycombe. Although the command's main area of responsibility and commitment is in Europe, it also controls operations and units on a worldwide basis. At present, this includes facilities in Cyprus, Gibraltar, Canada, Belize, Hong Kong, the Falkland Islands and Ascension Island.

The operations of Strike Command are controlled and conducted from a complex at RAF High Wycombe which was opened in April 1989, this replacing an Operations Centre that had been in use since before the Second World War. The older centre offered little protection from nuclear, biological or chemical attack, and was even vulnerable to accurate conventional weapons.

Construction of the new HQ began in 1982, with NATO funding some 55 per cent of the cost.

The main building is an underground concrete box, consisting of four floors, the lowest of which contains the life support systems, which provide air, water, sewage and electrical supplies in time of an emergency. Above this comes the communications and computer equipment, together with a meteorological complex and a systems control room.

The second-from-top floor contains the Operations Cells that organize the day-to-day activities of all the varied aspects of Strike Command. This includes such items as transport tasks, in-flight refuelling missions, air defence interceptors, maritime operations and logistics. More than 40 computer systems are employed, and wide use is made of close-circuit TV for briefing and information transfer. The top floor of this bunker is the domestic area, including sleeping accommodation, a first aid section and a restaurant.

NO 1 GROUP: STRIKE/ATTACK

Within the past year, the Headquarters of No 1 Group has moved from RAF Upavon in Wiltshire (which has been transferred to the British Army) to RAF Benson in Oxfordshire. This group is responsible for the some of the main 'teeth' of the RAF, controlling the Harrier- and Jaguar-equipped units based in the UK which are tasked with strike/attack operations and tactical support of the British Army. Further elements comprise two squadrons of Tornado GR.1A aircraft, equipped for reconnaissance missions but retaining a full strike capability. Complementing these strike aircraft are units equipped with helicopters, whose role is also to support the British Army in a land battle situation.

The Jaguar has now been in service since the mid-1970s, and formerly equipped several squadrons in RAF Germany, until replaced by the Tornado GR.1. Currently, it forms the equipment of three units based at RAF Coltishall, in Norfolk, these being Nos 6, 41 and 54 Squadrons. The main roles for the first and third squadrons are close air support, tactical strike and ground attack, while the primary responsibility of No 41 Squadron is tactical reconnaissance, with a secondary task of ground attack. In the event of war in Europe, the Jaguar units from Coltishall would be required to act as reinforcements for the Northern European Command of NATO. In connection with this, all three squadrons regularly deploy to forward operating bases in Norway and Denmark for training exercises. However, with the changed international situation, the Jaguar force is looking at the possibilities of being tasked for operations further afield. The three squadrons form part of NATO's Rapid Reaction Force, which acts as a 'fire brigade' organization capable of short-notice deployments to almost anywhere in response to an emergency situation,

The flight-line at RAF Coltishall, with Jaguar GR.1As of Nos 6, 41 and 54 Squadrons.

A No 54 Squadron Jaguar GR.1A between sorties. Note the practice bomb carrier under the fuselage.

mostly in connection with United Nations (UN) operations.

Elements of these squadrons comprised the Jaguar force that was sent to the Gulf region a few days after Iraq invaded Kuwait in August 1990, subsequently acquitting itself well in daylight strike operations. From September 1991, Jaguars and personnel from Coltishall were sent to Turkey, as part of a UN force to monitor and protect the Kurds in northern Iraq from attacks by the Iraqi Army, and this deployment continued unbroken through to April 1993, when the RAF's contribution to the UN force was taken over by units equipped with the Harrier GR.7.

However, the Jaguar force was not allowed to relax for long, as for a few months in the spring and early summer of 1993, the units at Coltishall were put on stand-by to deploy to the Adriatic region, in connection with the UN's operations in Bosnia and other areas of the former state of Jugoslavia, torn apart by ethnic strife and civil war. This stand-by turned into an actual deployment, when, on 16 July 1993, 12 Jaguars departed from Coltishall for Italy, to be based at Gioia del

A Jaguar GR.1A wearing a special green and white camouflage colour scheme for deployment to an Arctic location. Although devoid of unit markings, this aircraft is probably from No 41 Squadron as it is carrying the large BAe reconnaissance pod under the fuselage.

This Jaguar GR.1A carries the markings of No 6 Squadron.

Colle, alongside RAF Tornado F.3s, and other air-craft from western air arms.

Pilots for the Jaguar squadrons undergo conversion training with No 16 (Reserve) Squadron, the Jaguar Operational Conversion Unit, based at RAF Lossiemouth, on the Moray Firth, in Scotland. This unit was formerly known as No 226 OCU until mid-1992, when it was redesignated to keep alive a long-established squadron that had operated Tornado GR.1s in RAF Germany until its demise as a result of defence cutbacks. In addition to its main task of providing Jaguar pilots for the Coltishall squadrons, No 16(R)

Squadron also trains pilots for the Sultan of Oman's Air Force, as well as supplying the RAF's Jaguar air display pilot and aircraft each year. It is also responsible for the Jaguar Standardization Unit, which, as its name implies, regulates the operations of the RAF's Jaguar squadrons, and also those of the Oman Air Force. No 16(R) Squadron operates eight Jaguars, with equal numbers of GR.1A single-seaters and T.2A two-seaters, and has 14 staff instructors, two of whom operate with the Jaguar flight simulator.

To carry out its tasks, No 16(R) Squadron operates a number of courses, the principal one of

A Jaguar T.2A of No 16 (Reserve) Squadron rolls to take-off with full afterburner for another training sortie.

which is the Long Course, which caters for 14 *ab initio* students each year, and involves 61 airborne sorties, comprising 73 flying hours over an 18-week period. Ten students carry out refresher training on the Short Course annually, which is a compressed version of the features of the Long Course. Having qualified at one of the advanced Flying Training Schools at RAF Valley or RAF Chivenor, prospective Jaguar pilots commence their Long Course conversion with two weeks in the ground school, where they receive lectures on the Jaguar and its systems; this period is concluded with an examination. This is followed by a two-week period of sorties in the Jaguar flight simulator, before proceeding to the flying syllabus, which consists of a number of phases. The first of these is the conversion (or 'convex') phase, in which the trainee pilot gains experience to achieve solo standard. Return visits to the simulator are interspersed within the flying syllabus. Next comes instruction on instrument flying, before the student pilot moves on to the tactical phase. This covers formation and low-level flying, and then proceeds to the lengthy and intensive weapons phase. The course then progresses to simulated attack profiles, which combines previous tuition, and to tactical manoeuvring, often in the face of 'retaliation' by aggressor elements. Operations by night are also included.

Further courses run at RAF Lossiemouth are aimed at providing instructors for No 16(R) Squadron itself. Annually, four Qualified Weapons Instructors (QWIs) are trained, with 57 flying hours over a period of five months. Three Instrument Rating Examiners receive six hours of flying tuition in two weeks, while conversion courses to provide instructors for pilot training involve 20 hours of flying in seven weeks. Under current plans, the Jaguar is expected to remain in service until the turn of the century, when it is due to be replaced by the Eurofighter 2000. Thus No 16(R) Squadron will have a continuing role in providing new pilots for the Coltishall units, and running refresher courses for those with previous experience.

The Harrier, with its unique short or vertical take-off and landing capabilities, first entered service with the RAF in 1969. The main variant for many years, the GR.3, has now been withdrawn, and the No 1 Group Harrier units, based at RAF Wittering in Cambridgeshire, have largely re-equipped with the GR.7 variant, although a few GR.5s may still be in service, pending their conversion to GR.7 standard. The front-line unit at Wittering is No 1 Squadron, tasked with tactical support of the British Army in the ground attack role. Army officers are attached to No 1 Squadron to co-ordinate operations in this task. From time-to-time the squadron deploys to bases in Scandinavia in support of NATO exercises in that area.

The ability of the Harrier to operate away from large and therefore vulnerable airfields is frequently practised, if only at times on the more remote wooded fringes of RAF Wittering. To support these types of operations, a fleet of vehicles capable of carrying box-bodies is maintained. These bodies contain facilities that provide for engineering support, intelligence briefing and debriefing, communications to HQ command elements and to all dispersed aircraft 'hides', together with feeding and other domestic support for the air and ground crews. No 1 Squadron has taken part in the Operation 'Warden' deployment to Incirlik in Turkey, monitoring activities in the northern areas of Iraq.

RAF Wittering is the home base for the Harrier GR.7s of No 1 Squadron.

Harriers from Nos 1, 3 and 4 Squadrons adopted this light grey livery for the deployment to Turkey, to assist in UN operations in northern Iraq. No unit markings are carried.

Alongside No 1 Squadron at Wittering is No 20 (Reserve) Squadron, the Harrier Operational Conversion Unit, which until the middle of 1992 was known as No 233 OCU. As with other changes of a similar nature, No 20 Squadron was formerly a Tornado GR.1 unit based in Germany. The task of No 20(R) Squadron is to convert pilots to the specialized techniques of operating the Harrier in its assigned roles.

No 20(R) Squadron runs a number of courses, the main one of which is the GR.7 Long Course, which lasts for six months and includes some 75 hours of flying. This course is preceded by an initial conversion phase, which includes 15 sorties flown in the unit's Harrier T.4 two-seaters, and further sorties are flown in this variant during the Long Course. The T.4 version of the Harrier differs in many respects from the front-line GR.7, but with the approaching delivery of the two-seat Harrier T.10, the use of dual control aircraft is expected to increase markedly during the conversion course. Currently, much instruction is carried

The down-turned nozzles on this Harrier T.4 of No 20 (Reserve) Squadron induce spray to fly up from a damp runway.

A Harrier GR.7 of No 20 (Reserve) Squadron, carrying a PHIMAT defensive measures pod on the port outer pylon.

out from a chase aircraft flying in close formation with the student's machine. As with other modern aircraft, considerable use is made of simulators, particularly for training in emergency drill procedures. The unit also runs several other shorter courses, including training for weapons instructors, and refresher tuition for pilots with previous experience.

RAF Marham, in Norfolk, has become the home for two squadrons operating the GR.1A reconnaissance variant of the Tornado, these being Nos 2 and 13 Squadrons, who are expected to occupy the enclaves of Hardened Aircraft Shelters (HASs) formerly used by Nos 27 and 617 Squadrons. No 2 Squadron, who for many years provided the reconnaissance force for RAF Germany with such types as the Phantom and Jaguar, moved into RAF Marham from RAF Laarbruch with its GR.1As in December 1991, while No 13, who reformed with the GR.1A in early 1990, transferred from nearby RAF Honington in early 1994.

The GR.1A model is equipped for reconnaissance tasks with its unique linescan infra-red sys-

Line-up of Tornado GR.1As of No 2 Squadron at RAF Marham.

tems, in which images are recorded on standard video tape as opposed to film used hitherto. The new system enables the results of reconnaissance missions to be assessed immediately upon return of the Tornado, with the recordings being taken from the aircraft on landing to the Reconnaissance Intelligence Centre (RIC) for instant playback. Thus, time previously lost when 'wet' films were processed is now saved. The task of assessing the images obtained is far easier, with the information being presented on a standard TV screen, which can be viewed by several people at the same time, as opposed to the previous situation in which individual interpreters had to examine strips of film with magnifying equipment, prior to printing enlarged views. Although the pictures obtained by the conventional 'wet' film, as employed by the Jaguar and Canberra PR.9, are better in quality and definition, they can only be obtained during daylight, in good visual conditions, with resulting possible danger to the reconnaissance aircraft.

Each Tornado GR.1A squadron at RAF Marham has its own RIC, who pass the mission task to the aircrews concerned for flight planning and execution. The mission may involve gathering information by searching a designated area for certain targets; this was exemplified during the Gulf War when Tornado GR.1As were tasked with locating the elusive Iraqi 'Scud' missiles and their launchers. Other missions may involve gathering images at particular known locations, or flying along lines of transport, such as roads and railway tracks, to assess their availability. On return, the RICs analyze the results, and then pass their findings back to the tasking agency.

The equipment used at the RIC for assessing the tapes is known as the Imagery Analysis Work-Station. This has the ability to view the gathered material in a number of ways, one of which includes a fast 'run-through' of the whole mission, to form an overall picture. Particular sections can then be viewed in detail, with items of interest being 'frozen' for closer examination. Images can also be magnified, and improvements in contrast can be achieved by adjustments in the tonal range of the picture. Various copies of the original tape can be produced as required to suit the 'customers' concerned, and accompanied by written reports produced on the co-located keyboard and printer.

Although primarily tasked with reconnaissance missions, the Tornado GR.1As of Nos 2 and 13 Squadrons also retain most of the strike capabilities of the more widely-used Tornado GR.1s, except for the deletion of the Mauser 27 mm cannon and some items of external ordnance. Peacetime training for these two units has to cover both reconnaissance and strike missions,

and each squadron operates a couple of dual-control Tornado GR.1s for crew conversion. Particular attention is given to low-level flying by night, as the infra-red linescan sensors can operate in almost all conditions, by day and night.

In addition to its main obligation with front-line units, No 1 Group is also responsible for an important training element. This is the Tri-National Tornado Training Establishment (TTTE), which has been based at RAF Cottesmore since its formation in the early 1980s. The three countries involved in the Tornado programme (the UK, Germany and Italy) decided that a multi-national training programme should be created, and as such, this unit has functioned remarkably smoothly over the past 14 years. Since its inception, the TTTE has flown some 120,000 hours in the course of training approximately 2,500 Tornado aircrew.

The Station Commander (an RAF Group Captain) of RAF Cottesmore is also the Senior National Representative of the UK at the TTTE. He works in co-operation with the Senior National Representatives from Germany and Italy, who are officers of equivalent rank. As the operation at Cottesmore is a tri-national programme, there are a number of supporting organizations responsible for co-ordinating procedures and policies, particularly with regard to costs. These costs are shared by the three nations in proportion to their training requirements, and currently some 52 per cent of the students are from Germany, 37 per cent from the UK, with the remaining 11 per cent being from Italy.

Within the overall TTTE organization is the Tornado Operational Conversion Unit (TOCU), which is responsible for conversion training of pilots and navigators to the Interdictor Strike (IDS) version of the Tornado, for service with the RAF, the German Air Force, the German Navy and the Italian Air Force. The TOCU is commanded by a Chief Instructor (CI), appointed from each nation in turn. Within the TOCU is the Ground Training Squadron (GTS), and the Chief Ground Instructor is also a post rotated between the three member countries. Student pilots and navigators, who are converting to the Tornado IDS on the main training course, spend their first four weeks at RAF Cottesmore as part of the GTS. During this period, the syllabus calls for 70 hours of classroom lectures, plus 20 hours in video-driven self-study centres. Three hours are spent in a cockpit trainer, and 12 hours' training is conducted in the Basic Avionics Procedures Trainer and the Navigation and Attack Systems Trainer. These devices are replicas of the Tornado's cockpits and systems, and enable the students to familiarize themselves with the aircraft's sophisticated avionics. There then follows

An RAF Tornado GR.1 of the TTTE taxies past similar aircraft from Germany and Italy.

nine 'sorties', of 15 hours total duration, in the full-motion flight simulators, in which students can practise crew integration and emergency procedures.

The TOCU also comprises four flying squadrons, three of which are known as 'A', 'B' and 'C' Conversion Squadrons, these being commanded by German, British, and Italian officers respectively. The task of these squadrons is to train aircrew undertaking the main course (of which 15 or 16 are run each year) to have the ability to operate the Tornado IDS, both in handling the aircraft and its systems, by day and night. An important feature of the training at the TTTE is the full integration of the three nationalities; thus, for example, a British instructor may fly with an Italian student in a German aircraft.

Student pilots on the main course fly 29 sorties, involving 37 hours airborne; student navigators are airborne for 31 hours on fewer sorties. This flying training covers a period of nine weeks, and is divided into six phases. The first three phases cover basic handling, emergency procedures, navigation, formation flying, and instrument flying. The students then progress to sorties using the terrain-following radar, flown 'hands-off', initially by day, then later by night. The final phases involve simulated attack missions, although no weapons, either practice or live, are released or even carried.

The fourth flying squadron within the TOCU is 'S', or Standards Squadron, which is responsible for the training of instructors for the three Conversion Squadrons, and for checking and maintaining flying standards throughout the

The TTTE in operation: an RAF Instructor (left) *discusses details of the next training sortie with an Italian student pilot.*

Tornados of the TTTE generally operate 'clean', without any underwing stores. An RAF aircraft of 'B' Squadron is seen here in its landing configuration.

TOCU. The Commanding Officer of 'S' Squadron is of a different nationality to that of the TOCU CI at any one time.

To carry out the flying schedules, the unit is equipped with 35 Tornado IDS's, comprising 14 RAF aircraft, 17 German Tornados, and four machines from Italy. These aircraft are all from the early production batches, and lack in-flight re-fuelling probes and the laser ranger/marked target seeker fairing under the nose. They also fly 'clean', without underwing pylons or any external stores. The Tornados at RAF Cottesmore are flown intensively, and the engines on these air-craft have been downrated to extend their service lives. Ground support is the responsibility of the RAF, as is minor aircraft servicing. Major servic-ing of the TTTE Tornados is the responsibility of each contributing nation, and thus the German and Italian machines return to their home coun-tries for major overhauls. Although the Tornados at Cottesmore each carry the individual insignia of one of the four squadrons within the TOCU, they are all operated as a 'pool' of aircraft, and are used by any of the squadrons as required.

In addition to the main conversion course for *ab initio* aircrew, the TTTE provides refresher courses for aircrew with previous Tornado experi-ence, Competent to Instruct courses for TOCU instructors, and courses for Instrument Rating Examiners. Further RAF units based at RAF Cottesmore include the Tornado In-Service Software Maintenance Team, and the Tornado Maintenance School; this latter unit is responsible for the training of all RAF groundcrews who will work with the Tornado.

If and when the proposed Eurofighter 2000 enters service, it seems likely that a multi-nation-al training organization similar to the TTTE will be set up, to follow in the obviously successful steps of the operation at RAF Cottesmore.

Following their training at RAF Cottesmore, RAF Tornado aircrew then proceed to RAF Lossiemouth, which is the home of No 15 (Reserve) Squadron, the Tornado Weapons Conversion Unit (TWCU). Up to mid-1992, the Tornados of the TWCU (then based at RAF Honington in Suffolk) carried the markings of No 45 Squadron, a 'shadow' designation allocated to the TWCU. However, these markings were changed to those of No 15 Squadron to keep alive yet another early and long-established squadron of the RAF. No 15(R) Squadron moved to RAF Lossiemouth in late 1993.

Here, the student pilots and navigators learn to operate the Tornado GR.1 in its main role of strike/attack, through a phased training pro-gramme. The Long (or main) Course carried out by the TWCU is designed for *ab initio* RAF air-crews from the TTTE, and commences with a short period in the Ground School, with refresher training on the Tornado aircraft and its systems, together with lectures on weapons and electronic air warfare. Each phase in the flying syllabus at the TWCU is combined with a briefing, and training 'sorties' in the Tornado flight simulator. One of these simulator sorties involves the pilot and navigator 'swapping' seats, so that both may fully appreciate each other's tasks.

As already stated, the Tornados at the TTTE are flown 'clean', without pylons or external stores. The first two sorties with No 15(R) Squadron are familiarization flights, in dual-control aircraft, and are designed to introduce the crews to a much heavier aircraft, the Tornados of the TWCU being fitted with external fuel tanks, weapons, and underwing chaff and electronic countermeasures (ECM) pods. Student pilots fly with staff pilots and staff navigators on initial sorties, while student navigators fly with staff pilots, prior to student crews combining on later training details. Instruction covers formation, night and instrument flying, emergency procedures, and low-level and terrain-following operations down to 250 ft (76 m) above ground level (AGL), which is much lower than the minimum operating height already experienced at the TTTE.

The initial familiarization phase is followed by the weapons phase, which is divided into a number of sections. These cover lay-down bombing, in which ordnance is released during a low-level run at 200 ft (61 m), at 480 kts (890km/h), or loft-bombing, where the aircraft pulls up from a run-in, with the weapons being released in the climb to follow a trajectory to the target. For this train-ing, small practice bombs are used, either 6.6 lb or 31 lb (3 kg or 14 kg) in weight. A further type of attack is known as 'off-set' bombing, in which a well-hidden target is located by using a more visible feature nearby as an aiming point. Training in the use of other weapons is obtained by simulating such devices on the aircraft's computer, and altering the symbology presented to the aircrew via the cockpit displays.

Dive attacks, with use being made of the Tornado's Mauser 27 mm cannon for strafing, form a further element of the TWCU training syllabus. These sorties are usually flown in a dual-control aircraft, with the student pilot under the tuition of a staff QWI, and safety factors are paramount on these types of sorties. Night sorties form a further element in the training programme.

Although the Tornado GR.1 is primarily a strike/attack aircraft, the TWCU also provides training in air combat. This is to teach techniques in evasion, and also in defence and retaliation, as the aircraft can carry two air-to-air missiles (AAMs) on the inner underwing pylons. Two aircraft, both from the TWCU, carry out various air combat manoeuvres with each other, involving interceptions at 90° and head-on, amongst other scenarios. Aircraft are flown in different configurations and parameters of performance (i.e. with or without reheat), with varying types of AIM-9 Sidewinder AAMs. This training is carried out

A Tornado GR.1 of No 15 (Reserve) Squadron gets airborne. The pod on the port outer underwing pylon is a Marconi Sky Shadow ECM device, whilst a BOZ-107 chaff and flare dispenser is carried on the starboard outer pylon. The inner pylons carry large fuel tanks.

mainly over the North Sea, at a minimum altitude of 8,000 ft (2,438 m).

The Long Course concludes with five 'operational' sorties, which combine all the previous training into various scenarios, these sorties being planned and led by both staff pilots from the TWCU, and the students themselves. On completion of their training at the TWCU, pilots and navigators are posted (usually separately) to front-line Tornado units, as required. Once on a squadron, the training of aircrews is far from over. Instruction continues in the use of a wider range of weapons, formation flying, in-flight refuelling and more realistic training sorties.

Further courses run by the TWCU include refresher training for aircrew following a ground tour, together with courses for senior officers. Much of this training is tailored to suit the individual's previous experience. Training for flying and weapons instructors for the TWCU itself is also undertaken.

RAF Lossiemouth is also the home of the Tornado Standardization Unit (TSU), who monitor and check the operational and training standards of all RAF units that operate this type of aircraft. Thus, the highly qualified aircrew of the TSU are often away from Lossiemouth, evaluating the activities of RAF Tornado squadrons in the UK and Germany.

Support Helicopters

Five squadrons, together with an OCU, are equipped with three types of helicopters, and these elements form the UK-based support helicopters (SH) force, all being the responsibility of No 1 Group. The largest of the helicopter types, the Chinook, is currently being upgraded in the USA to HC.2 standard. When all these modified aircraft have returned to the UK, the capabilities of the SH force will be much improved. In addition, there are plans to expand the SH force, to cater for the changes in possible tasks that the RAF may be asked to undertake, particularly in support of UN operations. For more than 30 years, RAF Odiham, in Hampshire, has been the principal centre for RAF helicopter operations, and the base currently houses two squadrons, Nos 7 and 33, and No 27 (Reserve) Squadron, the Support Helicopter OCU, together with elements responsible for standards, trials and evaluation, and a helicopter servicing facility.

The role of No 7 Squadron is to provide medium- and heavy-lift helicopter support for the British Army with its fleet of some 16 Chinook HC.1/.2 twin-rotor helicopters. This involves working principally with 24 Airmobile Brigade and 5 Airborne Brigade. Over 50 fully-equipped troops, or small vehicles can be carried internally, whilst external loads can be transported suspended from three lifting points under the fuselage. Parachutists, both static line and free-fall, can also be deployed from the rear-opening ramp.

Part of No 7 Squadron operates in conjunction with the activities of Special Forces units, and a number of aircrew are specially trained and earmarked for these tasks. Also, No 7 Squadron is responsible for a two-aircraft detachment to

Chinook HC.1s of No 7 Squadron at RAF Odiham.

In addition to the Chinook, No 7 Squadron also operates one or two Gazelle HT.3 light helicopters.

Northern Ireland, in support of Army operations. In addition to the Chinook, the unit also operates one or two Gazelle HT.3 light helicopters for reconnaissance and communications duties.

No.33 Squadron, equipped with the Puma HC.1 helicopter, occupies a hangar and connected offices on the south side of RAF Odiham, away from the main complex of the base. This unit has a similar task to that of No 7 Squadron, i.e. sup-

port of Army units, but on a smaller and lighter scale. It operates casualty evacuation flights as required, and is also responsible for providing an aircraft and crew on stand-by for any emergency tasking that may arise. This stand-by is at two hours' notice, and is provided seven days a week throughout the year.

No 33 Squadron is divided into three flights, with the HQ Flight being responsible for adminis-

No 33 Squadron operates the Puma HC.1 medium-lift helicopter from RAF Odiham.

tration. 'A' Flight is connected with Allied Command Europe Mobile Force operations and overseas deployments, whilst 'B' Flight deals mainly with tasking within the UK. The squadron has been responsible for providing aircraft and crews for the Puma detachment in Belize (No 1563 Flight), but with the run-down of British forces in that location, this task may well soon end.

Formerly known as No 240 OCU, No 27 (Reserve) Squadron, the Support Helicopter OCU, adopted its new title in October 1993. No 27 Squadron formerly operated Tornado GR.1 aircraft from RAF Marham, until it was renumbered as No 12 Squadron in September 1993. No 27(R) Squadron is composed of four flights (the Puma Flight, the Chinook Flight, the SH Standards and Evaluation Flight, and the SH Tactics and Trials Flight), together with engineering and administrative elements.

The Puma Flight provides *ab initio* training for aircrew new to the aircraft, with three or four courses run each year, each of some 17 weeks' duration, with approximately 12 students on each course. Periods of instruction are spent in the Ground School, and trainee crews have to travel to Stavangar in Norway to use the Puma flight simulator located there. Pilots undertake 48 hours of flying training on the Puma, navigators are given 22 hours, and loadmasters 11 hours of instruction during the main Long Course. Other courses cover refresher training, and familiarization sessions for senior officers. The Puma Flight has the use of four or five aircraft for its training tasks.

With many Chinook HC.1s away in the USA for conversion to HC.2 standard, the shortage of this type of aircraft resulted in the suspension of training on this type within the Chinook Flight through 1993. During this period, a Course Design Team was at work, formulating the revised training syllabus required for the modified aircraft. With the Chinook HC.2s now entering service, training has recommenced, and use is made of the Chinook flight simulator located at nearby Farnborough, this having been reprogrammed to replicate the HC.2 variant.

No 27(R) Squadron is also responsible for the administration of the Support Helicopter Standards and Evaluation Unit. This unit, which reports to No 1 Group, is tasked with monitoring and evaluating the operational and training standards of all RAF support helicopter squadrons, as well as a small number of overseas air arms. The members of this unit are aircrew with experience on at least three or four different types of helicopter.

Although part of the Central Tactics and Trials Organization (CTTO), the Support Helicopter Tactics and Trials Flight (SHTTF) forms yet another element that is administered by No 27(R) Squadron at RAF Odiham. As with other CTTO elements, the SHTTF is responsible for evaluating new equipment, defining doctrines and formulating procedures and operational instructions relative to the support helicopter role. This is achieved through the work of a number of teams, covering the Puma and Chinook at Odiham, whilst the tactics and trials team responsible for the Wessex is located at RAF Benson. Members of the SHTTF visit RAF SH units to give presentations and advice on new equipment and procedures. They also brief staff officers on subjects connected with the SH force's task. Recent trials have been carried out in the use of Night Vision Goggles (NVGs), the effect of small-arms fire on helicopters, and techniques related to electronic warfare (EW). The SHTTF also conducts courses

A Wessex HC.2 of No 60 Squadron seen in a rural setting in Germany whilst taking part in an exercise in support of British Army units.

Elderly but still sprightly, a Wessex HC.2 of No 60 Squadron from RAF Benson comes in to land during a field exercise.

in helicopter tactics for crews from SH units.

1992 saw the emergence of an additional rotary-winged unit, this being No 60 Squadron (formerly providing communications flights in RAF Germany), which was reformed at RAF Benson with Wessex HC.2 helicopters. This squadron is tasked with providing helicopter support for Army elements both in the UK and in Germany. Part of it also acts as a conversion unit for the Wessex, and both *ab initio* and refresher courses are run to provide aircrew for units that operate this type in the UK and overseas.

At the time of writing, the unhappy situation in Northern Ireland continues to defy a solution, and the considerable Army presence in the Province has the support of two squadrons equipped with helicopters. No 230 Squadron, equipped with Puma HC.1s, reformed at RAF Aldergrove in 1992, having formerly been based at Gutersloh in Germany for many years. The long-standing helicopter unit based at RAF Aldergrove, No 72 Squadron, saw a reduction in the number of Wessex HC.2s that it operated, with some of the aircraft being transferred to RAF Benson for allocation to the reformed No 60 Squadron.

NO 2 GROUP: THE RAF IN GERMANY

With the momentous changes and upheavals that took place in the former Soviet Union and its erstwhile Communist allies in eastern Europe, the so-called Cold War between the Warsaw Pact and the western members of NATO was consigned to the history books. From this situation came the 'Options for Change' policies, and these have had a major effect on the assets of the RAF and of the British Army based in Germany.

Until recently, the RAF in Germany was administered by RAF Germany, a command organization similar to Strike Command that reported directly to the Air Board. The origins of this command go back to the Second World War, when the RAF formed the Second Tactical Air Force (2 TAF), to control the air assets that were operating in close air support roles on the Continent, a task that it carried out from the D-Day landings in Normandy in June 1944 to VE-Day in May 1945. The Allied victory led to 2 TAF being renamed the British Air Force of Occupation, but after a few years its previous title was reintroduced. No 2 Group formed part of Bomber Command from 1936 until 1943, when it was transferred to 2 TAF, and it served in Germany until it was disbanded in 1947. It was reformed in 1948, once again as part of 2 TAF, only to be disbanded again 10 years later.

2 TAF was retitled as RAF Germany in 1959. However, with the recent reduction in the number of RAF units based in Germany, the HQ structure was also changed, and this marked the demise of the last RAF Command HQ based overseas. RAF Germany was redesignated as No 2 Group, Strike Command, with effect from 1 April 1993, with its HQ at Rheindahlen, near Monchengladbach. In addition to housing the HQ of the this newly-reformed group, the complex at Rheindahlen, which was brought into use in the early 1950s, also accommodates the HQ of the British Army in Germany, along with a number of other HQ staffs of NATO commands.

For many years, the units of RAF Germany (and, more recently, No 2 Group) were integrated into the NATO command of the Second Allied Tactical Air Force (2 ATAF), which also included air force elements from the United States Air Forces in Europe (USAFE), Germany, Belgium and the Netherlands. The HQ of 2 ATAF (which should not be confused with the RAF's 2 TAF) was located at Rheindahlen. 2 ATAF was responsible for air assets in the northern half of Europe, whilst the central area of Europe was covered by the Fourth Allied Tactical Air Force (4 ATAF) from its HQ at Heidelberg, West Germany. Both of the ATAFs were integrated into HQ Allied Air Forces Central Europe (AAFCE), based at Ramstein Air Base.

However, the drastic changes to the political and military situation in Europe meant that the structure of NATO would have to be reorganized, and there have been significant reductions in the numbers of military aircraft and air force units amongst the member nations over the past two years. This has resulted in the closing of both 2 ATAF and 4 ATAF HQs, the responsibilities of these elements being absorbed by an expansion of HQ AAFCE, and these changes officially came into force on 1 July 1993, with AAFCE being retitled Allied Air Forces Central Europe (AIR-CENT). Further changes were planned for the beginning of 1994, when the area of responsibility of AIRCENT was due to be increased to include Denmark and northern Germany, both previously part of AFNORTH.

AIRCENT is commanded by a US four-star General, who is also in command of USAFE. The deputy commander is a Lieutenant-General from Germany, whilst the posts of director of operations and director of support are alternatively held by officers from the Netherlands and Belgium of Major-General rank. A number of RAF personnel are on the staff of AIRCENT, and an RAF support unit exists at Ramstein for these officers and other ranks. A Military Mission from France is attached to HQ AIRCENT, as is a liaison team from HQ Allied Land Forces Central Europe (HQ LAND-CENT). A similar liaison team from AIRCENT is located with HQ LANDCENT at Heidelberg. Despite all these changes, the operational squadrons of the RAF in Germany are still declared to NATO, although they remain under national control in peacetime.

Under the 'Options for Change' programme, five RAF squadrons in Germany were disbanded, and two airfields were closed, along with various other changes. The two air defence squadrons, Nos 19 and 92, flying Phantom FGR.2s from RAF Wildenrath, were disbanded, although they have reappeared as reserve squadrons within training units in the UK. Similarly, No 60 Squadron, which operated in the communications role with Andovers from Wildenrath, was also disbanded. With these changes, Wildenrath was handed back to German control.

Further east, the former Luftwaffe airfield at Gutersloh was transferred to the British Army in 1993. Prior to this, No 230 Squadron was moved to Northern Ireland with some of its Puma helicopters in May 1992, while the remaining Pumas were transferred to No 18 Squadron, also then based at RAF Gutersloh, to join that unit's reduced number of Chinooks. The two squadrons operating the Harrier GR.7, Nos 3 and 4, moved west from Gutersloh to RAF Laarbruch in November 1992, and No 18 Squadron made a similar move in the spring of 1993. The role of the Harrier in Germany is to provide offensive support for ground forces, with supply and tactical mobility being added by the Chinook and

Three Puma HC.1s of No 18 Squadron deployed for a field exercise in Germany.

A Chinook HC.1 of No 18 Squadron comes in to land whilst on an exercise in the field.

Puma helicopters, these forces forming part of the Allied Command Europe Rapid Reaction Corps. The helicopters of No 18 Squadron are also tasked with providing tactical support for the British Army.

The changed international situation resulted in a drastic reduction in the Tornado strike force within RAF Germany, with the Laarbruch Wing being eliminated. No 2 Squadron moved to RAF Marham in the UK in late 1991, to continue its traditional role of tactical reconnaissance with its Tornado GR.1As. The remaining Tornado GR.1-equipped squadrons at Laarbruch, Nos 15, 16 and 20, were disbanded as such in 1992, only to be reborn as reserve squadrons in the UK, with the tasks of conversion or training units. Over at nearby RAF Bruggen, the changes have been less noticeable, and the wing of four Tornado GR.1 squadrons, Nos 9, 14, 17 and 31, have continued in their role of strike/attack. Of these units, No 9 Squadron has been equipped with the ALARM anti-radar missile since the beginning of 1993, whilst No 14 Squadron is working up with the TIALD pod, for use in the laser-designation role. One element that did disband at Bruggen was No 431 Maintenance Unit, which had been responsible for the servicing of aircraft held by RAF Germany; in future, these aircraft will return to the UK for maintenance. On the plus side, new radar equipment was installed at Bruggen, improving the local air traffic control facilities.

Having for so many years trained and planned for a possible war in Central Europe, the RAF's units in Germany have more recently travelled much further afield, with many of the deployments being in support of UN operations. Tornados from Bruggen have been deployed to Saudi Arabia to enforce the UN no-fly zone in Iraq, south of the 32nd Parallel. At the other end of Iraq, Harriers from Laarbruch have been based at Incirlik in Turkey since April 1993, as part of the UN force monitoring the area north of the 36th Parallel. Aircraft from No 2 Group now use the range areas in the UK to a greater extent, in an attempt to reduce the level of aircraft noise in Germany and the Netherlands. In this context, use is also made of training facilities in Canada.

The RAF have maintained a presence at Gatow, in Berlin, for many years, and two Chipmunk T.10s are operated by the Berlin Station Flight. Throughout the Cold War, these aircraft were flown regularly over the then divided city, to maintain the Western Allies' rights to fly in that area. It is expected that these two aircraft will continue to be based at Gatow up to the RAF's withdrawal from the base at the end of 1994.

No 2 Group also has responsibilities in relation to range areas in Europe. The Italian Air Force base at Decimomannu in Sardinia is used by many NATO elements for air combat training on the nearby Air Combat Manoeuvring Instrumentation range, and for ground attack training on the bombing range at Capo di Frasca. Most RAF front-line units, from both the UK and Germany, deploy to 'Deci' from time to time to use the extensive range facilities, usually with the benefit of good weather in the area. To support these deployments, the RAF maintains a facility at Decimomannu to provide services such as engineering, movements, armaments, supply, catering

This Tornado GR.1 carries the markings of No 14 Squadron, one of four such units based at RAF Bruggen in Germany, as part of No 2 Group.

and administration. This RAF supporting facility reports to HQ No 2 Group at Rheindahlen.

A further range area is located at Nordhorn in the north of Germany. It is operated by the RAF, and is also used by several NATO air forces for bombing practice. Another RAF element within No 2 Group is the RAF Hospital at Wegberg, near Monchengladbach. No 2 Group is also responsible for an RAF training element in Germany, this being the School of Winter Survival, located at Bad Kohlgrub, in Bavaria.

Although much reduced in size, the elements of No 2 Group represent a mini air force, with long-range strike, tactical support, and helicopter transport assets, together with surface-to-air missile units of the RAF Regiment. The future extent of possible locations for deployments of the group's units seems far greater than has been the case over the past decades of Cold War confrontation.

NO 11 GROUP: AIR DEFENCE

The fighter aircraft and its pilot are probably one of the more glamorous and publicly well-known aspects of military aviation, and No 11 Group has a fine tradition to follow, for it was this group that controlled the RAF fighters based in the south-east of England during the Battle of Britain in 1940. Today this group continues with the same task, operating from its HQ at Bentley

Tornado F.3s of No 111 Squadron, seen here at RAF Valley whilst operating with STCAAME for air-to-air missile training.

No 43 Squadron operate Tornado F.3s from RAF Leuchars.

Priory in Middlesex, but is responsible for a far greater area, with the UKADR extending for over 1,100 miles (1,770 km) from north to south, equivalent in distance to that between Italy and Denmark.

With the withdrawal from RAF service of the Phantom FGR.2 in 1992, the front-line long-range air defence of the UKADR is, for the first time for several years, covered by one type of fighter air-craft, this being the Tornado F.3. The planned force of seven air defence squadrons was estab-lished by the end of 1990, with Nos 43 and 111 Squadrons at RAF Leuchars in Fife, Scotland; Nos 11, 23 and 25 Squadrons at RAF Leeming in Yorkshire; and Nos 5 and 29 Squadrons at RAF Coningsby in Lincolnshire. At RAF Leuchars, a couple of Tornados are detailed for quick reaction

alert (QRA) duty in response to any unauthorized intrusion into the UKADR. The aircraft are fully fuelled and armed, and this status is maintained for 365 days a year. Long-range support for this task is provided by tanker aircraft from No 38 Group, if required.

However, due to the changed international situ-ation, the 1993 Defence White Paper proposed reductions in the UK air defence force, with the number of active Tornado F.3s being reduced to 100 aircraft. It also proposed that No 23 Squadron at RAF Leeming should be disbanded in the spring of 1994.

Further air defence is provided by deploying Hawk T.1A aircraft from the Advanced Flying Training Schools (AFTSs) to forward bases, to act as a second line of resistance to any incursion.

A Tornado F.3 of No 29 Squadron gets airborne. (Denis J. Calvert)

These aircraft, which lack airborne interception radar, would operate visually, armed with two AIM-9L Sidewinder AAMs, and be flown by experienced instructors from the AFTSs.

Close-range defence is provided by Rapier surface-to-air missiles (SAMs), operated by squadrons of the RAF Regiment, at RAF bases and at airfields used by the USAF in the UK. More information on these units appears in Chapter Five.

In the spring of 1993, Tornado F.3s were deployed to Italy, in support of the UN's enforcement of a 'no-fly' zone over war-torn Bosnia. Eight aircraft, with their crews drawn from the three squadrons at RAF Leeming, were based at the Italian Air Force facility at Gioia del Colle, and this task was continuing at the time of writing, supported by TriStar tankers, also based in Italy.

Also based at Coningsby is No 56 (Reserve) Squadron, the Tornado F.3 Operational Conversion Unit. Until the middle of 1992, this unit was known as No 229 OCU, and its aircraft carried the markings of No 65 (Shadow) Squadron; but with the withdrawal of the Phantom from service at RAF Wattisham, the traditions of No 56 Squadron were transferred to operate the newer machines at Coningsby, albeit mainly in a training role.

As with other OCUs, the task of No 56(R) Squadron is the conversion of pilots and navigators to the standards required to fly and operate the Tornado F.3 in the air defence role. Pilots and navigators are 'paired' on arrival, and carry out their training together as far as possible throughout their time at the OCU. This training commences with a two-week 'lead-in' course, conducted in the Ground Training Flight (GTF). Here, basic training in air interception is given, involving features such as angles, ranges and other factors. In all, 12 exercises are carried out on the Micro Air Interception Trainer, a computer-based device on which simulated air interceptions can be conducted.

Following the lead-in course, the students then commence the main period of training in the GTF, with a three-week course that extends knowledge of both the Tornado F.3 and the air defence task. Lectures and presentations are generally carried out in the morning, with the afternoons being devoted to practical training. Extensive use is made of computer-based tuition, and considerable investment has been made in the GTF at Coningsby to this end in recent years, with software having been developed by both the RAF and civilian contractors. Lectures are carried out using large twin-screen TV projectors, and each student's table has two visual display units. On these, a variety of training programmes can be

presented, and various problems and questions can be posed, combined with a selection of possible solutions. These can be answered by the students via 'touch-screen' techniques, and their answers are instantly praised for being correct, or analyzed and corrected if in error. Overhead TV cameras enable the lecturer to present illustrations or diagrams directly onto the large screens, and presentation is further aided by the use of hand-held still video cameras.

Many further aids are also employed by the OCU for training, including the Cockpit Procedures Trainer, which simulates most of the systems functions of the Tornado F.3. Use is also made of cardboard replicas of cockpit layouts as an inexpensive method for training crews in the locations of the many cockpit controls and switches. One room contains the Keyboard Displays Trainer, with several positions that each contain parts of the instrumentation in the Tornado's cockpits. Here practical training is conducted in such areas as missile management, inertial navigation systems, radar warning receivers, and head-up displays.

The GTF contains two Tornado Air Interception Trainers (TAIT), in which both pilot and navigator are seated at replica cockpits either side of an instructor. Here lessons, usually of one-hour duration, and comprising some 10 air interception scenarios, are conducted, and the trainee crew is expected to act as a team to counter the posed threat. Seven such lessons are included within the GTF course, but the students will return to the TAIT several times as part of the various phases in the flying syllabus. During the third week of the GTF course, the students make use of the Tornado Mission Simulator (TMS), in which all flight procedures are carried out, commencing with strapping in and engine start, through to shut-down. Each of these TMS 'rides' lasts from one-and-a-half to one-and-three-quarter hours. There are six types of lesson carried out in the TMS, covering most situations, and particular attention is paid to the handling of emergency procedures by the trainee aircrews.

The students then commence their flying programme with the OCU, which runs two courses, depending on the experience of the personnel involved. The *ab initio* course is for pilots who have completed their advanced fast jet and weapons training at RAF Valley or RAF Chivenor, combined with navigators from the Air Navigation School at RAF Finningley. Each course usually consists of four crews (pilot and navigator), with a new course starting every eight weeks. Short courses are also run for aircrew who have previous experience and who are returning to flying following a ground posting, or who are changing flying roles. These courses are similar

The flight-line at RAF Coningsby, with Tornado F.3s of No 56 (Reserve) Squadron.

to the *ab initio* programmes, but the content of the various lessons is reduced. The programme of converting former Phantom aircrews to the Tornado F.3 has now been completed. No 56(R) Squadron has a nominal strength of 24 aircraft, and many of these are of the 'twin-stick' variety, with dual controls. To carry out the flying instruction, this unit can call upon some 50 instructors, divided equally between pilot and navigator roles.

The first part of the flying syllabus is known as the Convex Phase, with crews being introduced to the Tornado F.3; this phase is aimed mainly at the pilots. New pilots fly with the OCU's Qualified Flying Instructors (QFIs), then with OCU Staff Navigators, and finally with their 'paired' navigator. Practice is carried out in formation flying, night operations and instrument rating procedures, and students also continue to make use of the various training aids in the GTF, as described earlier.

Flight-line supporting equipment alongside a No 56 (Reserve) Squadron Tornado F.3.

Beyond this Tornado F.3 of No 56 (Reserve) Squadron are some of the Hardened Aircraft Shelters at RAF Coningsby.

Then follows the Basic Radar Phase, in which the crews start to familiarize themselves with the Tornado F.3's various weapons systems, and commence practising basic airborne interception techniques. This involves one fighter versus one target scenarios at medium, and then low levels, and these develop into one-versus-two 'battles' at medium and low levels. Interceptions from astern are practised, and these progress to head-on attacks, followed by reattacks from astern. For these scenarios, training sorties are carried out with the trainee pilot flying with an OCU staff navigator, or a student navigator flying with a staff pilot.

The next section of training at RAF Coningsby is the Applied Radar Phase, in which the basic tuition is taken to advanced levels, with many varieties of air interception scenarios and techniques. This involves radar interceptions being turned into visual air combat situations, with the aircraft being used to the airframe limits. Tactical missions are carried out at low-level, while supersonic sorties are conducted at high altitudes. The majority of air interception training sorties carried out by No 56(R) Squadron take place out over the North Sea, although other areas over the sea around the UK are used depending on weather conditions.

Following their training with the F.3 OCU, the aircrews are posted to the various air defence squadrons, although rarely together as the pairs that trained at Coningsby. At the squadrons, the interception training continues, with such scenar-

ios as two fighters versus multiple targets.

The Tornado F.3s are but part a greater system that is tasked with the air defence of the UKADR. To be fully effective, any air defence system must have the intelligence provided by comprehensive radar cover, as was so vividly illustrated in the Battle of Britain. This system has recently been greatly enhanced with the introduction into service of the Sentry AEW.1. Also, a great deal of investment has gone into updating the ground-based air defence radar stations.

The air defence radar system is known as the Improved UK Air Defence Ground Environment (IUKADGE), and this has seen many changes in recent years. The emphasis has been to get away from the large fixed installations with heavy radar heads in favour of smaller, more mobile units. These new radars are fully integrated with the command and control headquarters, with communications via multiple-pathed data links, which are resistant to the effects of electromagnetic pulses.

The UK is divided into two air defence sectors, with the division lying along the Parallel of 55° North, approximately level with Newcastle. Each sector is under the control of a Sector Operation Centre (SOC), the SOC for the Southern Sector being at RAF Neatishead in Norfolk, whilst the Northern Sector is controlled from RAF Buchan in Grampian. The SOCs are now housed in recently-built underground bunkers, with direct data links to the Air Defence Operations Centre, located within the Primary War HQ at Strike

Command HQ, RAF High Wycombe. Information can be exchanged with air defence radar systems in other NATO countries, and with the SACEUR HQ at Mons in Belgium. Each SOC has a number of responsibilities, including the command and control of assigned assets in its area, an evaluation of the threat, the planning of tactics and force dispositions, and the monitoring of activity.

Each sector has a reserve SOC at an alternative location, the Northern Reserve SOC being at RAF Boulmer in Northumberland, while the Southern Reserve SOC is situated at Ash, in Kent. Co-located with each SOC is a Control and Reporting Centre (CRC), whose function is to compile and disseminate the information that it has obtained and report this to the SOCs. Both sectors also contain a number of Control and Reporting Points (CRPs), which supplement the CRCs. Also, the CRCs and CRPs can control and co-ordinate the weapons systems, fighter aircraft and support aircraft (such as tankers) that it has at its disposal. The CRCs and the CRPs are equipped with radars and communication facilities to suit their tasks. Next in the chain comes the Reporting Points (RPs), which are equipped only with radars, and many of the these are located on the same sites as the CRPs or CRCs. The SOCs, CRCs and CRPs can exchange and view each others' displays via secure data links, and can communicate mass information with the Sentry AEW.1 aircraft, as well as with suitably-equipped ships. CRP/RP locations include Portreath (Cornwall) in the Southern Sector, with Benbecula and Saxa Vord (Shetland Isles), amongst others, being situated in the Northern Sector.

As stated earlier, the modernization of air defence radar in recent years has concentrated on providing mobile systems, as opposed to the older fixed (and vulnerable) installations. Various types of three-dimensional, phased array radars, operating at different frequencies, and designated as Types 91, 92 or 93, have been acquired from a number of manufacturers, and these are capable of being transported between dispersed, but prepared sites.

Further information on intrusions into the UKADR can be provided by the Ballistic Missile Early Warning System (BMEWS). This is a chain of three detectors, primarily tasked with the detection of attacks by intercontinental ballistic missiles, but they can also provide data concerning aircraft movements. The UK element of BMEWS is located at RAF Fylingdales, in Yorkshire, while the remaining parts of the chain are situated at Thule in Greenland, and Clear in Alaska. This system has been upgraded with new technology and equipment in recent years, and the three large spheres that protected the radar antennas, and which dominated the landscape of the

The navigator of a Tornado F.3 climbs out of the aircraft at the end of another sortie.

North Yorkshire Moors for so many years, have now been removed, to be replaced by a smaller, pyramid-type structure.

Complementing the radar stations are the seven Sentry AEW.1 aircraft, operated by No 8 Squadron from RAF Waddingtom, near Lincoln. This unit was declared fully operational in early August 1992, and the introduction of the Sentry

Mobile air defence radars such as this have replaced the former fixed installations.

No 8 Squadron operates the Sentry AEW.1 from RAF Waddington.

has seen a vast increase in the RAF's airborne early warning capabilities, when compared with the Shackleton AEW.2 that was previously operated in this role. The Sentry is not just another type of aircraft that fulfils a role, but is an integral part of the IUKADGE system, with data link communications to the air defence radar chain and to the Tornado F.3 units, amongst others, via the new Joint Tactical Information Distribution System.

The arrival of the Sentries at Waddington has necessitated a considerable amount of support work, with a large new hangar being constructed that is capable of housing two of the new aircraft. Contained in this hangar is a large, rail-mounted servicing gantry that can be rolled in to either side of the aircraft, together with an overhead crane system. Outside the hangar is a large parking apron, and the whole site is surrounded by security fencing, with strictly controlled access.

The training of the 17-strong crew of the Sentry has involved a considerable investment for the RAF, with two simulators being employed, one for flight-deck procedures and the other for tuition on mission tasks. The first two RAF crews for the Sentry were trained with the NATO AEW Force in Germany, and training then continued at Waddington with the Sentry Training Squadron, which is, in effect, an OCU for the type, to build up to an establishment of nine crews. The training of a Sentry crew occupies a period of some six months. The early part of this training programme was disrupted in mid-1992 as two RAF Sentries were deployed to Italy as part of the NATO elements tasked with UN surveillance duties connected with the civil war in the former Jugoslavia.

Another important element at RAF Waddington is the Mission Support Wing (MSW). Here, tapes for missions undertaken by the Sentries are prepared. These provide background information for display on the consoles in the Sentry, with such items as topographical data, airways, beacons and other navaids, danger areas, etc. The MSW is also responsible for evaluating tapes upon each aircraft's return from a mission, and for their storage.

Out of the Sentry's crew of 17, four are on the flight-deck, consisting of two pilots, a navigator and a flight engineer. The mission crew of 13 is commanded by a Tactical Director, and other positions include a Fighter Allocator, a Surveillance Controller and a Link Manager. There are also two Fighter Controllers, two Surveillance Operators, an Electronic Surveillance Measures (ESM) Operator and a Communications Operator. The crew is completed by three Technicians, covering communications, radar and displays. Most of these functions are self-explanatory, with the Technicians being responsible for maintaining various items of equipment in working order, as far as possible. The ESM Operators seek and listen for radar or electronic emissions, whilst the Communications Operator monitors and plots all transmissions received or heard.

There are nine consoles in the Sentry, arranged in three rows of three across the fuselage, the console displays in the RAF machines being in full-colour. Each console can operate independently of

One of the RAF's Sentry AEW.1s climbs away from RAF Waddington.

the others, displaying varying elements of the whole 'picture'.

Operation of the RAF's Sentries is integrated with the NATO Airborne Early Warning Force (NAEWF), and tasking for missions is issued from SACEUR on a day-to day basis. The NAEWF is equipped with about 18 Boeing E-3A Sentries, of similar layout to the RAF's E-3D model, and these aircraft are based at Geilenkirchen, in Germany. The NAEWF also operates three Boeing 707s, without the radar fittings, for crew conversion training and other duties. Both NAEWF and RAF Sentries have been involved in monitoring the civil war in Bosnia, flying surveillance missions over the Adriatic and neighbouring countries in support of UN operations.

Training for fighter controllers, for service on board the RAF Sentries and at ground stations of the IUKADGE system, is carried out at the School of Fighter Control, situated at RAF Boulmer.

No 11 Group is also responsible for what remains of the Royal Observer Corps (ROC). This organization originated in the 1920s, and throughout the Second World War served with distinction in the role of plotting and reporting aircraft movements. In the 1950s, the ROC's main role turned to the monitoring and reporting of nuclear explosions and radioactive fallout. Following a major reorganization in 1968, the ROC continued with the nuclear role, but also maintained its skills in aircraft recognition. These tasks were carried out from over 800 reporting Posts, located throughout the UK, which reported to 25 Control Centres.

ROC strength was about 10,000, the majority of whom were part-time volunteers, administered by a small, full-time cadre. The Commandant of the ROC was always a full-time serving RAF officer, of Air Commodore rank.

However, the changed international situation resulted in most of the ROC being 'stood down' in September 1991. At that time, MoD(Air) decided that a small cadre of ROC volunteers should be retained, against a possible future requirement within the Home Commands. A number of units remain, known as Nuclear Reporting Cells (NRCs), and these are located at various military HQs of all three Services throughout the UK. These NRCs are manned by about 220 officers and other ranks, under the command of the Senior Air Staff Officer within HQ No 11 Group, who has assumed the temporary role of Commandant ROC. HQ ROC was restructured, and the organization is currently administered by two full-time ROC officers, together with two civilian staff members. Along with many other defence-related elements, the future of the ROC is under review at the time of writing.

The Battle of Britain Memorial Flight: 'Lest We Forget'

A sure crowd-stopper at any air display, the Battle of Britain Memorial Flight (BBMF) is dedicated as a flying memorial to the many thousands of airmen who lost their lives whilst serving their country. It falls within the administration of No 11 Group and has been based at RAF Coningsby since 1976. It attends some 150 events each year, and it usually provides a formation consisting of the Lancaster, flanked by a Spitfire and the Hurricane, although the actual aircraft displayed depends on the event being attended and, of course, serviceability.

Currently, the BBMF comprises one Lancaster B.1, one Hurricane IIc, one Spitfire IIa, one Spitfire Vb and three Spitfire XIXs. The BBMF also operates a de Havilland Devon, dating from 1949, as a support aircraft, and a Chipmunk, which is used as a familiarization trainer in the operation of piston-engined aircraft with tail-wheel undercarriages. A recent addition has been a C-47 Dakota, which until early 1992 was in use with the Defence Research Agency (formerly the Royal Aerospace Establishment and Royal Aircraft Establishment) at Farnborough. With the retirement of the Shackleton from RAF service, the Dakota will be used to provide training for pilots of the Lancaster B.1, in the techniques required for handling a multi-engined aircraft with a tailwheel undercarriage. The Dakota will also act as a further support transport for the BBMF.

Apart from the Commanding Officer and the 18 ground crew, the pilots of the BBMF are all volunteers, and they all give up many weekends through the summer months to display and maintain the aircraft. The pilots attached to the BBMF carry out their display flying in addition to their normal duties through the week with the RAF, and many of them are based at RAF Coningsby, where they fly aircraft somewhat faster than those operated by the BBMF!

NO 18 GROUP: MARITIME OPERATIONS

The role of No 18 Group within Strike Command is broadly similar to that which it undertook when part of the formerly separate Coastal Command, i.e. the control of air assets operating in the maritime environment. Currently, No 18 Group is responsible for a variety of aircraft and tasks, ranging from long-range maritime patrols by Nimrods, maritime strike, providing target facilities for other units within Strike Command and also the vital tasks of Search and Rescue (SAR).

26 Nimrod MR.2Ps are in service at RAF Kinloss, operated by the four squadrons of the Kinloss Maritime Wing. (RAF Kinloss)

The various pods and antennas that adorn the Nimrod MR.2P are clearly visible on this example as it prepares to land.

All these activities are controlled from the Group HQ, located at Northwood, near London.

Following the 'Options for Change' programme, some changes occurred in the disposition of the Nimrod MR.2P fleet. The squadron based at RAF St Mawgan in Cornwall, No 42, was disbanded, and all Nimrods were located at RAF Kinloss in Scotland. Here, a number of aircraft were withdrawn from service, leaving 26 Nimrod MR.2Ps in use with the three based squadrons, namely Nos 120, 201 and 206, and the Nimrod OCU. However, the existence of No 42 Squadron was not allowed to die completely, as the Nimrod OCU, No 236, which redeployed from St Mawgan to Kinloss in 1992, was subsequently redesignated as No 42 (Reserve) Squadron.

The principal peacetime task of the Nimrod force is the surveillance of the sea areas that lie within the UKADR, monitoring both surface and sub-surface activities. Nimrods also form part of the SAR force, with one aircraft kept on short-notice stand-by for long-range search, and co-ordination of rescue forces in the area of any incident.

Apart from the primary tasks already mentioned, the Nimrod units compete with each other to find an aircrew that will represent the UK in the Fincastle Trophy competition, which is held annually between aircrews from the UK, Australia, New Zealand, and Canada, the trophy being awarded to the crew that displays the best expertise in anti-submarine warfare (ASW).

As already noted, the task of training aircrews for the Nimrod force is entrusted to No 42 (Reserve) Squadron, the Nimrod Operational Conversion Unit. As with the other OCUs, this unit runs a number of courses, the principal one of which is the Long Course, designed for *ab initio* training of personnel who are new to the Nimrod. Three of these courses are run each year, with each course lasting for six months and comprising two 13-place student crews. The training commences with eight weeks spent in the Ground School, with separate streams of training to cover the various tasks undertaken by a Nimrod crew. Use is made of Part Task Trainers, which are replicas of separate sections and workstations within the Nimrod, and 14 exercises are undertaken in the Nimrod Instrument Trainer, this being a replica of the Nimrod's flight-deck, with functioning instruments. Within the Ground School period, eight exercises are carried out in the Nimrod Dynamic Flight Simulator, with representative motion. Crews also attend RAF North Luffenham for aeromedical tests, and travel to RAF St Mawgan for survival training, both these items being in the Ground School schedule.

In week nine of the course, the trainees are brought together to form a 13-person crew, and will work and train as a team for the rest of their time with the OCU. Two weeks are then spent on the pilot conversion phase, which involves 23 hours of flying in eight sorties. Pilots are expected to 'go solo' (i.e. without an instructor on board) on the eighth sortie, with the two pilots on board each carrying out a couple of circuits in the left-hand seat.

The applied flying phase commences in week

11, and the syllabus calls for 80 flying hours over 15 flights. This phase concentrates on training the complete crew for the tasks undertaken by the Nimrod force, covering maritime patrol and surveillance, ASW and SAR, amongst others. One of the flights involves a deployment to RAF Akrotiri in Cyprus, and to Gibraltar, to provide an insight into overseas operations. This flying is interspersed with seven periods in the Flight Simulator, together with 13 exercises in the Maritime Crew Trainer (MCT), a static replica of the main fuselage of the Nimrod aft of the flight-deck.

On completion of their training with the OCU, the crew is posted amongst the three operational squadrons, to suit their requirements for crew positions. Pilots join the squadrons to act as co-pilots; they are promoted to aircraft captain on merit.

No 42(R) Squadron also runs a number of other courses. These include refresher training for those who have had previous experience of Nimrod operations, and who are returning to Kinloss after a ground posting or other tasks. Two of these refresher courses are run each year, with about five students on each receiving training over a two-month period. The training provided on the refresher course is adjusted to take account of the students' preceding experience, and includes nine airborne sorties, combined with five exercises in

the MCT. The conversion training of pilots and flight engineers destined to serve on the Nimrod R.1Ps of No 51 Squadron at RAF Wyton is also carried out by the OCU, as are ad hoc familiarization courses for senior officers. To provide all this training, the OCU has some 65 staff, some of whom are civilians, and three of the Nimrods based at RAF Kinloss are nominally set aside from the pool of aircraft for OCU activities.

Maritime Strike

For many years, No 18 Group has been responsible for two squadrons dedicated to the role of maritime strike, these being Nos 12 and 208 Squadrons, based at RAF Lossiemouth with Buccaneer S.2B aircraft. Under 'Options for Change', this element has been upgraded by replacing the venerable Buccaneers with a number of converted Tornado GR.1s. These have been modified for the maritime strike role, with the ability to carry the Sea Eagle anti-ship missile, in which configuration they are known as GR.1Bs. No 12 Squadron disbanded as a Buccaneer unit towards the end of September 1993, and No 27 Squadron, a Tornado GR.1 unit at RAF Marham, was renumbered as No 12 the following month. The new No 12 later transferred to RAF Lossiemouth. No 617 Squadron (the famous 'Dambusters' unit) made a similar move in the

Initially equipped with Tornado GR.1s (as illustrated), No 617 Squadron is receiving Tornado GR.1Bs for its new maritime strike role.

No 12 Squadron now operates the Tornado, having flown the Buccaneer for 24 years. Initially, No 12 have used the GR.1s previously flown by No 27 Squadron; it is due to receive the GR.1B variant for anti-shipping tasks. (Denis J. Calvert)

spring of 1994, as a replacement for the disbanded No 208 Squadron. No 27 Squadron has been reformed as a reserve training unit within Strike Command, taking over the tasks of No 240 OCU at RAF Odiham and trading in its Tornados for Chinooks and Pumas, and No 208 lives on as a Hawk-equipped reserve training unit at RAF Valley.

The demise of No 208 and its Buccaneers in the maritime strike role also brought about the retirement of the RAF's last operational Hunters, a handful of two-seaters having been used by Nos 12 and 208 Squadrons as continuation trainers for Buccaneer crews.

Search and Rescue

The deployment of SAR units and equipment underwent considerable change recently, and this process is still being carried out. The significant element in these changes was the decision to withdraw the Wessex HC.2 helicopter from the SAR role, although this process will not be completed until 1996. It is due to be replaced by the addition of six new Sea King HAR.3As, delivery of which will commence in late 1995 to supplement the existing Sea King force. Also, it was decided to reduce the number of bases at which SAR flights are located. This decision caused a great deal of public protest, but it must be borne in mind that the main role of the RAF's SAR helicopters is to provide cover for military aviation

activities, such as training and exercises, in the areas where these occur most. Thus, if military aviation is reduced in a particular area, as it has been as a consequence of recent changes in the international situation, then the need for military SAR assets also declines.

The main responsibility for the SAR of civilians rests with the Department of Transport, who can call on the assistance of a number of resources, one of these being the RAF's SAR helicopters. Happily, calls for the helicopters to assist in military aircraft accidents are few and far between, the vast majority of their tasks being in response to requests from the civilian authorities, such as the Coast Guard and the Lifeboat Service. The co-ordination of calls for assistance is handled by two Rescue Co-ordination Centres (RCCs), who also control the rescue operation and the services, both civilian and military, involved. These RCCs are located at Pitreavie Castle, Dunfermline, in Scotland, for the northern part of the UK, and at Plymouth in Devon to cover the southern half of the UK. In 1993 these two RCCs together dealt with over 2,100 incidents. There are plans to close the southern RCC in 1995, with the whole country being covered by the northern RCC, equipped with enhanced communications and other facilities.

Under the recent changes, 'B' Flight of No.22 Squadron, based at RAF Leuchars, was withdrawn in April 1993, and 'E' Flight of the same squadron was stood down at RAF Coltishall in

The Wessex HC.2s of No 22 Squadron will continue to operate in the search and rescue role until 1996.

mid-1994, at which time 'A' Flight of No 22 Squadron at RAF Chivenor re-equipped with Sea Kings. 'C' Flight of No 22 Squadron is not due to receive its Sea Kings at RAF Valley until early 1996. The Sea King-equipped flights of No 202 Squadron at RAF Leconfield, RAF Lossiemouth and RAF Boulmer remain unchanged, but 'B' Flight at RAF Brawdy closed in April 1994, and 'C' Flight at RAF Manston in Kent moved to RAF Wattisham in Suffolk shortly afterwards. Most of the SAR flights are on stand-by 24 hours a day, 365 days a year. The first female SAR helicopter pilot in the RAF, Flt Lt Nicola Smith, joined 'A' Flight of No 202 Squadron at RAF Boulmer in mid-1993.

The HQ elements of the two SAR squadrons were redeployed in 1992, with HQ No 22 Squadron departing RAF Finningley for RAF St Mawgan, as did the engineering support element for SAR helicopters. The SAR Engineering Squadron is responsible for the major servicing and modifications of both types of SAR heli-

No 202 Squadron operates the Sea King HAR.3 from four locations.

copters. HQ No 202 Squadron moved north from Finningley to its new base of RAF Boulmer, whilst the RAF Sea King Training Unit (SKTU) moved the short distance from RNAS Culdrose to RAF St Mawgan in April 1993.

The Search and Rescue Training Unit (SARTU) continues to be based at RAF Valley in Anglesey, and the close proximity of rugged coastlines and mountains make this an ideal location for the training of SAR techniques. This training covers pilots, navigators and loadmasters, together with Air Electronic Operators (AEOps) who will progress to the Sea King. A variety of courses are run at the SARTU, including basic tuition for SAR crews which forms part of their advanced flying training course at RAF Shawbury. Further courses at Valley cover specialized training for aircrew transferring to SAR units from other helicopters or from fixed-wing flying, training for students from overseas Services and familiarization instruction for senior officers.

A fundamental aspect of the SAR training that is conducted at SARTU is crew co-ordination and co-operation. The crew member who is lowered on the end of a 300-ft (91.4 m) cable, onto the deck of a violently rocking ship in raging seas, must have complete confidence in the winch operator in the helicopter above. Similarly, the pilot, who is blind to the activity directly below the helicopter whilst it is in the hover over the incident, must also rely on the winch operator for the accurate instructions required to position the aircraft. The task of winch operator is undertaken by the navigator or the AEOp.

Initial training is conducted over level areas, to establish basic SAR skills and procedures. Tuition in hovering and winch operation over small boats is carried out in nearby Holyhead Harbour. Activity then progresses to coastline locations, where crews encounter the problems caused by air turbulence around cliffs. Crews are required to plan the sequence of a simulated 'rescue', and full consideration must be given to the safety of the aircraft and of the crewman hanging on the winch cable below it. In a confined location, such as against a cliff face, an escape path for the aircraft must be planned, in the event of an emergency or an engine failure. The mountains of Snowdonia provide a further and dramatic location for SAR training, where the skills of the crew are enhanced to cater for the possible hazards that may be encountered, such as sudden changes in weather conditions, severe turbulence, aircraft performance and orientation.

All crew members destined for SAR operations pass through the SARTU, with the main course lasting 10 weeks and involving 60 hours of flying training, plus periods of ground tuition. Some 150 students are trained each year; on completion of

this training those who will fly in the Wessex proceed directly to No 22 Squadron, whilst the aircrew for No 202 Squadron transfer to the SKTU.

Although they will have trained on the Wessex helicopter at SARTU, the crews that transfer to No 22 Squadron, who also fly the Wessex at its dispersed flights, are not considered to be fully operational, and are thus required to undertake a further period of conversion training. This builds on the tuition already received at SARTU, and covers all aspects of SAR work with advanced techniques. This involves flying and winch operation by night, co-ordinating with other organizations in the SAR system (such as the Coast Guard, the Lifeboat Service, the RAF Mountain Rescue Teams and the emergency services), and the handling of casualties into and out of the aircraft. This continuation and conversion training with the squadron is checked and tested at regular intervals by Standards Officers, and is completed by the flight to which the individual crew member is posted.

Prior to its move to RAF St Mawgan in April 1993, the SKTU was based at RNAS Culdrose, also in Cornwall, for the previous 16 years, where it operated alongside the similar machines of the Royal Navy. The role of the SKTU is the conversion training of all RAF aircrew who will fly the Sea King with No 202 Squadron at its detached flights, following initial SAR training at the SARTU. A full Sea King crew, which consists of two pilots, an AEOp/winch operator and a loadmaster/winchman, are trained together on each course, which covers a period of some four months. The first two weeks of the course are spent in the ground school, whilst the flying training deals with general handling, together with day, night and instrument flying that is relevant to the SAR task. The course training culminates in a three-day SAR exercise. Further courses run by the SKTU deal with refresher flying for aircrew returning to SAR duties, and for instructors and senior officers.

Although having passed through the training programmes at both SARTU and SKTU, aircrew posted to No 202 Squadron face yet more tuition. This is designed to enhance their skills both as individuals and as a team, and to fully exploit the capabilities of the Sea King, particularly at night or in bad weather and poor visibility, with the increasing use of NVGs.

SAR missions are also carried out by helicopter-equipped squadrons based overseas, these being No 28 Squadron in Hong Kong, No 78 Squadron in the Falklands and No 84 Squadron in Cyprus.

A further significant element within the RAF's SAR organization are the six Mountain Rescue Teams (MRTs). They are based at RAF St Athan, RAF Valley, RAF Stafford, RAF Leeming, RAF

Leuchars and RAF Kinloss; these locations providing ready access to much of the remote and mountainous areas of the UK. Each MRT consists of about 25 to 30 members, a few of whom are full-time, whilst the remainder are part-time and undertake duty with the MRT in addition to their usual RAF tasks. All MRT team members are volunteers, and they all spend a great deal of their own spare time, particularly at weekends, training in the rescue role. All MRTs are equipped with suitable vehicles to travel over rough terrain, and they also have a range of equipment to assist in climbing to the scene of any incident, and to help in rescuing casualties. Each MRT has detailed knowledge of the local area, and all are on stand-by of one hour's notice throughout the year. On many inland rescue situations, the MRTs work in co-ordination with the SAR helicopters, and often the MRTs are the only agency that can successfully carry out a rescue, particularly in conditions of poor visibility.

Other No 18 Group units

RAF Wyton, near Huntingdon, was the home for a number of units that fall within the jurisdiction of No 18 Group. However, with the transfer of this station to the new Logistics Command as an HQ facility, these squadrons have had to find new homes. One of these is No 39 (1 Photographic Reconnaissance Unit) Squadron, which moved to RAF Marham in December 1993. This small unit could well be the last in the RAF to operate the venerable Canberra, and it has re-adopted the squadron number that was its identity for many

years, having for a period been known as No 1 PRU. It now has a dual title, as shown above. Its equipment is the Canberra PR.9, with an establishment of five aircraft (two of which are held in reserve), and five crews, each comprising a pilot and a navigator.

No 39 (1 PRU) Squadron has a variety of tasks, including low-level reconnaissance by day and night, medium- and high-level photography with vertical and oblique cameras, maritime reconnaissance, and aerial survey work. Low-level tasks are defined as being those missions that are carried out at altitudes between 250 ft (76.2 m) and 2,000 ft (610 m). The range of assignments the squadron is called upon to perform is wide, including surveying the area of aircraft accidents, and photographing damage caused by natural disasters and terrorist outrages.

Maritime reconnaissance involves the monitoring of shipping around the UK, with regard to possible pollution and illegal fishing, together with hydrographical surveys for the production of charts for the Royal Navy. The Canberra PR.9's thermal imaging capability with its infra-red (IR) linescan equipment offers better definition than that offered by the far newer Tornado GR.1A. One of the roles in which this equipment comes into its own is the surveying of areas for crop diseases, and the recent spread of Dutch Elm Disease amongst the woodlands of the UK was recorded by No 39 Squadron, with the IR cameras showing the difference between living and dead trees clearly.

Turning to the survey role, this squadron is currently undertaking a complete photographic sur-

The few Canberra PR.9s in service are operated by No 39 (1 PRU) Squadron from RAF Marham.

vey of the whole of the UK, for the production of new maps. This involves precision flying along parallel tracks, five miles (eight kilometres) apart, at 12,500 ft (3,810 m), and perfectly clear weather is required to achieve satisfactory results. Up to the middle of 1993, some 50 per cent of this task had been completed, after 18 months of work, and this photography was continuing at the time of writing. Similar survey work is also undertaken in (and paid for by) overseas countries.

Having for so many years flown various marks of the Canberra, No 100 Squadron, another unit within No 18 Group, commenced its transition to the Hawk in September 1991, and was fully-equipped with the smaller aircraft by the beginning of 1992. Like No 39 (1 PRU) Squadron, No 100 has also moved from RAF Wyton, having transferred north to RAF Finningley, near Doncaster, in the autumn of 1993. The general task of its Hawk T.1/.1As remains that of providing target facilities, in a variety of forms, for operational units of the RAF, other elements of the British Services and NATO forces. This covers items such as banner towing for air-to-air gunnery training, acting as 'silent' targets for all types of radar surveillance, and providing simulated targets for Rapier missile units. In the last task, the Hawk provides a greater degree of realism, being smaller, faster and much more agile than the Canberras previously used.

A frequent mission involves two or more Hawks acting as intruders to enable the air defence forces of Tornado F.3s, Sentry AEW.1s, and ground-based radar stations to practise their interception skills and procedures. Thus the Hawks of No 100 Squadron can often be found at Tornado F.3 fighter bases, as common briefing and debriefing forms a valuable part of air defence training. Due to the small size of the Hawk, a small cylindrical pod is sometimes carried under the fuselage which emits signals to enhance the radar signature of this aircraft, to assist in the training of *ab initio* radar operators. Some missions are flown in co-ordination with the Canberras of No 360 Squadron.

Training with air defence units also takes place in Cyprus, where No 100 Squadron frequently detaches about three Hawks to RAF Akrotiri to participate in the Armament Practice Camps (APCs). Hawks from this unit also detach to the Scottish bases of Kinloss and Lossiemouth to participate in Joint Maritime Courses, acting as silent targets for radar and defensive systems on Royal Navy and other NATO vessels. However, the future for No 100 Squadron is rather uncertain, as there are plans to turn the tasks of target facilities over to private contractors, and thus the unit may have disbanded by the end of 1994.

Turning to No 360 Squadron, this unit is distinctive in two respects: firstly, it is the youngest squadron in the RAF; and secondly, 25 per cent of its personnel are members of the Royal Navy, with every fourth of the squadron's Commanding Officers being from the RN. Formed for the first time in April 1966, No 360 Squadron has operated various marks of the Canberra in the same role since that date. The overall task of this unit is to provide electronic warfare (EW) training for the

No 100 Squadron is equipped with Hawk T.1s (as shown here) and T.1As, providing targets in various forms for training.

The Canberra T.17/.17As of No 360 Squadron are nearing the end of their service lives. (Denis J. Calvert)

British Services, primarily for the RAF, but also for the Royal Navy and Army. Amongst the squadron's 'customers' are air defence radar units, fighter squadrons, ships and SAM units. No 360's Canberras are excellent vehicles for EW training, having ample power available to transmit a variety of signals aimed at confusing and disrupting the radar equipment of units undergoing tuition or exercise. The Canberras emit signals that can jam or severely confuse a radar picture, present false targets, or, alternatively, hide real radar returns. The object is to present possible hostile scenarios to radar operators, in order that they may practice the procedures to overcome the EW 'weapons' that are being directed at them.

Communications are another aspect of military activity that can be disrupted, and No 360 Squadron also undertakes training tasks in this field, having the ability to jam actual, and issue 'spoof' transmissions, as appropriate. During exercises that often involve simulated attacks against the UK, Canberras from this unit fly ahead of the incoming strike aircraft, emitting signals to confuse and interfere with the defending radar displays. Sorties are mostly of two, to two-and-a-half hours duration, ranging from low-level to over 40,000 ft (12,200 m).

The squadron operates four Canberra T.17s and six T.17As, the latter model having updated avionics and an Omega navigation system. Normal crew is three, consisting of pilot, naviga-

Three Nimrod R.1Ps are flown by No 51 Squadron from RAF Wyton. Note the lack of the tail boom, and the numerous extra aerials.

tor, and AEOp. As with No 100 Squadron, however, the ECM training functions of No 360 Squadron may be transferred to private contractors by the end of 1994, thus marking the demise of some of the oldest aircraft in the RAF.

The remaining unit to be mentioned in connection with RAF Wyton is No 51 Squadron, with a complement of just three Nimrod R.1Ps. This unit is seldom in the limelight, and its aircraft are rarely seen as it carries out its quiet task of electronic intelligence-gathering. Very little information is available for publication on the activities of No 51 Squadron, but it is known that it took part in the Falklands conflict in 1982, and in the Gulf War of 1991. The squadron was reformed in 1958, and since then has carried out its current or similar roles, with Canberras and Comets being used before the arrival of the Nimrods. The squadron moved to RAF Wyton in 1963, and is due to move to RAF Waddington in January 1995, as the accommodation at Wyton is required for an alternative use, as already stated.

Another RAF station that falls within the remit of No 18 Group is RAF Manston, on the eastern tip of Kent. This is the home of the Defence Fire Services Central Training Establishment.

NO 38 GROUP: TRANSPORTS AND TANKERS

The title of No 38 Group will be remembered by many as that of the organization which provided spectacular set-piece 'battles' at numerous air displays in the 1960s and 1970s. Of course, this group had a far more serious purpose, being responsible for tactical operations, with elements comprising transport and close air support aircraft, together with helicopters. In fact, this group represented a complete small air force, with the assets and ability to rapidly respond to emergency situations. However in 1983, No 38 Group disappeared, the result of being merged into No 1 Group, within Strike Command.

Some nine years later, on 1 November 1992, No 38 Group was reformed, with its HQ at RAF High Wycombe, alongside HQ Strike Command. The task of the group is responsibility for the transport aircraft and air-to-air refuelling tankers of the RAF, involving 11 units based at four RAF stations in the UK. No 38 Group is also responsible for a number of other elements connected with the main transport role, together with the operation of RAF facilities on Ascension Island, in the South Atlantic.

Within No 38 Group, all transport aircrew are categorized in relation to each individual's ability, and on joining a squadron from an OCU, an individual would be of 'D' category. After six months with the squadron, he or she would then return to the OCU for a refresher course. This course lasts for two weeks, and involves at least four sessions in the simulator and four airborne training and checkout sorties, amongst other instruction. Upon completion, those on 'D' category would be expected to have graduated to 'C' category, which is the average standard that all aircrew members are expected to achieve and maintain.

After a period of one year, 'C' category aircrew are expected to undergo a further refresher course, either to confirm their 'C' status, or to advance to 'B' category, which is considered to be of above average ability. Those of 'B' category status can let 18 months elapse before they are required to go back to the OCU for the refresher course, and after a tour with a squadron they may be selected to be posted for training as an instructor with the Central Flying School. The highest category, 'A', is achieved by very few personnel, and the refresher course in this category need only be taken at intervals of two years. At the other end of the scale, a serious error may involve the individual being reclassified as 'E' category, which would involve periods of retraining to rectify the problem.

The principal base within No 38 Group is RAF Brize Norton, near Witney in Oxfordshire, which contains a number of units. The distinction of operating the RAF's largest and heaviest aircraft type falls to No 216 Squadron, which is equipped with nine Lockheed TriStars of four different variants. This unit claims the distinction of being the first military jet transport squadron to be formed in the world, having operated de Havilland Comet 2s and 4s between 1956 and 1975.

The current principal task for No 216 Squadron is to provide the air link to the Falkland Islands, via Ascension Island, and two services depart on this route each week, mainly operated by the TriStar C.2/.2A variants. Each leg of this route involves a flight time of about eight hours, and crews are changed (or 'slipped') at Ascension. A further regular service is the weekly flight to RAF Akrotiri in Cyprus, but in addition to these tasks, No 216's aircraft can be seen at any location worldwide where the three British Services operate and require airlift support. The large capacity of the TriStar means that it is particularly useful when supporting unit deployments and transfers, such as to and from Germany, and across the Atlantic to Canada. For these flights, the aircraft's crew would normally comprise a captain, co-pilot, flight engineer, loadmaster and four stewards. A ground engineer and two other personnel for servicing support are also carried if the aircraft is to be away from Brize Norton for any length of time.

One of the four TriStar KC.1 variants operated by No 216 Squadron from RAF Brize Norton, seen here in its landing configuration. The bump under the rear fuselage houses the Hose Drum Unit for air-to-air refuelling.

The K.1 and KC.1 variants of the TriStar provide a further task for No 216, that of air-to-air refuelling (AAR). This facility is exercised regularly in the various AAR areas around the UK, and is used to support the overseas deployment of RAF combat aircraft. Aircraft wishing to refuel from a TriStar join to formate with the tanker off the starboard wing, and then move to behind the centreline to take fuel, the operation being moni-tored and controlled by the flight engineer. Having received sufficient fuel, the recipient then formates off the tanker's port wing, prior to departing.

The squadron's tankers were heavily involved in the Gulf War, providing AAR support for the combat air patrols mounted by air defence units. In mid-1993, two tankers were deployed to Malpensa, in Italy, to support combat aircraft

The sole TriStar C.2A of No 216 Squadron. The C.2/.2As lack an air-to-air refuelling capability, hence the smooth line of the lower rear fuselage.

involved in the UN operations to enforce the 'no-fly' zone over Bosnia. No 216 Squadron has some 22 crews on strength, 10 of these being cleared for AAR operations.

The squadron has its own Training Flight, but conversion of pilots and flight engineers to the TriStar commences at London's Heathrow Airport. Here, under a contract with British Airways (BA), these crew members undertake a ground training course, which includes the use of the BA TriStar flight simulator. They then move to RAF Brize Norton to continue their training, with tuition in the Ground School combined with three local flying exercises. Flight-deck crew then commence route-flying under supervision, and must complete 12 sectors (a sector being, say, UK to Ascension Island) before they are considered to join a crew in the co-pilot's position. Five flight-deck crews are converted to the TriStar each year, and the above training programme lasts for some four months. There are plans to install the RAF's own TriStar flight simulator at Brize Norton in 1996.

Operating alongside No 216 Squadron at Brize Norton is No 10 Squadron, who have operated the VC-10 C.1 transport since 1966. This unit operates a number of scheduled routes, with two services a week to Washington DC in the USA, and weekly flights to Germany, Decimomannu in Sicily, and to Belize. The squadron has a heavy programme of flights in support of all three Services, and its aircraft can be seen all over the world. Such operations could include moving Royal Marines to Norway for winter exercises, Army units to Alberta in Canada for training on

the ranges there, transferring units to Kenya for hot-weather training, and changing garrisons at various overseas locations. The recent deployments of RAF combat aircraft to bases in Saudi Arabia, Turkey and Italy, in support of UN operations, has further added to this unit's workload.

No 10 Squadron is also tasked to provide special flights. Included in this category are aeromedical evacuation flights, and a crew is on stand-by for seven days a week to cover this task. The transportation of VIPs is a further role, and the squadron's aircraft can be converted to incorporate a luxurious interior to cater for members of the Royal Family. Other interiors can be provided for the carriage of the Prime Minister and government ministers, with their supporting staff and the press corps. Three of the squadron's crews, with a minimum of 'A' or 'B' category, are tasked with the carriage of high status VIPs.

In addition to its long-standing tasks of carrying passengers and freight, No 10 Squadron is now taking on the role of AAR. By the middle of 1993, two of the unit's aircraft had been converted, with the addition of wing-mounted Hose Drum Units (HDUs), to C.1K standard and it is envisaged that all 13 VC-10s will have been thus modified by 1995. Training for the new role is being carried out by the OCU at Brize Norton.

While No 10 Squadron is based on the north side of Brize Norton, a further unit equipped with VC-10s occupies facilities on the opposite side of the airfield. This is No 101 Squadron, who have now been operating the K.2 tanker version for the past 10 years, and the K.3 variant for slightly less. With the demise of No 55 Squadron and its

A VC-10 C.1 of No 10 Squadron, as yet unconverted to the additional tanker role.

One of No 101 Squadron's VC-10 K.2 tankers commences its take-off run.

Victors in the autumn of 1993, No 101 Squadron is now the sole tanker-only unit in the RAF. The unit has two main tasks: the support of Tornado fighters and Sentry AEW aircraft of No 11 Group in air defence operations, and the AAR support of aircraft on exercises and overseas deployments. This can involve not only aircraft of the RAF, but machines from other air forces that are equipped with refuelling probes that are compatible with the RAF's hose-and-drogue system. It is expected that No 101 Squadron will also operate the K.4 variant of the VC-10, when they enter service in 1994.

No 101 Squadron was heavily involved in the Gulf War, and at one time all nine of the unit's VC-10s were deployed to the area, the only RAF squadron to completely move to that theatre of operations. More recently, the squadron has been tasked to support the various deployments of RAF combat aircraft, in support of UN operations in the Iraq and Bosnia areas. This has involved VC-10 tankers being deployed for extended periods to bases in Cyprus, Turkey and Italy, with intensive tasking.

RAF Brize Norton is also home to the VC-10

A VC-10 K.3 on approach to landing. Note the underwing HDUs, and the central HDU denoted by the fitting under the rear fuselage.

OCU. Formerly known as No 241 Operational Conversion Unit, this element has now adopted the title of No 55 (Reserve) Squadron, to perpetuate the unit that, until October 1993, flew the venerable Victor tanker, the last of the 'V' bombers, from RAF Marham. No 55(R) Squadron is responsible for two main streams of conversion training, with one course covering the air transport role, to provide crews for service with No 10 Squadron. The other course concentrates on training for the AAR role, to teach aircrews the techniques required by No 101 Squadron.

A more recent development is the provision of training to qualify the air transport (AT) crews of No 10 Squadron with the additional task of AAR, now that the former VC-10 C.1s are being converted to C.1Ks. This modification particularly affects the flight engineer position, thus involving different procedures for this crewmember. Also, with the impending introduction of the VC-10 K.4 variant, thought is being given to running a short course to cater for this model, due to detail variations between the tanker versions of the VC-10. Studies are being carried out with the aim of combining these courses into a single stream of training, to provide VC-10 crews that are dual-qualified in both AT and AAR roles, although this may not occur until the mid-1990s.

No 55(R) Squadron trains six crews each year for the AT role, and a similar number of crews for AAR tasks; both of these courses last for 23 weeks. The unit has the use of two VC-10 flight simulators, one being optimized for AT operations, the other for AAR. Trainee crews, comprising pilot, co-pilot, navigator, and flight engineer (plus a loadmaster for the AT role), stay together throughout their training. Pilots on the AT course undertake some 44 hours of individual flying training, within a total course flying time of about 85 hours. Crews training on the AAR course are airborne for some 65 hours.

In common with other OCUs in the RAF that train aircrews on large aircraft, No 55(R) Squadron does not have any dedicated aircraft of its own. One VC-10 of No 10 Squadron is normally allocated to the OCU for training purposes; if further aircraft are required, they are obtained by 'borrowing' VC-10s from both Nos 10 and 101 Squadrons, as required, depending on the type of training being undertaken. Also, AAR training has to be carefully co-ordinated with other relevant RAF units, to provide realistic instruction for all concerned.

In addition to training crews for the two VC-10 units, No 55(R) Squadron also includes the RAF Air-to-Air Refuelling School. To this element come all aircrew in the RAF that operate aircraft types that are AAR-capable. This covers such types as the Tornado (all variants), Jaguar,

Harrier and Nimrod. Training mainly consists of ground lectures, covering the procedures and techniques involved in both receiving and dispensing fuel, and course lengths vary, depending on the aircraft type.

As with other OCUs in the RAF, No 55(R) Squadron runs a number of other courses connected with its main tasks. These include refresher courses, and training for nursing staff who will fly in the VC-10, to learn the layout of the aircraft. It also administers the No 38 Group elements responsible for standards and evaluation of operations by the VC-10 and TriStar units at Brize Norton.

No 1 Parachute Training School (PTS) has been based at RAF Brize Norton since 1976, having moved from nearby RAF Abingdon. The current task is to teach parachuting techniques to those relevant elements in the British Services who need to operate with these skills. This includes, of course, the Parachute Regiment, together with the Special Air Service (SAS), the Royal Marines, the RAF Regiment, 5 Airborne Brigade and units of the Territorial Army (TA), amongst others. The unit is run by RAF officers, and all the parachute jumping instructors (PJIs) are drawn from the RAF Physical Education branch.

No 1 PTS is divided into three squadrons, one of which is responsible for all basic training, whilst the Free-Fall Training Squadron (FFTS) covers the more advanced techniques. Free-fall parachuting is used by the military to deploy personnel from a high altitude, sometimes with oxygen, their parachutes being opened at low level to avoid detection. The RAF 'Falcons' Free-Fall Parachute Display Team, who delight thousands of spectators each year with their expertise of parachuting skills, is part of the FFTS. The third squadron is responsible for organizing the training programme, aircraft availability, support, etc. Detachments from No 1 PTS are located with the SAS at Hereford, the Royal Marines Special Forces at Poole in Dorset, 5 Airborne Brigade at Aldershot and with TA units throughout the UK. These detached personnel and PJIs carry out continuation training with the relevant units.

No 1 PTS runs 15 different courses, the principal one of which is the four-week basic training session for Regular servicemen, with 12 of these courses being run each year. Each course accommodates 64 trainees. Further courses are allotted for TA training, and for refresher tuition for Regular troops. Other courses cover such items as training and refresher tuition for PJIs and other instructors, dispatching from helicopters, descents into water, free-fall parachuting, and other related subjects. Some of the high-altitude free-fall parachute training takes place in France, or at El Centro in California, to take advantage of the usually fine weather at these locations.

One of the hangars at Brize Norton is used by the PTS for ground training, and thus contains various structures at differing heights, from which the students can practice the art of landing safely from a parachute descent. The technique of exiting an aircraft is practised from a mock-up of a Hercules fuselage.

To qualify for parachute 'wings', the trainee must carry out eight descents. The first of these is from a large tethered balloon, similar to the wartime barrage balloon. The gondola beneath the balloon carries a PJI and about four or five trainees, who jump from a height of 800 ft (244 m). The rest of the jumps are from aircraft, usually the Hercules, with the eighth descent being undertaken at night, with full combat kit and equipment. Much of the training is carried out at the dropping zone located at RAF Weston-on-the-Green, a grass airfield situated north of Oxford. Parachute packing (together with collection and repacking after use) is now carried out by a private company, under contract, and it is planned that the operation of balloons for parachute training will also be contracted out.

The other main RAF transport base is RAF Lyneham, near Chippenham in Wiltshire. This large station houses a variety of units in the support and operation of a single aircraft type, the Lockheed C-130K Hercules. Four squadrons, together with a reserve squadron that functions as the Hercules OCU, fly the 60 aircraft that are assigned to the base. These are operated on a 'pooled' basis, and are used by the units as required for their particular tasks. Thus, an aircraft may be flown in the morning on a route detail to a base in Germany and back, and in the afternoon the OCU will use the same aircraft for local flying training.

The four front-line units at Lyneham, Nos 24, 30, 47 and 70 Squadrons, all undertake route-flying in support of RAF, Army and Royal Navy activities worldwide. They were very heavily committed during the Falklands conflict, and more recently, in the Gulf War with Iraq. At the time of writing, these units continue to be tasked intensively, supporting the deployment of RAF combat aircraft in Saudi Arabia, Turkey, and Italy, in support of UN forces which are endeavouring to counter the situation in Iraq and the civil war in Bosnia. To give some idea of the effort required in supporting such deployments, the transfer of six Tornado F.3s to Italy in the spring of 1993 involved the mounting of some 60 sorties by the Hercules force. These sorties include positioning the empty aircraft from Lyneham to RAF Leeming (the Tornados' base), where they were loaded with the required equipment, spares, tools, etc., and then flying these cargoes to Italy. The empty aircraft then returned to Lyneham for any first-line servicing required, and to change crews, before repeating the cycle.

Five Hercules from the Lyneham Transport Wing, with C.1Ps leading and at the rear; the central and each wing aircraft are the longer C.3P variant.

Hercules C.1P, with its rear loading ramp partly lowered.

Further route tasks for the Lyneham units involve the long-standing commitments to the Falkland Islands, Belize, and Hong Kong, together with the support of training operations at Goose Bay in Canada, and in Alaska. The participation of RAF Tornados and other types in the 'Red Flag' exercises at Nellis AFB in Nevada provides further support work for the Hercules. Also, the Lyneham units compete in the 'Volant Rodeo' series of competitions amongst airlift units from various nations, which are run by the USAF, and the RAF has achieved some success in these events.

Further tasks involve humanitarian relief flights, and in recent years many sorties have been flown into such places as Ethiopia, Somalia and Sarajevo, where there is the added danger of hostile fire from the factions fighting in the area. To undertake all these tasks, each of the squadrons can call upon about 20 crews.

In addition to the principal route-flying tasks, the squadrons at Lyneham have other roles, although these are not shared by all of them. Nos 24 and 30 Squadrons train to operate in the AAR role, and five Hercules are permanently fitted-out with the equipment required for this task. The main purpose of these operations is to provide AAR facilities in the area of the Falkland Islands, particularly for the Tornado F.3s that are based at RAF Mount Pleasant. Two Hercules C.1Ks, together with three crews, are detached from Lyneham to form the equipment of No 1312 Flight, based at RAF Mount Pleasant. Crews are

drawn from Nos 24 and 30 Squadrons, and a tour of duty at this remote location in the South Atlantic lasts for about six weeks.

Nos 24 and 30 Squadrons also undertake low-level flying training, again in connection with the commitment in the Falklands, as resupply sorties are flown to South Georgia, with loads being dropped from low altitudes. This training involves the dropping of packs weighing up to 200 lb (91 kg), these being dispensed through a door on either side of the aircraft's rear fuselage.

Different tasks add to the route-flying duties of the other two squadrons at Lyneham, namely Nos 47 and 70. This is known as Transport Support, and involves operations affiliated with the Army, in particular 5 Airborne Brigade, covering the provision of air mobility, the dropping of paratroops and their associated equipment, and resupplying Army units at deployed locations. These tasks involve training in the art of low-level flying, defined as 250 ft (76 m) AGL, and operating into (and out of) small airfields in confined locations. Training is undertaken in the dispensing of large loads out of the open rear ramp of the Hercules.

About two-thirds of the crews on these squadrons are cleared for low-level operations, and aircrew who join these units would expect to spend six months to a year on route-flying tasks before undertaking a low-level conversion course with the Hercules OCU, involving all five crew members. A recent innovation has been the introduction of NVGs, and a few crews have been trained in the use of this equipment. No 47 Squadron has an additional role in the support of Special Forces, with a small number of crews being trained for these operations. A typical training exercise in support of parachute forces would involve the use of 15 Hercules, nine of which would carry some 500 paratroops, with the remaining six carrying supporting stores and equipment. The paratroops would be dropped from about 800 ft (244 m) in peacetime training, but lower altitudes would be used in wartime. It would be the aim for all 15 aircraft to pass over the dropping zone within a slot-time of five minutes.

A large amount of the servicing of the Hercules fleet is carried out at RAF Lyneham, with this task being divided between two elements, known as 'A' and 'B' Servicing Flights. These form part of RAF Lyneham's Engineering Wing, which employs some 1,300 personnel. Major overhauls are undertaken by Marshalls at their Cambridge (Teversham) Airport facility.

Conversion training of the five-strong crews for the Hercules is carried out at RAF Lyneham by No 57 (Reserve) Squadron, the Hercules Operational Conversion Unit (HOCU). Formerly known as No 242 OCU, this unit adopted its new title in 1992 under the policy of keeping alive the identities of long-established RAF squadrons. No 57 Squadron formerly operated Victor tankers from RAF Marham until it was disbanded in June 1986.

Courses are run by the HOCU to cover the five crew positions, these being pilot, co-pilot, navigator, flight engineer, and loadmaster. For those who are joining the Hercules force for the first time from the various training schools, the first element involves eight weeks of instruction in the Ground Training School (GTS), dealing with a variety of subjects that are relevant to the operation of the Hercules. Included in this eight weeks are four days spent at RAF North Luffenham for medical checks, and three days of sea survival training which is carried out at RAF St Mawgan.

Following the GTS element, crew training then moves to the Hercules Conversion Squadron, which annually runs about five courses, involving some five or six crews. These courses last for two-and-a-half months, and include some 35 hours spent on the simulator for the flight-deck crew. Flying training involves local circuit-flying, asymmetric flying, instrument landing system approaches, night and instrument flying, emergencies and formation flying. Longer sorties involve training (and checking by qualified instructors) on flights using the airways and navigational beacons in Europe, and trans-Atlantic missions and training flights within the USA. These flights are co-ordinated with actual support and resupply flights, carrying both passengers and cargo, in order to prevent aircraft flying around empty whilst on training details. One element of this training is aimed at the responsibilities of the co-pilot, with regard to the vast amount of paper-

A Hercules C.1P of the RAF's Lyneham Transport Wing turns onto its landing approach.

work involved in such operations.

The Simulator Squadron has three Hercules flight simulators at RAF Lyneham, and they are in operation for 16 hours each day. All flight-deck aircrew are required to carry out an exercise in the simulator every two months. This involves at least one hour's briefing on a scenario, followed by an exercise of at least two hours' duration. A number of overseas air forces who also operate the Hercules purchase time on these simulators for training their crews, and thus visiting aircraft of this type from various air arms are often to be seen on the Lyneham flight-line.

Having successfully completed the conversion course, the aircrew are then posted amongst the four squadrons, to suit their particular requirements for crew positions. Pilots usually join a squadron as a co-pilot for one tour, and then move to one of the other squadrons at Lyneham to function as a Hercules captain. Crews rarely fly together as the same five-person team, due to leave, sickness, etc.

A further unit within No 57(R) Squadron is the Support Training Squadron (STS), which is mainly responsible for training the TS roles applicable to Nos 47 and 70 Squadrons. During a five-week course, members from these squadrons (usually with a fair degree of experience of route-flying) are given instruction in low-level tactical operations, dropping loads at low level from the rear ramp, formation flying, and the use of NVGs. After a period of six months, crews return to the STS for a reinforcing course of one week's duration. A total of 24 crews undergo the TS course each year.

Training for the AAR role of the Hercules is carried out by the Tanker Training Flight (TTF), a unit within the STS. Crews from Nos 24 and 30 Squadrons undergo a four-week course which covers the procedures required to dispense fuel from the Hercules, and also to receive fuel from other tanker aircraft. Training for this task is conducted around the UK, in order to prepare the crews of both tankers and receivers for the characteristics of AAR from the Hercules, prior to their deployment to the South Atlantic. Fighter affiliation training, in which the Hercules acts as a target for fighter interceptions, is also carried out by the TTF, again in connection with the Falklands tasks.

To carry out this varied array of training and conversion courses, No 57(R) Squadron can call upon the services of some 120 staff instructors. The quality of instruction and training achieved by the HOCU is subject to periodic checks by the Standards Evaluation Unit from HQ No 38 Group, and inspectors from this unit can arrive at Lyneham on a no-notice basis to scrutinize any aspect of instruction carried out by the unit.

RAF Lyneham is also home to another important element within the transport force, namely the United Kingdom Mobile Air Movements Squadron (UK MAMS). Its primary function is to organize terminal facilities at Lyneham, covering both passengers and freight, for the Hercules squadrons, together with their loading and unloading. This task is the responsibility of the Base Air Movements Flight (BAMF), an element within UK MAMS and permanently based at Lyneham. The BAMF operates on a shift system, and is available 24 hours a day, 365 days a year, to handle any cargo or passengers through the terminal facilities at RAF Lyneham. It is responsible for processing all passengers, and their luggage, and for loading freight onto (and off) the Hercules. Co-ordination of the many factors involved in the carriage of passengers and cargo is the responsibility of a section called Load Plans, who check that the tasking request can be met in terms of size, weight and suitability for the Hercules.

A further unit within the UK MAMS is the Mobile Air Movements Flight (MAMF), members of which are deployed to any location in the world where transport aircraft of the RAF are operating, and which requires the support of air movements personnel where none normally exist. This also includes supporting the TriStar and VC-10 transports based at RAF Brize Norton, and any civil transport aircraft that the MoD may charter, in addition to the Hercules squadrons from Lyneham.

A classic example of the MAMF's role was in the build-up to the Gulf War, with personnel from the unit being deployed to nine locations in the region, in order to establish airheads to receive the flood of supplies being sent into that theatre of operations. These deployments included personnel from the UK MAMS, together with specialist cargo-handling equipment, fork-lift units, and suitable vehicles. Many valuable lessons were learnt in the Gulf conflict, particularly in relation to operating in a tactical situation with minimal facilities at unprepared sites, and also in carrying out operations under NBC conditions. These lessons have now been incorporated in current training programmes.

Personnel and equipment from the MAMF are also used to reinforce the existing movements units that operate at such locations as Cyprus, Hong Kong, Ascension Island, the Falkland Islands and in Germany, if the flow of RAF traffic exceeds the handling capacity of these local elements. The deployment of UK-based combat aircraft to an overseas location would involve a large amount of supporting transport flights. Thus, staff from the MAMF need to co-ordinate with the combat units involved, to be aware of the nature and volume of spares, tools and other relevant equipment that needs to be transported.

Further tasks for the MAMF involve the setting up of movements facilities for the RAF, pending the arrival of a more permanent movements unit. Instructions for the handling of helicopter loads, including underslung cargoes, are provided for personnel from all three Services. Also, MAMF personnel may be deployed to any location at short notice, to organize the handling of aircraft loads. An example here would be the movement of a replacement engine for an aircraft that has become unserviceable with a faulty powerplant, and the recovery of the failed unit.

Members of the MAMF have been involved in all the humanitarian operations that the RAF has undertaken in recent years. More recently, its personnel have been assisting the airlift of supplies into Sarajevo, in Bosnia.

The MAMF is composed of 14 teams, each of six members, and these personnel are liable to be deployed as required, either as a team or separately. Their tasks and locations are recorded on comprehensive wall displays in the UK MAMS Operations Centre. These personnel must be able to drive and operate the specialist cargo-handling equipment, and must also be medically fit to travel to anywhere in the world. The UK MAMS has a personnel strength of more than 300, over 80 of whom are with the MAMF.

RAF Benson has been the home of the Queen's Flight (and formerly the King's Flight) since 1939, and ⠀'s unit continues to operate an intensive progr⠀ me of flights in support of the activities of h⠀⠀yal Family. It also transports senior membe⠀⠀ the British Government, high-ranking

Service officers and visiting heads of state. To carry out these tasks, it is equipped with just five immaculately maintained aircraft: three BAe 146 CC.2s and two Wessex HCC.4 helicopters.

The RAF formerly included several units who operated in the communications and light transport role. In line with various cuts in defence spending, these units were steadily disbanded over the years, and the demise of No 60 Squadron in 1992 has left just one squadron carrying out this task. This is No 32 Squadron, based at RAF Northolt, to the west of London, who were reformed in 1969 by the retitling of the Metropolitan Communications Squadron.

The principal task of No 32 Squadron is the transport of VIPs to destination throughout the UK and Europe, and occasionally further afield. These passengers can include members of the Royal Family, the Prime Minister, members of the government, civil servants and high-ranking Service officers, amongst other VIPs. Further passengers may include RAF and other Service personnel who may need to travel rapidly between locations due to service requirements. Also, aeromedical evacuation flights are carried out by this unit. Aircraft from No 32 Squadron were deployed to the Gulf region in 1990/91 to operate communications flights, and the movement of politicians and officials connected with European Community activities adds to the current workload.

In terms of numbers of aircraft operated, No 32 Squadron was one of the largest units in the RAF. However, the recent planned withdrawal of the Andover from RAF service has meant a reduction of aircraft types operated from three to two: the

Three of these BAe 146 CC.2s form the fixed-wing equipment of The Queen's Flight at RAF Benson.

No 32 Squadron's four BAe 125CC.1s were retired in March 1994.

BAe 125 and the Aerospatiale Gazelle. No 32 Squadron operated a number of Andover CC.2s for several years, and these were joined in 1992 by three Andover E.3s, transferred from No 115 Squadron at RAF Benson. All of the Andovers had been withdrawn from RAF service by the spring of 1994.

The squadron currently operates eight BAe 125 twin-jet executive transports, comprising two CC.2s and six CC.3s. The crew of the '125 consists of three; pilot, co-pilot and an air steward, and normal passenger capacity is seven. Four Aerospatiale Gazelle light helicopters are also operated, for short-distance flights and tasks to non-airfield sites. In 1992, the squadron gained the distinction of being the first flying unit in the RAF to employ the services of the first full-time female pilot in the RAF, when Flt Lt Julie Gibson BSc commenced her duties as a co-pilot.

Operating alongside No 32 Squadron is the Northolt Station Flight, which is equipped with two PBN Islander CC.2 aircraft for light communications flights.

One element of No 38 Group that no longer exists is No 115 Squadron, who were disbanded in the autumn of 1993. This unit flew four Andover E.3s on calibration duties to check navigational equipment and landing aids at British military airfields. However, this operation has been contracted out to Hunting Air Services (a division of Hunting Aviation plc), who now operate the four Andovers from East Midlands Airport. RAF personnel are still involved in calibration duties on these aircraft, although the flight-deck crews are civilian.

THE RAF OVERSEAS

Apart from the elements within No 2 Group in Germany, the RAF maintains a number of units and facilities in other parts of the world, all of which are the responsibility of Strike Command.

Belize

The RAF (together with the Army) has maintained a variety of forces in Belize since the 1970s, to counter a possible threat from the neighbouring country of Guatemala. The main strike element was No 1417 Flight, equipped with Harrier GR.3s, which provided close support for the British Army units in the region. The GR.3s were retained for the Belize operation, as they had a reconnaissance capability. However, with the easing of relations with Guatemala, the British Forces in Belize are to be run-down, and thus the Harriers were withdrawn in July 1993, with No 1417 Flight being disbanded.

Further RAF support for the Army is provided by Puma helicopters operated by No 1563 Flight, based at Belize International Airport. This airport is also the supply airhead for transport flights from the UK, and RAF units are protected by a detachment of the RAF Regiment, equipped with Rapier SAMs. At the time of writing, it is not known for how long, or to what extent, the British Forces presence will be maintained in Belize.

Cyprus

During the 1960s, and into the 1970s, RAF Akrotiri was one of the largest bases operated by the RAF, and contained squadrons operating bomber, fighter, transport and helicopter types. Cuts in defence spending, combined with the policy of concentrating forces in central Europe, steadily reduced the establishment at Akrotiri, and for many years the sole flying unit based in Cyprus has been No 84 Squadron. This unit is equipped with the venerable Wessex, but these are different from other examples of this helicopter flown by the RAF, being ex-Royal Navy machines. These are designated as HC.5Cs, and No 84 Squadron is the only RAF unit to operate this variant.

The squadron's principal task is SAR, operating

in support of the continued RAF activity at Akrotiri and in the area. Additional tasks include fire-fighting, VIP transport and liaison, and troop-carrying. Although the numbers of based RAF aircraft have been drastically reduced, the base is often very busy with RAF machines, as all fighter units frequently deploy from the UK to carry out APCs, together with other RAF units providing associated target facilities. In addition, many other units deploy to Cyprus for exercise purposes, and the airfield acts as a useful staging post for transport aircraft en route to Middle and Far East destinations. Akrotiri also played a major role in supporting the RAF elements that were deployed to the Gulf area in 1990 in response to the invasion of Kuwait by Iraq.

On a lighter note, the 'Red Arrows' aerobatic team usually deploy to Akrotiri during the winter months, in order to perfect their display routine by taking advantage of the better weather conditions.

In addition to the Wessex-equipped squadron, further RAF personnel serve at the Joint Headquarters establishment, and at a number of signals units. The RAF Regiment are represented on the island by No 34 Field Squadron. SAR operations are organized by the Rescue Coordination Centre, situated at Episkopi, while medical facilities are provided by the Princess Mary's Hospital.

Hong Kong
RAF elements have been based in Hong Kong since the Second World War, including fighter units that were based at RAF Kai Tak until the late 1960s. In recent years the RAF has operated helicopters from the airfield at Sek Kong, and Kai Tak has become the large international airport for the colony. A small team of RAF personnel are still stationed at Kai Tak to handle the movement of such RAF types as the Hercules and VC-10 transports.

At Sek Kong, No 28 Squadron operates its Wessex HC.2 helicopters in various roles, including SAR, fire-fighting, anti-smuggling patrols, surveillance for illegal immigrants, and assistance in disaster relief. A Gurkha Brigade HQ is based at Sek Kong, and No 28 Squadron also provides troop-carrying capacity and training support for the Army and for the local Police Force. It is expected that the RAF presence will continue to be based in Hong Kong until 1997, when the British Forces are due to withdraw and the colony handed over to the Chinese.

Ascension Island
For over 10 years this remote island in the Atlantic Ocean has provided a vital link in the supply chain that extends from the UK to the Falkland Islands. The RAF team at RAF Wideawake is responsible for handling the various flights, dealing mainly with transport operations to and from the South Atlantic. RAF Wideawake falls within the responsibility of the recently reformed No 38 Group, within Strike Command.

Falkland Islands
Ever since the conflict with Argentina in the spring of 1982, the RAF, along with other elements of the British Services, have maintained a significant presence at this remote South Atlantic location. A new airfield, together with a supporting complex, was bought into use at RAF Mount Pleasant in 1985. The air defence of the area is entrusted to No 1435 Flight, equipped with four Tornado F.3s which replaced the previously-used Phantoms in 1992. The fighters are supported by two Hercules C.1K tankers, which form the equipment of No 1312 Flight. These aircraft, with three crews, are detached from the strengths of Nos 24 and 30 Squadrons at RAF Lyneham.

Two types of RAF helicopter are based at Mount Pleasant, these being the Chinook HC.1 and the Sea King HAR.3, and both are operated by No 78 Squadron. This unit provides helicopter support for the other British Service elements in the region, together with SAR cover. Short-range air defence is provided by a squadron of the RAF Regiment, equipped with the Rapier SAM. This unit provides round-the-clock cover with radar, and is drawn from RAF Regiment short-range air defence squadrons stationed in the UK and Germany. Further RAF elements include signals units, and movements personnel to handle cargo and passengers.

Goose Bay, Canada
In Labrador, Canada, a team of RAF personnel is stationed at Goose Bay to support the increasing numbers of RAF aircraft that use this base. Due to objections from the public and congestion in UK and European airspace, several aircraft deploy to Goose Bay to practise low-level flying in areas of sparse population. This mainly involves units equipped with the Tornado GR.1. Also, several aircraft, such as Tornados and Jaguars, transit through Goose Bay on their way to, or from, Nellis Air Force Base in Nevada, where they participate in the 'Red Flag' or 'Green Flag' exercises, staged by the USAF. These types of combat aircraft may be accompanied by VC-10s, TriStars, Hercules and Nimrods, providing AAR, transport and SAR support.

Goose Bay is situated in a remote location, with very severe extremes of climate. In winter, the temperature can fall to –30°C, or even as low as –60°C with the wind chill factor. In these conditions, aircraft have to moved into hangars when not in use, and care has to be taken when handling equipment outside due to frostbite. In contrast, the short summer can produce temperatures up to +30°C, but this hot weather is accompanied by hordes of flies and mosquitoes.

OTHER STRIKE COMMAND-RELATED UNITS

There are a number of units and organizations that are not the responsibility of any of the RAF's numbered groups, but are instead directly administered from HQ Strike Command at RAF High Wycombe. Still more elements do not directly report to Strike Command, but are controlled from various departments within the MoD. These are included in this chapter as their tasks are closely connected with the activities of front-line units.

Tactics and Trials

Within Strike Command is the Central Tactics and Trials Organization (CTTO), which is responsible for evaluating equipment and developing tactics and operational procedures for the RAF. As its title implies, the CTTO, which is based at A&AEE Boscombe Down in Wiltshire, is responsible for testing, examining and conducting trials on equipment, and for formulating and recommending the tactics required in the use of various operational aircraft, together with the weapons systems that they carry. In addition to conducting analyses of these systems, the CTTO is also responsible for the related instructional and procedural manuals. To undertake these tasks, the CTTO works in liaison with front-line RAF squadrons, and with manufacturers and suppliers of defence equipment.

The CTTO is divided into a number of divisions, some of which operate their own aircraft. Based at Boscombe Down is the Strike/Attack Operational Evaluation Unit (SAOEU), which operates small numbers of the Tornado GR.1/.1A and the Harrier GR.7, together with a Jaguar T.2 and a Harrier T.4. The SAOEU concentrates on conducting trials and developing operational tactics connected with the strike version of the Tornado, and the close-support role of the Harrier.

A similar element exists for the air defence role, with associated development tasks being undertaken at RAF Coningsby by the Tornado F.3 Operational Evaluation Unit (F.3OEU); as to be expected, this OEU is equipped with a small number of Tornado F.3s. Two further elements are the Support Helicopter Tactics and Trials Flight, based at RAF Odiham (see earlier in this chapter), and the Electronic Warfare Operational Support Establishment, which is currently located at RAF

Three of the types operated by the SAOEU from Boscombe Down; (L-R) Harrier T.4, Tornado GR.1 and a Harrier GR.7.

This Tornado F.3 is from the F.3 OEU based at RAF Coningsby.

Wyton, although it is planned that this unit will move to RAF Waddington in the autumn of 1995. These last two units 'borrow' relevant and suitable aircraft types from RAF units as and when required, and their tasks are generally revealed by their titles.

In July 1993 an overall organization was created which incorporated the elements of the CTTO, described above. Known as the Air Warfare Centre, it also absorbed other units, such as the Air Defence Ground Environment OEU and the RAF Cranwell-based Department of Air Warfare.

Institute of Aviation Medicine

Strike Command is also responsible for the RAF Institute of Aviation Medicine (IAM), which is based at Farnborough, in Hampshire. The IAM exists to conduct research into the medical effects of aviation-related activities on RAF personnel, and to examine the influences that these effects may have on operational effectiveness, and on safety. This work is not only conducted on behalf of the RAF, but also applies to the Army and Royal Navy, and to civil aviation.

Strike Command Air-to-Air Missile Establishment

In order that the highly-trained aircrew of the RAF maintain their expertise, they must continue to practise the various tasks that they may be called upon to undertake. One of the most spectacular of these is the firing of AAMs, and all units of the RAF that operate aircraft which are

capable of carrying these weapons are required to practise their techniques at regular intervals. For this purpose, Strike Command operate a unit to organize the firing of AAMs, and to evaluate and report on the results of these activities.

This unit, which is based at RAF Valley in Anglesey, is the Strike Command Air-to-Air Missile Establishment (STCAAME), which reports directly to the Command HQ, and whose task is aptly described in its motto 'By Practice We Validate'. The missile firings take place in a large range area located in Cardigan Bay, and are carried out in co-ordination with two other elements. These are the Defence Research Agency airfield at Llanbedr, from which the various targets are operated, and Aberporth, where the Range Control is situated.

The origins of STCAAME go back to the mid-1950s, and since then such types as Swifts, Hunters, Javelins, Lightnings and Phantoms have undertaken missile firings in this area, with earlier British missiles like the Firestreak and Red Top. Today, the principal AAMs used are variants of the American AIM-9 Sidewinder and the BAe Sky Flash.

Although the main users of the facilities at STCAAME are the Air Defence squadrons that operate the Tornado F.3, other types that are missile-capable, such as the Harrier, Jaguar, and Tornado GR.1, can also be seen at RAF Valley. The air defence units undertake three different types of practice exercise to enhance their expertise in the use of AAMs. One of these includes QRA procedures, which involves a no-notice scramble by fully-armed and fuelled aircraft. A second exercise is similar to the QRA scenario, but with a slightly longer notice of activation. Both of these exercises involve the aircraft departing from their home bases and are intended to fully evaluate the ability of the participating squadron to undertake these types of operation.

After take-off, the aircraft fly to the Cardigan Bay range, equipped with operational missiles fitted with live warheads. These are then expended against suitable targets over the range, after which the aircraft land at Valley. Here, STCAAME examines and reports on the results of the missile-firing, although this information can at times be somewhat limited, due to the short-notice nature of the exercise.

The main type of exercise undertaken at STCAAME is the Missile Practice Camp. In these, five or six aircraft from a squadron deploy to Valley for up to two weeks, with full crews, and support and servicing personnel, to supplement the permanent staff attached to STCAAME. The facilities at Valley include accommodation for the visitors and hangars for the aircraft, along with spares and other technical support, together with, of course, supplies of the appropriate missiles.

A number of different targets are employed at Llanbedr, the most common of which is the Jindivik, the design of which originates in Australia. This is a pilotless, radio-controlled drone, which in fact acts as a tug for various towed devices that are the actual targets for the missiles' warheads. It is fitted with cameras and telemetry that record and transmit information that can be analyzed to evaluate the missiles' performance. The modern AAM is a highly-sophisticated (and expensive) item of equipment, and thus the use of telemetry that simulates the characteristics of these weapons is often employed. The Jindivik is powered by a small turbojet engine, and its performance is therefore somewhat limited.

To simulate high-speed targets, the rocket-powered Stiletto target is employed, being air-launched from a Canberra aircraft. This target can fly at just below the speed of sound at medium and low altitudes, and is also used in the Cardigan Bay range. The Stiletto is also capable of speeds in excess of twice the speed of sound, at altitudes of over 50,000 ft (15,240 m); but the Cardigan Bay range is too small to accommodate these high-speed, high-altitude target profiles, and thus this type of missile training takes place in a larger range area to the north-west of the Outer Hebrides.

Following the firing of any missile, a full report is compiled, this being a complete analysis of all relevant details. This would include all aspects of the performance of the firing aircraft, its crew, the aiming and launching procedures, and of the missile itself. Information is gathered from films taken by the participating fighter, from cameras carried in the Jindivik and also from chase aircraft, together with telemetry data produced by various electronic sensors. Details obtained from radar-tracking records are also taken into account in order to produce a complete picture of the missile-firing sequence.

With the high cost of these weapons, the number of firings per year is limited for each squadron, and thus the maximum possible amount of information is collated with the aim of improving future techniques. The facilities provided by STCAAME were used extensively prior to the Gulf War in 1990/91, when RAF crews practised their procedures in the use of AAMs.

RAF Movements School

Although based at RAF Brize Norton since 1972, the RAF Movements School (RAFMS) does not, in fact, form part of No 38 Group; instead, it is an MoD-sponsored unit that is directly tasked by the Department of Logistic Operations (RAF). Its role is to provide movements and mobility training for personnel from all three Services, and also for personnel from certain overseas forces. Within the RAF, this training is provided for Supply Branch officers specializing in movements, and for other personnel as trade training within Trade Group 18 (Movements). The task of movements mainly covers the safe and correct methods that must be employed in the loading of cargo into RAF (and occasionally civilian) transport aircraft. It also covers the management and administration of the carriage of cargo and passengers.

To carry out this training, the RAFMS has the use of a hangar at Brize Norton which contains a number of freight load simulators. These include mock-ups of the C.1 and C.3 variants of the Hercules, fitted with roller-conveyer freight-handling equipment, together with an actual fuselage section of a withdrawn VC-10. Available for load-training are a wide range of 'cargoes', including packing cases of many different sizes, liquid drums, pallets, and several other 'awkward' items. Further up the scale for training in possible loads to be moved are the fuselage and wings from an early Harrier, together with a retired Wasp helicopter. Additional training is conducted in three computer-equipped classrooms.

The RAFMS runs some 24 different courses each year, and annually trains about 1,300 students. In addition to the practical cargo-handling already mentioned, training is also provided in many related functions. These include the management of cargoes and passengers, reservations, load-planning, load-trimming, aircraft utilization, the use of computers for these tasks, and paperwork. Courses are run to cater for the different transport aircraft types within the RAF, and refresher training is provided to cover new items of equipment that are relevant to the movements and mobility tasks.

Tactical Communications Wing

The motto of the Tactical Communications Wing (TCW) – 'We speak everywhere' – has proved to be most apt in recent years. The TCW was deployed to the Falklands in 1982, and was fully-committed in the Gulf War of 1991. Its role is to provide tactical communications that are capable of rapid deployment in support of RAF aircraft and operations at any location. The TCW is directly tasked by Strike Command and has its own supply and administrative elements, with its HQ at RAF Brize Norton being supported by No 38 Group. It is on a constant stand-by of 72 hours' notice, to deploy as required.

The TCW is divided into two main squadrons, one being the Field Communications Squadron (FCS), which, in turn, is divided into various flights covering mobile and strategic communications, and air traffic control facilities. The second unit, the Base Support Squadron (BSS), is composed of several elements, which provide engineering, maintenance, training and standards support, with workshops that can undertake both repair and development functions. The whole unit has about 300 personnel, and operates some 180 vehicles to carry out its tasks.

In time of war the TCW has a number of defined tasks. These involve providing communications to support deployed RAF squadrons, the NATO Rapid Reaction Force, Harrier units in the field, out of area operations, and general communications support, particularly in respect of repairing damaged communications equipment. These operations can involve the establishment of a network of secure communications, linking an HQ unit with its deployed elements, other command HQs, and with the UK. Much of the TCW's equipment is installed in vehicles such as Land Rovers, and can be rapidly brought into use at deployed sites. A communications centre would involve the erection of tents and aerials, linked to the specialized vehicles.

A further task for the TCW is to provide equipment to fill any gaps in the IUKADGE air defence radar system, to cover items that may have failed. For this task, the TCW has the use of its own portable Type 99 radar system, formerly used by the Argentine forces during the Falklands conflict, but 'liberated' by the British in 1982.

Modern technology is playing a greater part in military communications, with equipment utilizing digital data links and fibre optics being ever more widely used. Of course, satellites play an important part in such communications, and the TCW employ a number of VSC501 dish aerials to link with the Skynet system.

The TCW is also responsible for providing air traffic control (ATC) facilities at any 'bare' airfields to which RAF aircraft may be deployed or operate from. For this, the unit can deploy portable Watchman ATC radars, with associated consoles and communications equipment. Even approach and runway lighting can be provided, with modern, rechargeable units that can be activated by radio signals, thus obviating the need to lay wiring across landing areas.

In peacetime, the TCW has responsibilities to respond to any sudden overseas contingencies, and has provided tactical communications to support the RAF relief operations in Somalia and Bosnia. It also deploys local communications equipment to assist at sites of aircraft crashes or other accidents and emergencies. The TCW carries out its own training, particularly in relation to mobility and deployment in the field. A one-month-long field training course is undertaken, covering STO procedures, first aid and activities under NBC warfare conditions, amongst other related features.

Joint Air Transport Establishment

Occupying a complex of offices and two hangars on the south side of RAF Brize Norton, the Joint Air Transport Establishment (JATE), although primarily connected with air transport, is responsible to, and controlled by, the Central Staffs of the MoD. The Commandant of JATE is always an officer of Colonel rank from the Army, whilst the Deputy Commandant is an RAF Wing Commander. The officers and other personnel serving with JATE are drawn from all three Services, and the unit also employs several civilian staff.

JATE is tasked with the examination, development, trials and testing of procedures, techniques and equipment related to air transport operations and airborne assault. It is also responsible for providing a design advisory service for new equipment that may be transported by, or dropped from, both fixed- and/or rotary-wing aircraft. Additional tasks for JATE cover the investigation of malfunctions of parachutes or other equipment connected with aerial dropping or delivery, and problems with underslung loads on helicopters. The preparation of Operations Manuals related to air transport activities, together with the training of instructors connected with the above tasks, are also the responsibility of JATE.

To carry out the above tasks, JATE is divided

into a number of sections, with varying responsibilities, as follows:

Air Portability Section: Responsible for providing an advisory service on all aspects related to the internal air transportation of passengers, cargo, vehicles, weapons, etc., in fixed- or rotary-wing transport aircraft. Studies are also conducted into cargo-handling and restraining equipment.

Helicopter Section: Primarily tasked with providing clearance for external or underslung loads to be carried by helicopters, in order to produce information on the correct preparation and rigging of cargoes to be lifted.

Airborne Trials Section: This section is responsible for developing techniques for the delivery of men, together with their personal equipment and weapons, by parachute or by abseiling from helicopters.

Aerial Delivery Section: Mainly responsible for carrying out Service trials and development of parachute and other systems connected with the air-dropping of all types of equipment, including vehicles, guns, equipment and supplies. The Ultra Low-Level Airdrop system is also the responsibility of this section.

Flying Section: To enable the various Sections of JATE to carry out their tasks, this section is allocated the use of a Hercules transport, drawn from the fleet based at RAF Lyneham. The crew that forms this section are all highly experienced personnel, having completed tours with the TS squadrons.

A number of other sections within JATE operate in support of the above functions. These include an Engineering Section and a Design Drawing Office, together with printing and library elements, and a Training Section.

Whilst all the front-line squadrons, together with the principal training and supporting units within Strike Command have been described in this chapter, it should not be regarded as a complete directory of all the many elements that combine to keep a modern air force functioning. There are other units that carry out many tasks, covering administration, training, maintenance, research and development, to name just a few, that support the front-line units.

CHAPTER TWO

Personnel and Training Command

THE ORIGINS OF this new command can be found in a government study called 'Prospects', which, amongst other items, recommended that there should be a reduction of some 20 per cent in the staffs of MoD HQ elements. This recommendation was in line with the reductions in front-line units under the 'Options for Change' programme. It further proposed that many of these HQ functions should be moved out of London. The result was that the existing Support Command, which itself had been formed by the merging of Maintenance Command and Training Command between 1974 and 1977, should be split into two new commands, one of these being Personnel and Training Command.

This new command officially came into operation on 1 April 1994, and operates from a new HQ office complex that has been built alongside existing facilities at RAF Innsworth in Gloucestershire. RAF Innsworth has been the home for a number of years of the RAF Personnel Management Centre, and its duties have been absorbed into the new Command HQ. Staff from the offices of the Air Member for Personnel (AMP) have moved from London to Innsworth, whilst further staff have also arrived from the former HQ Support Command at RAF Brampton in Cambridgeshire. The new HQ has a staff of some 1,500, over half of whom are civilians. With this influx of personnel, work has been undertaken to expand the existing Messes at Innsworth with extra accommodation and to provide additional married quarters.

As its name implies, Personnel and Training Command is responsible for training members of the RAF, and this covers recruitment, selection, and most of the many aspects of training. Once trained, the command's obligations to the individual do not stop, for it is also responsible for many aspects of a serving member's career. These include career management, postings, conditions of service, resettlement and pensions. Other facets, such as legal matters, medical services and chaplaincy functions also form part of the command's activities. In addition, it is responsible for various aspects relating to the reserve forces of the RAF.

The first contact that prospective officers, airmen and airwomen have with the RAF is through the RAF Careers Information Offices (CIOs), 63 of which are located throughout the UK. The CIOs are administered by the Directorate of Recruiting and Selection, which was formerly the responsibility of the AMP, but is now part of the new Personnel and Training Command. The CIOs provide information to prospective members on the requirements of entry to the RAF, and advise on the situation regarding vacancies. With the recent reductions in the size of all the Services, vacancies are currently very limited, but the situation could improve when the present organizational changes have settled down.

INITIAL OFFICER SELECTION AND TRAINING

The correct selection of suitable personnel to serve as officers, and as non-commissioned officer (NCO) aircrew, is an important element before an individual commences the long and expensive training process. The responsible operation of the current and future generations of high-technology aircraft and weapons systems requires that personnel be of the highest calibre, and the RAF sets high standards of selection that are strictly adhered to. The selection process is carried out at the Officers and Aircrew Selection Centre (OASC), which for many years was based at the famous Battle of Britain airfield of Biggin Hill in Kent. In 1992 the OASC moved into a new complex at RAF Cranwell. The OASC also forms part of the Directorate of Recruiting and Selection and processes some 8,000 candidates each year.

The OASC is divided into two selection boards, each of which comprises a number of boarding teams. The Air Board is responsible for assessing the suitability of candidates for service as officers or NCOs in aircrew duties, whilst the Ground Board studies the qualities of applicants who seek a commission in one of the many ground branches of RAF service. Candidates who seek cadetships, bursaries or RAF scholarships are also selected by the Air or Ground Boards as appropriate, and interviews by visiting headmasters or professors are also employed.

Most of the selection courses run at the OASC are of four days' duration, although those for ground branches, medical candidates or re-entry personnel are one day shorter. All courses are of a similar pattern, commencing with aptitude tests, which are designed to assess the individual's ability to co-ordinate physical movements, reasoning, mental agility and the ability to solve various problems. All tests are carried out on micro-computers, and print-outs are produced to enable the OASC staff to assess the individual's performance. Candidates seeking aircrew positions undertake some six hours of aptitude testing, whilst those for other branches undergo about three hours of such tests. They are followed by medical examinations, which are more extensive for aircrew candidates.

The next stage is the individual interview which is carried out by the boarding teams mentioned earlier. These teams consist of a Wing Commander and a Squadron Leader, and the interview lasts for some 45 minutes. Candidates for the medical and dental branches will also undertake further interviews. This is followed by a review of the individual's progress so far. Those who fail to meet the required standards at this stage may be offered alternative chances to join the RAF, or they are free to depart from the OASC.

Those who have succeeded in the above tests that have formed Part One of the selection process now embark on Part Two. This involves acting in syndicate teams of five or six and undertaking practical exercises over an obstacle course. No leader is appointed for these teams, and it is therefore up to each individual to contribute to the task of carrying out the exercise. This is followed by a discussion period and further sessions involving exercise planning as a team, and a further exercise in which the individual must act as a team leader to undertake a particular task. Part Two of the selection process concludes with a final interview to establish all the details of the candidate's application.

The boarding officers of the OASC then consider the individual's performance in the various tests and exercises. Their preferences of career and the needs of the various elements of the RAF are also taken into account. The final selection is undertaken by the Board President who will notify the applicant of the result within three weeks of their testing.

With the announcements in the late 1980s that women were to be allowed to train as pilots and navigators in the RAF, the variety of tasks that can be undertaken by both sexes has widened even further than many people would have dreamt possible just a few years ago. Indeed, there are now very few areas of activity within the RAF that are not open to women.

Those candidates who are successful in passing the OASC course and who accept the position in

The impressive College Hall at RAF Cranwell.

the RAF that has been offered to them then return to RAF Cranwell to undergo initial officer training. This is carried out by the Department of Initial Officer Training (DIOT), which undertakes the basic training of all those who aspire to serve in the RAF as a commissioned officer. There are various types of entry to become an RAF officer, as follows:

(a) Direct Entry: These are candidates who enter from civilian life without a degree. Whilst at DIOT they are known as 'Officer Cadets' and they are commissioned on graduation.
(b) Graduate Direct Entry: Known as 'Student Officers', these candidates have obtained a degree and are commissioned when they begin their DIOT course. However, should the candidate fail the DIOT course, the commission must be given up.
(c) University Air Squadron Entrant: These cadets have had their university education sponsored financially by the MoD on the condition that they will serve in the RAF when they graduate. Whilst at university, they are commissioned with the rank of Pilot Officer. A similar type of entrant is the University Bursar, who is also sponsored whilst at university, although such entrants do not receive their commission until they arrive at the DIOT. These candidates are also known as 'Student Officers' and the commission will be lost if they fail the DIOT course.
(d) Serving Airmen/Airwomen: These entrants can come from all trades and various ranks, and prior to attending the OASC they may have been interviewed by a Station Commissioning Board. Commissions as officers in various branches are open to serving airmen between the ages of 35 to 45, and these entrants are also known as 'Officer Cadets' during their training at DIOT.

The DIOT currently has the capacity to train some 960 officer cadets annually, in six Entries, each having a strength of about 160. However, the reduced personnel requirements of the RAF in the 1990s will mean that there will probably be only four Entries per year, each comprising some 120 to 150 cadets, for the foreseeable future. Some 40 per cent of RAF cadets are destined for aircrew positions, 15 per cent are for General Duties and Ground Branches, 20 per cent are engineers, 17 per cent are administrative roles, six per cent are for supply roles and two per cent will go to security duties. Some 10 students in each Entry may come from a variety of overseas countries.

Female officers undertake their initial training, from the age of 18, at the Initial Officer Training Course at RAF Cranwell alongside their male colleagues, after which they are further trained according to their selected branch of specialization. Some 12 per cent of all entrants are women.

Training at the DIOT is carried out in flights, each of which consists of some eight to 10 cadets, whose ages range from 17 to 45 (or even older, on rare occasions). Each flight should, ideally, comprise a wide range of ages and experience, combining cadets, both male and female, who will undertake a range of duties with the RAF and overseas air arms upon graduation.

The DIOT has been subject to some reorganization in recent months, in line with the general reduction in RAF strengths. It currently consists of two main Training Squadrons, and the Specialist Entrant and Re-entrant Squadron (SERE). These units are supported by the Regiment Training Squadron with responsibility for drill training, the Leadership Training Squadron, which runs four-week induction courses for flight commanders, and the Academic Training Squadron, which is responsible for checking and maintaining the required standards of instruction within the DIOT. Further support is provided by the Defence Studies Team who examine current aspects of military affairs. The DIOT as a whole has a staff of some 100.

The duration of the principal syllabus at the DIOT, aimed at officers seeking full commissions in the RAF, was increased in 1992 from 18 weeks to 24 weeks, and is divided into three phases. The first of these extends for four weeks and seeks to introduce new cadets to the disciplines and standards of Service life. This includes instruction in physical education, drill, general duties and English. The second phase encompasses leadership training, together with skills in communicating, general Service knowledge and self-discipline; this covers a period of nine weeks. The third phase of the syllabus consolidates previous instruction, and covers confidence, military awareness, character development, pride and leadership. Talks are given on a wide range of subjects related to their future RAF service. A small amount of air experience flying is also provided, this being a new feature in the DIOT training. For this and other tasks, a new unit, the RAF College Air Squadron, has been formed at Cranwell, equipped with four or five Bulldog T.1s.

This third phase is the most important of the syllabus, and includes short exercises and two camps to test leadership. The second of these camps takes place at RAF Barkston Heath, to the south of RAF Cranwell, and is known as Exercise 'Peace Keeper'. The scenario covers the command and control of an RAF station through transition to war procedures, and in a war situation. Field service conditions are in force, and the trainees operate in full NBC kit.

Trainee officers undergoing combat field instruction with the DIOT.

The progress of each cadet through the DIOT course is monitored throughout the syllabus and he or she is advised of their strengths or weaknesses at the various stages of the training programme. Those who fail to achieve the required standards may repeat various stages, or may be recommended for suspension. For those who succeed, the syllabus culminates in the graduation parade and dinner, a most memorable occasion.

The SERE Squadron runs courses for officers who are re-entering the Service, and for officers who intend to specialize in branches such as medical, nursing, dentistry, legal matters and chaplaincy. Six courses, each of eight weeks' duration, are run each year, with up to 24 cadets on each course.

Other courses run at the DIOT include a short introduction for university cadets, initial officer training for Reserve officers, introductory courses for Volunteer Reserve members and staff training for DIOT flight commanders.

Once a person has graduated, they then move to one of the many RAF establishments that will train them for the specialized tasks required in their chosen career. However, with the recent reductions in the size of the RAF, and despite the fact that some personnel have left the Service voluntarily, whilst others have, sadly, been made redundant, there are currently more personnel than there are positions for them to fill. This is particularly apparent in the aircrew branches and many prospective pilots and other aircrew members are having to wait, or 'hold', to give it the Service term, until a training place becomes available and the situation stabilizes. The training programmes have been reduced to match cutbacks in the front-line, but when the current changeable situation settles down, it is expected that there will be a need to increase the relative rates of recruitment and training.

The specialization that an RAF officer conducts his or her career within is known as a branch, and these cover the wide range of activities that are required for the day-to-day running of the Service. Some (although not all) of these branches are:

General Duties (Air) Branch
General Duties (Ground) Branch
Air Traffic Control
Fighter Control
Intelligence
Engineer Branch
Supply Branch
Administration Secretarial Branch
Education Branch
Catering Branch
Physical Education Branch
RAF Regiment Branch
Provost Branch
Dental Branch
Medical Branch
Chaplain Branch
Legal Branch

The RAF operates a number of training establishments throughout the country, dealing with various aspects of the above branches. In line with cutbacks in the front-line units, the training elements of the RAF have also seen reductions, and these changes are continuing at the time of writing, affecting both flying training and ground-based tuition. Some of these training units train only officers, whilst others are responsible for the trade instruction of other ranks. A number of training schools provide tuition for all ranks, depending on the subject(s) being taught.

BASIC FLYING TRAINING

The responsibility of operating highly-sophisticated, complex and therefore expensive aircraft such as the Tornado or the Sentry requires aircrew who have been trained to the highest possible standards. This training covers many aspects, as will be described in this section, and a prospective pilot must be prepared for his or her training to last for some three to four years from joining the RAF to being posted to an operational unit.

Aircrew for the RAF can come from various sources, the nature of which dictates the first elements of their flying training. About 25 per cent of entrants to be pilots are university students who have been financially sponsored by the RAF with a University Cadetship. Whilst at university, these cadets undertake flying training with one of the 16 affiliated University Air Squadrons (UASs), which also provides an insight into Service life. However, these activities must not

interfere with their university studies and the cadets must obtain the appropriate degrees and standards of education that the RAF requires of its applicants. The names and locations of the UASs are as follows:

Aberdeen, Dundee & St Andrews UAS: RAF
  Leuchars
Birmingham UAS: RAF Cosford
Bristol UAS: Colerne
Cambridge UAS: Cambridge Airport
East Lowlands UAS: RAF Turnhouse
East Midlands UAS: RAF Newton
Glasgow & Strathclyde UAS: Glasgow Airport
Liverpool UAS: RAF Woodvale
London UAS: RAF Benson
Manchester & Salford UAS: RAF Woodvale
Northumbrian UAS: RAF Leeming
Oxford UAS: RAF Benson
Queens UAS: RAF Aldergrove
Southampton UAS: A&AEE Boscombe Down
Wales UAS: RAF St Athan
Yorkshire UAS: RAF Finningley

These 16 UASs are, between them, affiliated with over 70 universities, colleges and polytechnics in their local areas. Together, they have an established flying membership of 725, for which task they are equipped with a total of 79 Bulldog T.1 training aircraft, with tuition being provided by 76 instructors. Most of the UASs have establishments of four or five Bulldog aircraft, with similar numbers of Qualified Flying Instructors (QFIs). However, London UAS is larger, with

Bulldog T.1s of London UAS are seen here at their home base of RAF Benson.

nine aircraft, and eight QFIs. A further element within the UAS organization is the Royal Military College Air Squadron (RMCAS), based at Shrivenham, near Swindon in Wiltshire, although this unit does not operate any aircraft. Members from the RMCAS can join the RAF on similar conditions to those from the other UASs.

Whilst with a UAS, the cadet receives some 100 hours of flying tuition on the Bulldog, over a period of three years, and each summer the squadron normally deploys from its home base to another RAF station for its annual camp, of one month's duration. Cadets who aspire to be navigators can obtain 60 hours of flying training with their UAS, whilst cadets for ground branches can also volunteer for some 40 hours of tuition. Flying student places on the UASs are also available to members of the RAF Volunteer Reserve.

The HQ of the UAS organization is located at RAF Cranwell, where it forms a department within the RAF College. The staff of HQ UAS have a varied range of responsibilities, such as supervision of flying and ground training, organization of summer training camps, liaison with the various universities, supervising maintenance on the Bulldog aircraft (along with the Chipmunk T.10s operated by the Air Experience Flights for the Air Training Corps and Combined Cadet Force cadets), and general administration of the prospective RAF members within the Cadet and Bursar schemes. The RAF College Air Squadron also falls within the jurisdiction of HQ UAS.

A further source of RAF aircrew is the Flying Scholarship programme, under which the RAF pays for prospective pilots to receive 30 hours of flying training with a civilian flying club, up to the standard required for a Private Pilot's Licence. This scheme accounts for some 50 per cent of pilots who are accepted for training with the RAF.

Yet another method of entry for RAF aircrew, covering some 25 per cent of applicants, is the Direct Entry method, in which those who intend to take a Short Service commission are accepted although they have little or no previous flying experience. In order to establish whether the entrant has the co-ordination and aptitude to commence pilot training, these entrants are required to undertake screening and elementary flying tuition. The qualities that are required for pilots are not present in all applicants, through no fault of their own, and with the cost of pilot training running into millions of pounds, those who may not make the grade must be identified at an early stage in order not to waste resources. Many applicants who fail to attain pilot status often transfer to other branches of aircrew training, or to ground specialities.

For many years this elementary flying tuition was carried out by the Elementary Flying Training Squadron (EFTS), which was based at RAF Swinderby, near Lincoln, operating Chipmunks. A similar unit, the Royal Navy EFTS, operated Bulldogs from RAF Topcliffe as an element of No 1 FTS at RAF Linton-on-Ouse, its task being elementary screening and flying training. In the early-1990s the government proposed to combine the RAF and RN EFTSs, and to contract out the operation, with a private company being chosen to own and operate the aircraft, and to provide elementary flying and ground tuition.

In October 1991, Invitations to Tender were issued by the MoD to 15 companies, and eight of these submitted bids. In early 1993, it was announced that Hunting Aircraft plc had been successful, and this company was subsequently contracted to operate the new Joint Elementary Flying Training School (JEFTS), being responsible for supervisory, instructional, air traffic control (ATC) and engineering support staff, with these being supplemented by flying instructors from the RAF and the Royal Navy. The first courses commenced in July 1993, and these closely follow the former programmes that were undertaken by the previously separate EFTSs. Direct Entry students for the RAF undertake 54 hours of elementary flying training over a 16-week period, before proceeding to either Nos 1 or 3 Flying Training Schools (FTSs). For this training, Hunting has purchased a fleet of Slingsby T.67M Firefly Mk 2 aircraft, and the JEFTS operation is carried out at RAF Topcliffe, as an element within No 1 FTS.

Currently, the RAF has two Basic Flying Training Schools, these being No 1 FTS at RAF Linton-on-Ouse, just north of York, and No 3 FTS at RAF Cranwell, near Sleaford in Lincolnshire. After many years with the Jet Provost, both these units are now fully-equipped with the Tucano T.1.

Each FTS is divided into three squadrons, numbered 1, 2 and 3, each of which is subdivided into two flights. The six flights are designated by letters 'A' to 'F', and each accommodates one course, of some eight to 12 student pilots, who stay with their respective flights for the duration of the course, for 10 months. There are between 15 to 18 instructors on each squadron. The first six weeks of each course are spent in the Ground School, with an intensive programme of lectures and studies. Topics dealt with cover physical education, principles of flight, combat survival, aircraft instruments, navigation, meteorology, aircraft technical systems, avionics and general service training. In the classrooms, blackboards and chalk have long since given way to modern visual aids, such as computers, video projectors and mock-ups of cockpit layouts, together with cutaway sections of aircraft engines, instruments

Both of the Basic FTSs are now fully equipped with the Tucano T.1; this is the flight-line of No 3 FTS at RAF Cranwell.

and systems. With the introduction of the Tucano, a Cockpit Procedures Trainer (CPT) has been installed at both bases. This is much less sophisticated than a full flight simulator, but it enables the student to become familiar with the layout of the Tucano's cockpit, and various problems can be presented on the CPT's instrumentation from the instructor's console.

The RAF has also purchased five Tucano Flight Simulators (TFSs), with two being installed at both Nos 1 and 3 FTSs, whilst the remaining TFS has now been relocated with the Central Flying School at RAF Scampton, having formerly been installed at RAF Church Fenton.

One week is then spent under examination of progress so far, followed by a week of 'rough' survival training out on the Otterburn Range in the north of England, or some other similarly remote location. Here, leadership and organizational skills are assessed. During week nine of the course the student is debriefed on progress thus far, and any remedial work is carried out to rectify earlier shortcomings. When the trainee pilot has reached week 11 in the course, he or she is then transferred to one of the six flights.

The student then commences flying training on the Tucano, with the main Long Course, for pilots from the flying scholarship scheme, involving 109 hours of airborne tuition, this being interspersed with 28 hours spent in the TFS. A shorter course, of 92 hours flying and 18 hours in the simulator, is run for those who have a minimum of 30 hours of airborne experience with one of the UASs, a civilian flying club, or who have carried out the JEFTS course. The course covers all aspects of

flying training, including general handling, emergencies, flying at night or in poor weather, formation flying, and procedural flying within the national ATC system. Students undertaking the Long Course would be expected to have the ability to carry out their first solo flight in the Tucano after just over 11 hours of tuition, although this figure can be reduced if the instructor thinks that the trainee has achieved the required standard. The training time to solo standard is some three hours less for those on the Short Course.

Both of the Basic Flying Training Schools have Relief Landing Grounds (RLGs) nearby for use in the event of the circuits at the main locations becoming overloaded with training traffic. Thus, No 1 FTS has the use of RAF Church Fenton, which is situated 15 miles (24 km) to the south of RAF Linton-on-Ouse, while RAF Barkston Heath acts as an RLG for No 3 FTS, being some five miles (eight kilometres) to the south-west of RAF Cranwell.

In addition to the basic flying training carried out at Nos 1 and 3 FTSs, pilot training for the RAF is undertaken at one other location. In 1982, the European and NATO Joint Jet Pilot Training (ENJJPT) programme was set up, with the aim of combining pilot training for some NATO member countries in the USA, in an operation run by the USAF. This is carried out by the 80th Flying Training Wing at Sheppard Air Force Base, located near Wichita Falls in Texas. The RAF nominates six pilots each year to participate in this programme, with candidates being selected from those who have had previous flying training with one of the UASs, and who are likely to progress to fast-jet flying. The course at the ENJJPT lasts for some 13 months, and involves 120 hours of tuition on the Cessna T-37B, a twin-engined jet trainer with side-by-side seating for the instructor and student. This is followed by a further 130 hours of training on the supersonic Northrop T-38A Talon, again a twin-engined aircraft, but with its two seats in tandem.

Pilots for the RAF are classified into three groups, with Group One being fast-jet aircrew destined for the Tornado, Harrier and Jaguar. Group Two covers pilots who will fly multi-engined aircraft, while helicopter pilots fall within Group Three. Following the initial 109-hour (or 92-hour) programme, the Group One trainees undertake a further 38 hours of flying training, plus five hours in the simulator, over a period of 13 weeks. This acts as a lead-in to the advanced section of their training, which is carried out on the Hawk at RAF Valley or RAF Chivenor.

Group Two pilots carry out an additional training programme at Nos 1 or 3 FTSs, covering 31 hours of flying in seven weeks, before transferring to the advanced element of their tuition, which is undertaken on the twin-engined Jetstream T.1 at RAF Finningley. The prospective helicopter pilots of Group Three leave the initial section of training on the Tucano after 65 hours on the Long Course (or 50 hours on the Short Course) and then move to RAF Shawbury for specialized advanced helicopter training on the Gazelle and Wessex.

ADVANCED PILOT TRAINING

Following the 'streaming' process, the next stage for the prospective fast-jet pilots of Group One is advanced flying training on the Hawk T.1, and they head for RAF Valley in Anglesey, home of No 4 FTS, or to RAF Chivenor in north Devon, which is the base for No 7 FTS. The procedures for the advanced training of these pilots underwent a radical change in the autumn of 1992. Prior to this, trainees went to No 4 FTS for conversion from the Jet Provost or Tucano onto the faster regime of the Hawk. This was followed by a move to one of the two Tactical Weapons Units (TWUs), either No 1 TWU at RAF Brawdy or No 2 TWU at RAF Chivenor, to apply weapons training, tactics and delivery to fast-jet flying. This training was carried out on the Hawk, which equipped both of these units.

With the 'Options for Change' policy, the requirement for front-line combat pilots was reduced, and this resulted in a major change in the training programmes. No 1 TWU closed, along with RAF Brawdy, and No 2 TWU at RAF Chivenor was renamed No 7 FTS. The new programme, introduced under the title of 'Mirror Image Training', set out to combine the previous functions of three bases into two, with obvious savings in aircraft requirements and costs. One aim of the new programme is to keep pupils with the same instructors, on the same base, as far as possible throughout both the training on the faster Hawk aircraft, and the application of weapons that follows. Thus Valley added training in weapons and tactics to its existing task of fast-jet instruction, whilst the reverse situation applied at Chivenor, with advanced fast-jet flying training being taken on in addition to tuition in tactics and weapons delivery.

Both Nos 4 and 7 FTSs are each divided into two squadrons, both of which are organized along identical lines, with the same tasks. One purpose of this arrangement is ease of administration, but another important aspect is the degree of competitive edge that will be stimulated between trainee pilots on different squadrons.

Up to mid-1992, the two squadrons that comprised the flying element of No 2 TWU at Chivenor were Nos 63 and 151, and the based Hawks carried the markings of these units. Both were designated as 'shadow' squadrons and they would become operational units in time of war. With the demise of the Phantom in RAF Germany in the early 1990s, the identities of the two units that operated this type became available and these have been reformed at Chivenor as reserve squadrons. Thus, from late-1992, the Hawks of No 7 FTS have had their markings changed from Nos 63 and 151 Squadrons to Nos 19 (Reserve) and 92 (Reserve) Squadrons respectively.

In recent years the flying elements at RAF Valley, within No 4 FTS, were identified as Nos 2 and 3 Squadrons (not to be confused with the front-line squadrons of the same numbers). But as with the allocation of disbanded squadron numbers to No 7 FTS, so No 4 FTS found its squadrons being retitled. Thus No 2 Squadron was redesignated as No 234 (Reserve) Squadron, with No 3 becoming No 74 (Reserve) Squadron, and the Valley-based Hawks subsequently carried the identifying marks for these units. Further change occurred in April 1994, when No 234(R) Squadron was redesignated No 208(R) Squadron, following the retirement of the last Buccaneers in service with No 208 Squadron.

Formerly, the basic T.1 variant of the Hawk was mainly operated at Valley, whilst the weapons-capable T.1A was to be seen at Chivenor and Brawdy. With the changes in 1992, and the closure of Brawdy, many T.1s moved to Chivenor, with T.1As taking their place at Valley. To complement these changes, the Hawk simulator at Valley was modified to represent the T.1A cockpit.

One of the Reserve squadrons within No 7 FTS at RAF Chivenor is No 92, whose markings are seen here on a Hawk T.1A.

Upon arrival at Valley or Chivenor, the trainee pilot is given a flight in a Hawk as a 'taster' of things to come. He or she will then embark on five weeks of study with the Ground Training Squadron, which is divided into two flights, these being the Ground School Flight and the Simulator Flight. Over 120 hours are spent on 'academics', covering such items as aircraft operations, technical aspects of the Hawk, aerodynamics, meteorology, pilot navigation, survival training and aviation medicine. A further 53 hours are spent on General Service Training studies, including ground defence, physical education and leadership. Eight 'sorties', each of approximately one hour's duration, are 'flown' in the Hawk simulator, covering general procedures and emergencies.

The student then moves to one of the two flying squadrons on each base, where he or she will spend the next seven months. Further time is spent in the Ground School, including over 20 'sorties' in the Hawk simulator. The flying syllabus covers 100 hours airborne and is divided into three phases. The first of these, known as the Conversion Phase, concentrates on general handling of the Hawk and includes such items as circuit flying, aerobatics, stalling, spinning, practice forced-landings and instrument flying; this phase involves a total of 35 flying hours.

This is followed by the Applied Phase which deals with navigational exercises, night sorties and formation flying, and involving 33 hours airborne. Then comes the Weapons Phase, including

combat manoeuvres, simulated attack sorties and air defence profiles, with 32 hours of flying. Air-to-air gunnery practice is carried out against towed banner targets. Although it is intended that Valley and Chivenor operate along identical lines, aircraft and crews from Valley detach to Chivenor for one week during each course. This is to enable them to practise air-to-ground strike profiles on the range at Pembrey in South Wales, for which Chivenor is conveniently situated, there being no similar facility near to Valley. Should the airfield circuit at RAF Valley become congested (after, say, a period of bad weather that has restricted flying), students can use the RLG situated a few miles away at RAF Mona.

The changes that were introduced in the training of fast-jet pilots have produced significant savings, in that 20 fewer Hawks and 28 less instructors are now required to carry out the training programmes. Also, the students' course flying time has been cut by 30 hours, representing obvious reductions in costs.

Each course can accommodate up to 10 trainee pilots, with new courses starting at about seven-week intervals. Annual throughput is about 65 new pilots. Following the successful completion of their training at Valley or Chivenor, fast-jet pilots are awarded their coveted 'wings' insignia, and are then posted to one of the dedicated reserve squadrons for conversion training onto the Harrier, Jaguar or Tornado.

However, the constant demands to reduce

spending on defence, combined with the reduced needs for aircrew has meant that the advanced training programme for fast-jet pilots is again under review. It was announced in December 1993 that RAF Chivenor is due to close for flying training by October 1994, and the advanced training task is to be centred at RAF Valley. In order that students from RAF Valley can utilize the Pembrey Range, detachments will be made to RAF St Athan, where additional facilities are to be provided. The effect that this change will have on the disposition of the reserve squadrons currently at Chivenor and Valley has yet to be determined.

MULTI-ENGINE TRAINING

Not all trainees who graduate from the Basic Flying Training Schools want, or are suitable to be, pilots of high-speed fighters or strike aircraft. Also, at various periods, the RAF may not have any vacancies in these roles, and this was most noticeable following the 'Options for Change' programme, when a number of Tornado-equipped squadrons based in Germany were disbanded, thus creating a surplus of experienced crews in the Group One category.

For pilots in Group Two who aspire to fly somewhat slower but larger aircraft, the next stage following basic flying training is advanced tuition with No 45 (Reserve) Squadron, an element within No 6 FTS, based at RAF Finningley, near Doncaster. Formerly known as the Multi-Engine Training Squadron (METS), the unit is equipped with the Jetstream T.1 and it runs a

number of courses, each depending on the previous experience of the trainee.

The longest course is the Advanced Flying Training (AFT) Course, which is of 20 weeks' duration. Here, students from Nos 1 or 3 FTSs, having completed their basic tuition on the Tucano, are introduced to a larger and slightly more complex aircraft. The first phase, which lasts for five weeks, is spent in the Ground School, with instructions in multi-engine characteristics, techniques and performance, aerodynamics, avionics and flight planning, amongst other items. Whilst at the Ground School, the students get their first exercise in the Jetstream Instrument Trainer (JIT), which is a replica of the cockpit of a Jetstream, with fully functioning instruments but without the dynamic action of a full simulator.

Following the Ground School phase, two exercises, each of 90 minutes' duration, are carried out in the Jetstream Dynamic Simulator (JDS). Here, the student is introduced to the cockpit checks and to the effects of the controls, which the JDS reproduces realistically. Items covered include procedures for take-off, climbing, descending and landing, combined with emergencies caused by failures of equipment or fires. Only when the two exercises in the JDS have been completed does the trainee embark on the flying exercises.

There then follows a sequence of 34 flying exercises, interspersed with exercises undertaken in the JDS and the JIT. Various flying exercises throughout the syllabus cannot be undertaken until the relevant JIT and JDS exercises have been

No 45 (Reserve) Squadron uses the Jetstream T.1 for the advanced training of future pilots of multi-engined aircraft.

completed satisfactorily. The trainee is required to undergo 18 exercises in the JDS, most of which are of 90 minutes' duration.

As with the ground-based training sessions, the flying exercises are mostly of 90 minutes duration. The trainee progresses through general handling of the aircraft, flying circuits at Finningley, asymmetric flying with one propeller feathered and various simulated emergencies. After over 11 hours of dual tuition, on Exercise No 9 the trainee undertakes his or her first solo flight on the Jetstream, lasting one hour and covering local flying and circuits. This is followed by a series of instrument flying exercises, with an Instrument Rating Test being carried out on Exercise No 14. The flying programme is then expanded to cover navigational flights at various levels to other airfields for circuit training, followed by the Intermediate Handling Test in Exercise No 22. The emphasis then turns to night flying, and also to use of the civilian airways and navigational beacons, with instrument approaches to civil airfields. This culminates in an exercise sortie, using the international airways system, to land at an overseas destination. Then comes low-level flying and revision of previous exercises, with the Final Handling Test, taken on Exercise No 35, bringing total flying time on the AFT Course to 50 hours.

A similar, though shorter, course is run for pilots who have previous experience on fast jets or other types, and who are transferring to larger, multi-engined aircraft. This is known as the Multi-Engined Cross-Over Course, or MEXO, and like the AFT Course, it consists of three streams of exercises, these being flying, time on the JDS, and also time on the JIT. Some 30 hours of flying training is accumulated in 20 exercises, combined with co-ordinated training periods on the JDS and JIT. The MEXO syllabus is similar to the AFT Course, but compressed in time, being completed in 10 weeks.

A further course run by No 45 (Reserve) Squadron is the Jetstream Refresher Course, aimed at officers who are returning to multi-engined flying after a ground-based appointment. This course lasts just five weeks, the first of which is spent in the Ground School. Then follows four weeks of flying exercises, with a total of 15 hours airborne in nine sessions. Yet another course is of 12 weeks duration, with training given to QFIs by instructors of the Standards Squadron.

A significant point in RAF history was made in June 1991, when the first full-time female member of the Service to receive her pilot's 'wings' graduated at RAF Finningley following her course with the then METS. Upon completion of their advanced flying training, Group Two aircrew graduate with their 'wings', and then transfer to the appropriate Strike Command training unit to convert to the various front-line multi-engined types.

TRAINING HELICOPTER PILOTS

RAF Shawbury, near Shrewsbury, is the home of No 2 FTS, which is responsible for training helicopter pilots for the RAF, as well as pilots for overseas air arms, under contract. RAF pilots move to Shawbury following a shortened basic flying training course on the Tucano. No 2 FTS also converts RAF pilots who have previous experience on fast jets or multi-engined aircraft to the different skills required of helicopter pilots.

As with other RAF training establishments, the first period of tuition at RAF Shawbury is spent in the Ground School, on a course lasting some four weeks. Classes are composed of equal numbers of trainee pilots and navigators, who receive instruction together on such topics as meteorology, technical and aerodynamic aspects of helicopter flight and navigation. One room within the Ground School includes various sections from a Gazelle helicopter, to enable students to familiarize themselves with the mechanics of the machines that they will eventually fly. The joint training of pilots and navigators is designed to promote crew teamwork. Further Ground School activities include a daily, one-hour session of physical education, and a day spent on medical instruction. Students also travel to the Royal Naval Air Station at Yeovilton in Somerset for instruction in underwater escape techniques.

No 2 FTS is divided into two squadrons, Nos 1 and 2, with No 1 being responsible for the basic course of training for prospective helicopter pilots. For this task, it employs the Gazelle HT.3 light helicopter, which has now been in service in this role at Shawbury since the 1970s. The course for pilots involves over 85 hours of flying over a period of four months. On most flights, trainee navigators are accommodated in the rear seat of the Gazelle, thus continuing the crew training scenario, but on some lessons in the syllabus, the emphasis is on navigator training, and so he or she moves to the front, left-hand seat. Topics covered in the flying training syllabus include familiarization with the Gazelle helicopter, elementary handling, autorotation, transition from vertical to horizontal flight, hovering, flying backwards and sideways, and engine-off and forced landings. Landing and manoeuvring in confined spaces, low flying, instrument and night flying, formation flying and navigational exercises form further parts of the course.

Use is made of suitable locations such as clearings in wooded areas within the vicinity of RAF

The Gazelle HT.3 is used by No 2 FTS at RAF Shawbury for helicopter pilot training. (Bob Munro)

Shawbury, with the full co-operation of the local landowners concerned. The mountainous areas of Wales are relatively nearby, and thus flying in this type of environment forms a valuable part of the training syllabus. The basic syllabus concludes with handling tests, checks and examinations of both student pilots and navigators, to ensure their suitability to move on to the advanced phase.

Advanced helicopter flying training is undertaken by No 2 Squadron of No 2 FTS, using the venerable Wessex HC.2 helicopter. Here, the concept of crew operation of a larger, passenger and cargo-carrying helicopter is taught, with the pilot, navigator and loadmaster acting as a team. The advanced syllabus involves over 60 hours of flying over a period of three months, and expands on the items covered in the basic syllabus. Troop-carrying exercises are often carried out, in co-operation with local Army units. A period of training with the Search and Rescue (SAR) Training Unit, based at RAF Valley, forms part of the syllabus of advanced helicopter flying training. Having successfully completed their training at RAF Shawbury, helicopter aircrew then either return to RAF Valley to continue SAR training, or proceed to RAF Odiham to convert to the Chinook or Puma types operating in the support helicopter role.

CENTRAL FLYING SCHOOL

The Central Flying School (CFS) has the distinction of being the oldest military flying school in the world, having been first established at Upavon in Wiltshire in June 1912 as an element of the Royal Flying Corps. Today, the CFS continues with its primary task of training flying instructors who will serve in the various other training schools within the RAF. It is also responsible for training flying instructors for the Army and the Royal Navy, as well as various overseas countries.

The HQ CFS is located at RAF Scampton, near Lincoln, the famous bomber base from which No 617 Squadron flew to carry out the raids on the dams in Germany in 1943. Here, the CFS Flying Wing consists of various squadrons, each responsible for training instructors for differing tasks. These elements include the Ground School, the Bulldog Squadron, the Tucano Squadron and the Refresher Squadron.

Suitable instructors for the RAF are selected with care. Candidates can apply for instructional duties after at least one tour with a front-line unit, whilst others may be selected by the Commanding Officers of their units to go forward as an instructor. The suitability of candidates for instructional duties is discussed at periodic conferences held by the Commandant CFS, along with other staff officers. They consider reports on the candidates' previous service, together with information from the RAF PMC at RAF Innsworth, and the wider requirements of the RAF. Although a pilot may have exceptional skills at handling an aircraft in all circumstances, he, or she, may not possess the qualities and skills required when it comes to instructing a nervous student.

As with most RAF aircrew training units, the first period of any training course is spent in the Ground School, with most of the student instructors spending four weeks of tuition on such items

The crew of a Bulldog T.1 of the CFS's Bulldog Squadron prepare for another training sortie. These aircraft are used to train instructors for the UASs.

as academics, features of the Bulldog and Tucano aircraft and techniques of instruction. Use is made of a CPT and a TFS. Time is also spent covering safety and survival equipment, and on medical testing at RAF North Luffenham.

Trainee instructors then move to one of the flying squadrons. The role of the Bulldog Squadron is to train instructors who will serve with the UASs. Often, these instructors are chosen from slightly older or more mature candidates, as they will be operating in the slower regime of the Bulldog's flight envelope. The course with the Bulldog Squadron lasts for 17 weeks, and covers three phases. The first of these is the Conversion Phase, where the students learn to fly the Bulldog; this involves just over 15 hours of flying training, comprising dual tuition combined with solo and mutual flying, in which the student 'gives back'

training to the instructor. The Basic Phase involves nearly 29 hours of flying, and here the trainee instructor starts to learn the techniques of instructing.

Finally, the student carries out the Advanced Phase, covering 35 hours airborne, bringing the total flying time required for the Bulldog course to nearly 80 hours in as many sorties. Trainee instructors are tested after each phase to assess progress. Having successfully completed the final handling test, the trainee would then be posted to one of the 16 UASs as a QFI.

The Tucano Squadron has the task of training instructors for future service with the Basic (Nos 1 or 3) FTSs. Younger pilots are usually selected, when compared to those who go to the Bulldog Squadron. They must have a minimum of one tour with a front-line squadron; however, pilots with

The CFS Tucano Squadron's flight-line at RAF Scampton.

exceptional ability (known as 'creamies') may be selected to go for instructor training directly from completing advanced flying training with Nos 4 or 7 FTSs.

Following Ground School training, students with the Tucano Squadron follow a similar path to those in the Bulldog unit. After a Conversion Phase, which involves 22 flying hours, the Basic Phase covers a further 25 hours airborne. Here, instructional skills are taught, with CFS staff acting as basic flying training students. The trainee instructors are expected to adapt their teaching style and methods to suit the particular student, to achieve the best results. The Advanced Phase includes formation flying, aerobatics, navigation, spinning, night flying and low-level flying, all combined with training to instruct successfully. This phase covers some 45 hours of flying, and each phase is followed by an assessment test.

Instructors are graded according to ability, and the initial grading following training is a probationary 'B2'. A proficiency test has to be taken within six months, to proceed to grade 'B1', which is the minimum grade normally expected of instructors. Tests have to be taken annually, to maintain grade, while above average instructors can be regraded as 'A2', for service with the CFS staff or Examining Wing. Further regrading can achieve an 'A1' status, but these instructors are very rare and of exceptional ability.

The Refresher Squadron of the CFS has the role of providing refresher flying training to previously-trained QFIs, who are returning to a flying appointment after a ground posting. To carry out its tasks at RAF Scampton, the CFS fleet consists of some 10 Bulldogs and over 20 Tucanos.

The CFS also provides instructor training for a number of overseas air arms. These trainees must first undertake a five-week course (including one week in the Ground School, followed by 15 hours

of flying) to familiarize them with operations in the UK environment. They then proceed to one of the squadrons for the full training course.

The Examining Wing of the CFS is responsible for monitoring standards of all the elements of the CFS, whilst its agents are attached to most training units in the RAF to carry out the same task. Members of the Examining Wing occasionally visit overseas air arms to study their training methods, and the CFS often hosts visitors for the same purpose.

The CFS at RAF Scampton also acts as a parent unit for the RAF's famous formation aerobatic team, the 'Red Arrows'. This team consists of nine pilots, three of whom are changed each year, together with a team manager, who also acts as a commentator, and supporting ground crew. The team operates ten Hawk T.1/.1As, slightly modified to suit their aerobatic role. The 'Red Arrows' perform about 100 displays each year, and carried out a tour of the USA in the autumn of 1993.

Following the end of a season's displays, three of the team's members are changed, and training for the new team commences, initially with small formations and then progressing to larger presentations. Training usually is transferred to Cyprus in the early spring, to take advantage of the clearer Mediterranean weather. Only after the team has been assessed as being proficient at their programme of display flying are they allowed to commence public performances.

Not all elements of the CFS are located at RAF Scampton. The CFS Hawk Squadron detachment operates from RAF Valley, to train instructors for advanced flying training with Nos 4 and 7 FTSs. They also train fast-jet instructors for the Royal Navy and a few overseas air arms. RAF Shawbury is the home for the CFS Helicopter Squadron, which is responsible for training Qualified Helicopter Instructors (QHIs) for all three British

Immaculate formation flying by the nine Hawks of the 'Red Arrows' display team.

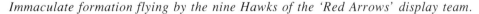

Services. This unit carries out its instructor training on the Gazelle HT.3s, which are shared with No 2 FTS. Trainee QHIs commence their training with the usual Ground School sessions, followed by a 15-hour conversion course onto the Gazelle. The main course of QHI involves over 70 hours of tuition, which includes information being passed 'both ways' between instructor and trainee.

NAVIGATOR TRAINING

Training for navigators is undertaken at the Air Navigation School (ANS), part of No 6 FTS at RAF Finningley, in an intensive course lasting for more than a year. Candidates can come from the OASC at RAF Cranwell, or can transfer from other branches of the RAF, and must be between 18 and 26 years of age, with five 'O' levels or similar academic qualifications.

In 1992 a new syllabus for training navigators was introduced, with Bulldog T.1, Tucano T.1 and Hawk T.1 aircraft arriving at Finningley to replace the venerable Jet Provost. Also, two new wings, the Basic Navigation Wing (BNW) and the Advanced Navigation Wing (ANW) were formed within the ANS. Trainee navigators first attend RAF North Luffenham for a period of Aviation Medicine Training, and then embark on a series of training modules. Module One covers Academic and Flying Introduction, lasting nine weeks, with many classroom sessions, together with 15 hours of flying in the Bulldog. In this module, the student is introduced to the basic principles of flying, use of the radio combined with airfield procedures, and basic navigation and map-reading in the local area.

This is followed by one week spent on a Combat Survival Exercise, conducted under realistic conditions in a remote area of the UK. Low-level navigational training is then undertaken in Module Two, with classroom tuition and 30 hours of flying in the Tucano over a period of 10 weeks. Module Three involves Systems Management and Radar, which introduces the trainee to airborne radar. Extensive use is made of simulators, along with 16 hours flying in the Dominie T.1, with sorties being conducted at low level. This culminates in an overseas mission for an initiation in international ATC procedures.

Trainees are then subjected to a Leadership Training Exercise, following which they are 'streamed' for their future roles, be it on fast jets, multi-engined aircraft, or support helicopters. The decision as to which role the trainee navigator undertakes depends on personal choice, but is also influenced by recommendations from a conference of the ANS instructors, combined with the wider needs of the RAF at any particular time. Those navigators who will transfer to the support helicopter force then move to RAF Shawbury to continue their training there.

Navigators for fast-jet flying then carry out further radar training in the Dominie, covering 26 hours flying, but this time at low level through remote hilly areas. Up to this stage, the various elements of the training programme have been the responsibility of the BNW. The remainder of navigator training is dealt with by the ANW. Fast-jet navigators continue their training with a 10-week module, during which some 16 hours are flown on navigational exercise in the Hawk. Further 'streaming' then places fast-jet navigators in modules specializing in air defence or strike/attack roles, with 19 hours being flown in the Hawk over a 10-week period. This completes training for navigators destined for Tornado units, during which they will have flown over 122 hours in 60 weeks (including leave periods).

This Bulldog T.1 is used for part of the syllabus of navigator training by No 6 FTS at RAF Finningley.

The Dominie T.1 has seen many years of service in the navigator training role. All are based at RAF Finningley with No 6 FTS.

Navigators for multi-engined aircraft continue their training in the Dominie, with enhanced instruction that includes over 50 hours of flying in a 28-week period, which concludes their course at the ANS of 115 hours flying in 59 weeks. The ANW also covers refresher training for navigators who may be returning to flying duties after a ground appointment, and for those who may be switching from fast-jet to multi-engined aircraft, or vice-versa. A further task for the ANW is the training and standardization of Navigator Instructors at the ANS. In all, 12 navigator training courses are run each year, although the intervals between commencement can vary slightly due to holiday periods such as Christmas, etc. In recent years, increasing numbers of women have undertaken training as navigators.

Once the trainee navigators have completed their course at RAF Finningley, they are posted to the various reserve squadrons for type conversion, be it fast-jet or multi-engined. In the spring of 1991, the first woman in the RAF to qualify for a position on the flight-deck of an RAF aircraft received her navigator's brevet following training at RAF Finningley.

AIRCREW TRAINING

Apart from pilots and navigators, there are a number of other important tasks that RAF aircrews undertake, all of which are vital to the smooth running and success of the mission being carried out. The training of these aircrew members takes place at RAF Finningley at the Air Electronics, Engineer and Loadmaster School (AEELS), the title of which conveys the roles that are taught in this establishment. The AEELS forms part of No 6 FTS.

Prior to entering the above school, RAF personnel who intend to become aircrew members must first undergo a seven-week course with the Airman Aircrew Initial Training Course (AAITC), also located at RAF Finningley. Candidates can come from Direct Entry, via selection at the OASC at RAF Cranwell, followed by recruit training at RAF Halton, or can have transferred from another trade and been recruited as NCO aircrew. Once at the AAITC, the trainees commence an intensive and rigorous syllabus of training, covering such subjects as RAF law and regulations, management of both personnel and resources, and the ability to display leadership. The course is mentally and physically demanding, and the students are assessed for their self-confidence and motivation through activities such as public speaking and the competence to organize tasks and resolve problems. Drill and Physical Education are important elements of the course, which includes several days spent on exercises on the Yorkshire Moors or in the Otterburn Training Area in the north of England. Whilst participating on the AAITC, all students are required to live on base for the full duration, even if they are married. Each course consists of about 26 to 32 candidates, and on the successful completion of the programme, the trainee is promoted to Acting

Sergeant, and must have the potential to be appointed to Senior NCO rank before moving on to more specialized aircrew training.

Air Electronic Operators

There is a requirement for seven Air Electronic Operators (AEOps) in the Nimrod maritime patrol aircraft, with further places being available in the Sea King SAR helicopters. With the recent entry into service of the Sentry AEW aircraft, there is an additional requirement for these specialized personnel.

The training programme for AEOps is divided into a number of sections, the first of these being the Common Phase, lasting for a period of 26 weeks. Much emphasis is given to instructions in mathematics and science, forming a basis for the main instruction on communications, maritime, underwater, acoustic and electronic warfare, and radar. Periods are spent on a Synthetic Communications Procedures Trainer, involving practical exercises, these leading to airborne exercises in the Dominie. Once the Common Phase has been completed successfully, the trainee AEOp is selected for further specialist tuition. Crews in Nimrods are divided into 'dry' and 'wet' sections. The 'dry' crews are responsible for above-surface radar operations, whilst the 'wet' operators concentrate on underwater sonar disciplines.

The 'dry' AEOp (Radar) then spends a further 27 weeks in the Ground School, undergoing advanced tuition in radar and EW procedures, employing such equipment as the Searchwater radar and the 'Yellow Gate' ESM. To this is added instruction in communicating with the Morse Code, together with typing and equipment operation, combined with further sorties in the Dominie.

Trainee 'wet' AEOps (Sonar) undertake 19 weeks of training on such subjects as acoustics, sonobouys and oceanography, together with the passive and active characteristics of surface and underwater vessels. Computer-enhanced training aids are employed, together with visits to RAF and Royal Navy units. Once the relevant training phases have been successfully completed, the trainees are awarded their AEOp's brevet, although the final confirmation of this award depends on further satisfactory progress at an OCU.

Air Engineers

Modern multi-engined aircraft are highly complex machines, and thus the role and expertise of the Air Engineer (AE) crewmember is vital. The main responsibility of the AE is to monitor and operate all the various systems, covering the basic airframe and powerplants, together with hydraulics, electronics, avionics and fuel management. More recently, many transport-type aircraft have been equipped to operate as air-to-air refuelling tankers, and thus these systems have now been added to the AE's workload. The environments, both internally and externally, are also on the list of tasks for the AE, with responsibility for pressurization, oxygen and air conditioning, along with any problems that icing may cause. With all these systems, the AE must be able recognize and analyze any faults or failures that may occur, and then take the appropriate remedial action, as far as is possible.

As with the AEOps, candidates for the AE role are NCOs, and can be Direct Entrants or transfers, who must then pass through the seven-week AAIT Course at RAF Finningley. The prospective AEs stay at this station for their specialized role-training, which covers a period of 43 weeks, and is divided into four phases. The first of these covers basic academics, commencing with mathematics and science, and continuing with detailed studies of aircraft components and systems, this phase being of 18 weeks duration. The second element of an AE's training is known as the Applied Phase, and commences with a one-hour flight in a Bulldog for familiarization. Further flying is then undertaken in the Dominie, with these sorties being co-ordinated alongside navigator training to fully utilize resources. The trainee AE carries out 13 flying exercises, each of three hours duration, to fully familiarize the student in the airborne tasks of a co-ordinated aircrew.

The third Phase in AE training is Advanced Academics, covering a period of nine weeks, which develops and advances the student's knowledge and expertise. Time is spent on various systems to be found on the Hercules transport, including electronics and the Allison engines. Use is then made of the Air Engineer Procedures Trainer (AEPT), a full replica of the cockpit of a large four-engined aircraft, based on the flight-deck of a Nimrod. Here, all the various systems are reproduced in full working order, with inputs and situations controlled by a computer. Thus various problems and scenarios can be introduced by the instructors, with the aim of teaching the student the ability to recognize and rectify the situation that has arisen. Use is also made of a full-size aircraft, this being one of the airframes that remain from the abortive Nimrod AEW.3 project. This aircraft has been stripped of all the internal avionics, but retains all the flying systems. Although no longer airworthy, the engines are still in place, and the aircraft can be taxied if required. This Nimrod, now known as a Ground Instructional Aircraft (GIA), provides the trainee AE with a realistic training aid, with all

This Nimrod still carries the nose and tail radomes from its abortive AEW role. It is now used as a Ground Instructional Aircraft (GIA) for the training of Air Engineers at RAF Finningley.

the various 'bugs' that can afflict a complex airframe. Operation of the various systems, such as pressurization, anti-icing, fuel flows, heating, and many others can be practised in the GIA. Although primarily used to assist in AE training, the Nimrod GIA is also used by student navigators and loadmasters in their training programmes.

The final phase in the training of AEs involves simulator instruction in the AEPT, with the student converting the previous tuition into practical skills that can be assessed. The student undertakes 39 hours of training in the Air Engineer's position, together with 30 hours operating in the co-pilot's seat, with the aim of completing 13 exercises of ever-increasing complexity. Once the training at Finningley has been successfully concluded, the AE insignia is awarded on graduation, but is only confirmed after satisfactory performance at the operational conversion stage that follows, onto aircraft types such as the Nimrod, Hercules, VC-10, TriStar or Sentry.

Air Loadmasters

Another vital crewmember in a number of aircraft is the Air Loadmaster (ALM), who is responsible for a wide range of tasks within the main cabin of transport aircraft, or in support helicopters, covering both cargo loads and passengers. The ALM must be able to organize the distribution and securing of all types of cargo loads, with particular regard to dangerous items such as explosives or chemicals. When carrying passengers in RAF transport aircraft, it is the ALM's responsibility to

ensure that they are briefed on safety and emergency procedures, and that suitable catering is provided. On long-distance flights with passengers, in aircraft such as the VC-10 or TriStar, the ALM is responsible for the supervision of any Air Stewards/Stewardesses who may be in the crew to assist him or her. It may be that an aircraft is retasked during a mission, and the ALM will then have to reorganize the interior of the aircraft with regard to seating, stretchers, roller conveyors, etc. The ALM may also have to liaise with overseas authorities.

In support helicopters, the ALM is known as a crewman, and is responsible for similar tasks to those in fixed-wing transports, albeit on a smaller, but, at times, a far more rigorous scale. Support helicopters would, in time of war or in emergency operations, be dispersed into small self-contained and self-supporting flights, often functioning in remote areas under spartan conditions. On such operations, the ALM is responsible for the safe and efficient carriage of fully-equipped troops, and stores such as ammunition and vehicles. Also, the external securing and carriage of underslung loads of all types, together with casualty evacuation, form part of the ALM's tasks.

Only after having obtained much experience on fixed-wing transports or support helicopters may male ALMs volunteer for places as winchmen on the SAR helicopter force. Often, the winchman is lowered to the casualty, who may be badly injured, to administer first aid and assist in the rescue, making it a role that may not be suitable for the faint-hearted.

As with AEs and AEOps, ALM trainees must first successfully pass through the AAIT Course, following which they commence a 12-week training syllabus for their new branch of service. This starts with a Basic Phase of over five weeks, with tuition in such subjects as mathematics, aviation medicine, principles of flight, aircraft systems; together with studies into weights and measures, and the handling, loading and restraint of cargoes.

There then follows three periods of training, each of approximately one week's duration. Survival instruction is given for both land and sea situations, combined with an exercise carried out in a remote location under realistic conditions. Training in first aid is provided at RAF Halton, where students have to achieve standards that are acceptable to the Health and Safety Executive. Leadership training to an advanced level involves a suitably challenging project which the students have arranged, planned and organized themselves during the preceding weeks.

Once the Basic Phase has been satisfactorily completed, students are 'streamed' for further specialist instruction in procedures relevant to either fixed- or rotary-wing aircraft. Students for fixed-wing types receive further training applicable to the safe operation of transport aircraft, with regard to cargo and/or passenger loads, and covering items such as route operations and catering. Trainee ALMs for helicopters are instructed on such topics as the principles of flight, and the systems and servicing of rotary-wing aircraft. ALMs with previous experience pass through the Streaming Phase if they are returning to flying duties or switching between fixed- and rotary-wing aircraft. On the successful completion of the Streaming Phase, which is of three weeks duration, the trainee ALM is posted to the appropriate OCU for further training on type. Only when this has been completed satisfactorily is he/she awarded the LM brevet.

OFFICER TRAINING FOR GROUND DUTIES

Two of the main elements of organization at all RAF stations cover engineering and supply functions, and the training of officers for these branches is undertaken at RAF Cranwell. This training is carried out by the Department of Specialist Ground Training (DSGT), in a large building known as 'Trenchard Hall'. Until 1 April 1993, the DSGT was a department within the RAF College; since then it has reported directly to the Command HQ. Engineer and supply officer training is also provided for selected civil servants from the MoD, and for members of certain overseas air forces.

Training for engineering officers involves a number of phases, the first of which is known as Engineer Officer Training One (EOT1); this lasts for 20 weeks, with up to nine EOT1 courses being run each year. The last three weeks of the EOT1 course are spent with the Servicing Instructional Flight (SIF), which is located in a hangar on the eastern side of the airfield at RAF Cranwell. This hangar contains a number of Hunter single- and two-seat aircraft, as well as a Jaguar GR.1, and although these machines are not airworthy, they still retain their engines, and are capable of being taxied. The SIF is organized along the lines of an active, front-line squadron, and is designed to provide practical training for engineering officers in as near a realistic manner as possible. Various problems, with a tight time-scale, are presented to the trainee officers, and the training includes the fitting of external stores and weapons, with inert examples of these items being available for use.

EOT1 provides enough training to enable the officer to act in a command capacity, and following its completion, the trainee officer is posted to an operational environment to complete one tour of duty, usually of two or three years duration. They then return to RAF Cranwell for EOT2, the second phase of their training at the DSGT. The first five weeks of this course are a common management module, following which the trainees are streamed into various specialist sections covering such items as aeromechanics, avionics, and communications, training in which lasts for some 12 to 15 weeks. Further pre-employment courses linked to EOT2 deal with areas such as propulsion, weapons, aircraft fatigue, etc. The DSGT also runs advanced courses aimed at experienced engineering officers who are destined for senior appointments.

The DSGT also trains officers for the supply branch, with a similar system to that used in the training of engineering officers. The first element, Supply Officer Training One (SOT1), gives initial supply training over a 12-week period, following which the trainee is posted to an operational unit. They then return to RAF Cranwell for SOT2, for advanced training to more senior positions.

The Administrative Wing is a major element in the organization of most RAF stations, and often includes numerous subordinate squadrons and flights. Officers for the administrative branch are trained for four specializations, these being Secretarial, Education, Catering and Physical Education. Secretarial officers, having completed the DIOT course, then undertake some 13 weeks of training at RAF Hereford, although this operation is due to move to RAF Halton in mid-1994. Their first tour of duty at an RAF station would be in elements dealing with such topics as accounts, personnel management, housing, works,

Although not airworthy, these Hunter aircraft are still serving the RAF with the Department of Specialist Ground Training at RAF Cranwell.

families, or general duties.

Education officers carry out a few weeks of specialist training at the RAF School of Education at RAF Newton, followed by their first posting to a training or educational position. Those officers who intend to follow the catering specialization proceed, from the DIOT, to the RAF School of Catering at Aldershot for a familiarization course, following which they are posted to a junior position in a station's catering squadron. These RAF schools, both of Education and Catering, are also due to move to RAF Halton in the mid-1990s.

Physical Education officers receive four weeks of instruction at the RAF School of Physical Training at RAF Cosford, followed by two weeks of elementary parachute tuition at RAF Brize Norton, before their first posting to the Physical Education Flight on an operational station.

There are many other streams of training for RAF officers. These include courses for the RAF Regiment at Catterick (moving to RAF Honington in 1994), for fighter controllers at RAF Boulmer, air traffic controllers at RAF Shawbury, the RAF Police at RAF Newton (and later at RAF Halton), and intelligence duties at RAF Wyton. Much of the training for service in the Medical Branch and Dental Branch is carried out at RAF Halton. Chaplains of various denominations carry out a course of general service training at RAF Cranwell, as do prospective RAF Legal Officers.

STAFF TRAINING FOR OFFICERS

Further training for officers is carried out at the RAF Staff College (RAFSC), located at RAF Bracknell, in Berkshire. For over 70 years, this establishment has undertaken training of officers

to enable them to fulfil appointments to staff and command positions; a task which continues to this day. A variety of courses are run, catering for a range of experience and appointments.

The work carried out during Initial Officer Training (at RAF Cranwell) is continued and reinforced by a four-week Officers Command Course, aimed at junior officers to improve their performance in command positions. This course is currently carried out at RAF Henlow, under the control of Bracknell. The work is further consolidated with a correspondence course. Junior Squadron Leaders are trained during the Basic Staff Course, over a period of four weeks, with the qualities required to suit them for appointments applicable to their rank.

Each year, about 90 officers of senior Squadron Leader or junior Wing Commander rank undertake Advanced Staff Training, to equip them to operate effectively as commanders of squadrons or RAF stations. Yet further training is given during the 10-month-long Advanced Staff Course, which covers such items as the application and effect of air power, international politics, military subjects, leadership, management, and joint Service operations. However, the courses and activities at the RAFSC are currently the subject of a comprehensive review, and it is probable that changes will be implemented in due course.

INITIAL TRAINING FOR AIRMEN AND AIRWOMEN

The public image of the RAF is mainly generated by the activities of front-line units as reported in the popular media outlets, or through more serious study in the pages of the many aviation mag-azines now available. This can cover such items as heroic SAR operations by the crews of heli-copters, mercy supply flights by Hercules trans-ports to drought-stricken areas of the world, or the more public performances by the 'Red Arrows' and other RAF aircraft at numerous air displays throughout the country in the summer months.

However, the efficient undertaking of these activities would be greatly reduced without the support of fully-trained ground crews, and other ground-based supporting personnel, all of which requires an extensive and comprehensive ground training organization. This training covers a vast range of subjects, affecting personnel directly connected with aircraft operations, the servicing and maintenance of aircraft, electronics, weapons, communications and ground equipment. Further training covers the numerous administrative and other supporting tasks that are required to keep the RAF functioning.

Training for the RAF was established by Lord Trenchard from the very beginning in 1918, with the setting up of a number of training schools covering various trades. One of the more famous of these was the RAF Apprentice Training School, which was established at RAF Halton, near Aylesbury, in 1920. This famous school con-tinued to supply apprentices for the RAF for 73 years, but due to changes in requirements, com-bined with the demographic situation, it closed in the middle of 1993, with the passing-out of No 155 Entry.

The ground training elements within RAF Personnel and Training Command have been the subject of an extensive review for some while, along with most aspects of the RAF, as a part of the 'Options for Change' programme. This review has resulted in various changes in the ground training organization, and the remodelling process will continue to be carried out until well into 1995.

For all airmen and airwomen, their first posting on joining the RAF is the School of Recruit Training, and this unit is now established at RAF Halton, having moved during 1993 from its home for many years, RAF Swinderby, near Lincoln. The school's task is to transform the raw civilian recruit into a disciplined and reliable member of the RAF, and this is the only entry point into the RAF for all ranks other than officers. The course lasts seven weeks, during which time the recruit is taught general service knowledge with an overall picture of the RAF, drill and parade procedures (the infamous 'squarebashing'), physical educa-tion, and the care of personal kit and uniform. Further subjects covered involve ground defence and small-arms training, NBC warfare, first aid and fire-fighting. The basic rank for the new entrant is aircraftsman or aircraftswoman. There are procedures to enable those who find the RAF not to their liking to leave by mutual agreement. Those who successfully complete their initial training at Halton take part in a graduation parade before a senior officer of Group Captain rank or above.

TRADE TRAINING FOR AIRMEN AND AIRWOMEN

Following recruit training, the new recruit is then posted to one of the ground training establish-ments for tuition in one of the many trades that the RAF offers and requires. The preferred trade that the recruit seeks will have been established during the initial interviews at the CIO, and efforts are made to ensure that these choices are met, providing that the new recruit satisfies the minimum educational requirements, and subject to vacancies being available in the chosen trade. Should the initial choice of trade be unavailable, alternative trades are offered, but should these not be acceptable, in some cases the entrant may be given a free discharge from the RAF.

There have been significant changes in the training system for ground trades in recent years, and the previous classifications of Apprentice and Direct Entry Technician have now been eliminat-ed. The current system involves two streams of tradesperson: Mechanics or Technicians. The Mechanic stream is the larger of the two, and this commences with a basic trade training course, lasting from four to six months. The partially-trained Mechanics then transfer to operational elements, to further refine their skills, and they would remain in this type of job for their Service engagement, up to a maximum of nine years. This does not mean that Mechanic-grade tradespeople cannot advance, as some will be able to transfer to Technician grade by personal effort and upon recommendation by their Commanding Officers.

Entrants for the Technician stream must pos-sess certain educational qualifications, depending on the trade being pursued. This stream under-takes the same basic training as the Mechanic stream, and would then also transfer to opera-tional training. However, after some two years, and subject to their performance thus far, they can return to the training school for further tuition in their trade. This additional training can last for one to one-and-a-half years, and with these skills there is possible promotion to NCO or Warrant Officer rank.

Personnel are trained in some 150 different subjects, and the specialized trades which they then follow are classified as falling within 18

Trade Groups (TGs). The classification of Mechanic or Technician does not apply to all trades. The following list covers both Technician and Mechanic streams, as appropriate, and the current TGs cover the following subjects:

TG1:   *Airframes; Propulsion; Weapons.*
TG2:   *Aircraft Electrical; Avionics; Synthetic Trainers.*
TG3:   *Ground Electronics; General Electrical.*
TG5:   *General Engineering; Ground Support; Aerial Erector.*
TG6:   *Mechanical Transport; Driver.*
TG8:   *RAF Police; RAF Regiment Gunner; Fireman; Kennel Assistant.*
TG9:   *Air Traffic Control.*
TG10: *Administration; Physical Education; General Duties.*
TG11: *Communications.*
TG12: *Aerospace Systems Operator.*
TG13: *Painter and Finisher; Survival Equipment Fitter.*
TG14: *Air Photography Processor; Air Cartographer; Ground Photographer; Photographic Interpreter.*
TG15: *Various Medical Trades.*
TG16: *Dental Technician; Dental Hygienist.*
TG17: *Accounting; Secretarial; Data Analyst; Personnel Administrator.*
TG18: *Supplier; Movements Operator.*
TG19: *Catering Clerk; Chef; Steward/Stewardess.*
TG21: *Musician.*

For the past 73 years, RAF Halton has been the home of No 1 School of Technical Training (SoTT), but under the recent review of RAF ground training this unit is in the process of moving to RAF Cosford, near Wolverhampton. This complicated task commenced in September 1993, and will take over one year to complete. The first element to move from Halton to Cosford was the Propulsion and Survival Equipment Training Squadron, to be followed by the Aircraft Training Squadron, and the Electrical Training Squadron. These units are responsible for training personnel in skills required in TGs 1, 2 and 13. Training for TGs 1 and 2 was also carried out at RAF Cosford by No 2 SoTT. RAF Cosford will see a significant expansion as it absorbs the various elements from RAF Halton, and when the transfer of No 1 SoTT has been completed, the training of airframe and aero-engine skills will be concentrated at one location. The move of No 1 SoTT will result in the disappearance of the unit title of No 2 SoTT at RAF Cosford.

For the last 22 years Cosford has also been the home of the Joint Services School of Photography, whose task is to train personnel from all three Services in the skills required for processing film from reconnaissance and survey photography, and the servicing of airborne cameras. Ground photographers for all three Services are also trained at this School.

The RAF School of Physical Training has been based at RAF Cosford since 1977, its task being the training of physical education instructors and coaches. This school has benefited from the construction of new facilities, which were opened in early 1993. This new complex contains two large gymnasia and a swimming pool, together with other supporting facilities.

Further changes under the Ground Training review will involve the transfer of a number of instructional elements into the vacated areas at RAF Halton. Secretarial and Supply training will move from RAF Hereford, together with the Airmen's Command School (ACS), and this move is due to be completed by the middle of 1994, upon which RAF Hereford will be closed. Also moving to RAF Halton in a similar timescale will be the RAF School of Education, transferring from RAF Newton, near Nottingham. This unit includes the Training Development Support Unit, whose role is to provide training for the RAF's instructors and designers of training aids and programmes. A further unit that will move from RAF Newton to RAF Halton in 1994/95 will be the RAF Police School.

The ACS is responsible for running two General Service Training Courses. One of these is to prepare airmen and airwomen who have been provisionally selected to be promoted to Corporal rank; the other takes the process a step further, being aimed at Corporals who aspire to become Sergeants.

Additional training for NCOs is carried out at RAF Scampton, home of the Trade Management Training School (TMTS). Here, courses are run to provide tuition in the techniques required for supervisory and junior management positions throughout the RAF. These cover the management of airmen and airwomen to undertake tasks related to flight-line duties, airframes, powerplants, electronics, weapons and safety equipment, amongst other items. NCOs are trained in the economical use of manpower, motivation and clarity of instructions, along with considerations regarding quality assurance and health and safety regulations.

The TMTS has the use of six Hunter aircraft, both single- and two-seat versions, to assist in their training tasks. As with the aircraft used for officers' ground training at RAF Cranwell, these aircraft are non-airworthy, but can be taxied if required. Some 600 Junior Technicians are trained to Corporal standard each year; similarly, approximately 400 Corporals receive tuition

A two-seat Hunter T.7 of the TMTS at RAF Scampton is seen here being used in an aircraft handling training session.

for future service as Sergeants.

No 4 SoTT has now been instructing members of the RAF in a number of trades at RAF St Athan for over 55 years, since it was formed in 1938 with the initial task of training fitters and mechanics specializing in airframe and engine work. In the middle of the Second World War, the school switched to the training of aircrew, with over 20,000 Flight Engineers passing through the unit. In the early-1950s, the training of airframe and engine fitters resumed, until 1977, since when the school has concentrated on the tuition of ground engineering trades. This school has not been affected by the recent review of RAF ground training, mentioned earlier.

Currently, No 4 SoTT has four main tasks, covering the basic trade training of both airmen and airwomen within Trade Groups 3, 5, 6, and 13. These tasks cover driving, general engineering, transport maintenance, and painting and finishing. The unit also operates a civilian training school for the tuition of apprentices over a four-year period in the skills of aircraft engineering. Within these main tasks are numerous specialized courses of varying lengths.

To achieve the above tasks, the school is divided into four squadrons, two of which, the Training Support Squadron and the Course Design Squadron, provide training aids and lessons, set examinations, maintain a reference library and compile reports, to mention just a few tasks.

The Engineering Training Squadron (ETS) cov-

ers a wide range of subjects, with training being provided in workshop, electrical, and mechanical engineering skills, specializing in ground support equipment and transport. Tuition for painting and finishing trades, along with welding, sheet metal-work and machining is also provided. Courses are also run for officers and NCOs in engineering management. In 1992 the Aircraft Battle Damage Repair Training Flight was transferred from RAF Abingdon to RAF St Athan, to fall within the responsibility of the ETS, which has the capacity to instruct some 660 trainees each year.

The Armed Forces of the UK operate vast numbers of vehicles of all types and sizes, and thus the Driver Training Squadron (DTS) fulfils an essential task in training and examining the many drivers required. As well as instructing RAF drivers, the DTS's 170 staff also instruct members of the RAF Regiment, RAF Police, and some drivers of the Royal Navy, with an annual throughput of some 3,000 trainees. Specialized training is given in the operation of such vehicles as coaches, fire/crash/rescue tenders and cranes, amongst others, and the DTS fleet of 134 vehicles covers over two million miles each year.

The Civilian Technical Training School (CTTS) at RAF St Athan is responsible for the training of apprentices for the MoD in the trades of aircraft and propulsion engineering. The normal intake is 36 apprentices a year, with a course that covers four years of tuition.

A further CTTS is situated at RAF Sealand, the

main task of which is the training of civilians for technical work within the co-located No 30 Maintenance Unit. Apprentices commence with two years training in the CTTS, this being followed by a further two years improver training with one of the production wings. Training is also provided for other supporting elements of the RAF, and for various government departments, including short courses on work with computers.

RAF Locking, near Weston-super-Mare, is the home of No 1 Radio School (RS), which is responsible for training personnel in the skills required to function as ground electronics mechanics and technicians, involving a variety of tasks within TG 3. This training is given to airmen and airwomen who have recently joined the RAF, and also to existing personnel who are advancing from Mechanic to Technician level. Courses are run for both Service and civilian trainees, and for service personnel from NATO, Commonwealth, and other countries.

The training provided at No 1 RS is directed to provide personnel for the RAF with sufficient skills to enable them to repair and maintain the vast array of electronic equipment used by the Service. The school provides practical training for personnel to be able to undertake the correct servicing procedures, with detailed instruction being given for over 100 different electronic installations currently in use with the RAF. This includes such items as ground communications, radios of all types, radar equipment, flight and other simulators, data transmission equipment and computers.

AIR TRAFFIC CONTROL

RAF personnel who operate in the control towers of RAF airfields, and at other military air traffic control (ATC) centres are trained for their future tasks at the Central Air Traffic Control School (CATCS), which has been based at RAF Shawbury in Shropshire for many years. This unit used to operate its own small fleet of aircraft, such as Vampires, and, more recently, Jet Provosts, but much more use is now made of computers and simulators.

Students at the CATCS are trained to be able to operate in a variety of ATC functions, on a course that lasts for 17 weeks and involves much classroom study, together with sessions on simulators. These provide realistic situations and problems that the students are required to control and resolve. The average number on each course is about 16 students and this often includes Royal Navy personnel and trainees from overseas.

Following successful completion of their training, the student is posted to an RAF station as an ATC assistant. Here, they would be required to

requalify for each of the various functional positions, due to the fact that no two airfields are alike in layout. Once the required standard for a particular function has been achieved, a Certificate of Competency is awarded, which indicates that the individual is licensed to operate solo at that position. Other tasks within the control centre require requalification.

On completion of their initial tour at an RAF airfield, ATC personnel return to the CATCS at RAF Shawbury for a six-and-a-half week course that covers procedures employed at an Area Control Centre. This is then followed by further tours at any RAF air traffic control facility.

As can be seen in this chapter, the training organization operated by the RAF is a vast undertaking. The great range of courses offering basic, refresher, familiarization, continuation, post graduate and other forms of training are aimed at providing the Service with suitably qualified personnel at all levels. The effectiveness of this training is borne out by the professional manner in which the RAF carries out its various tasks around the world.

ADDITIONAL ELEMENTS

Medical

The Royal Air Force Nursing Service was formed in 1918, just two months after the RAF itself was first formed. In June 1923, the Royal Assent was given to rename this Service as the Princess Mary's Royal Air Force Nursing Service (PMRAFNS), by which title it is still known.

There are three methods of entry to the PMRAFNS, these being as Commissioned Officers, Staff Nurses or Enrolled Nurses. All of these entrants must be registered with the United Kingdom Central Council for Nursing Midwifery and Health Visiting. The PMRAFNS is a fully integrated element within the RAF. Officers within the Nursing Service hold the Queen's Commission, and complete either Short Service or Permanent Commissions. Other ranks can join the medical service for engagements of varying lengths, with possibilities for career development and promotion.

The principal centre for the medical services of the RAF is the Princess Alexandra Hospital at RAF Wroughton, near Swindon in Wiltshire. This hospital is jointly staffed by the Army and the RAF, and its role is to serve the units of these two Services in the southern part of the UK. This hospital also acts as the reception centre for aeromedical flights that are inbound to the UK, via RAF Brize Norton which is less than one hour away by road, or a few minutes by helicopter. The hospital is equipped to deal with most of the many and varied aspects of medical matters, and works in co-operation with other hospitals in the local area. Treatment is provided for NHS patients when required.

In line with the rest of the RAF, the medical facilities of the PMRAFNS have been reduced in recent years. The RAF hospital at Ely in Cambridgeshire was handed over to the local civilian health authority, and the hospital at RAF Nocton Hall, near Lincoln, has been reduced in status, and now deals mainly with out-patients. However, other medical facilities remain, and principal overseas locations include the RAF hospitals at Wegburg in Germany, and at Akrotiri in Cyprus. The RAF also operates the Defence Services Medical Rehabilitation Unit, located at Headley Court, near Leatherhead, in Surrey.

Four medical units are located at RAF Halton, the principal one of which is the Princess Mary's Royal Air Force Hospital. First established in 1919, its primary role is the treatment of casualties from the uniformed Services in time of war, and the training of staff for this task is the main peacetime activity. Containing some 200 beds, it equates to a district general facility, and possesses a range of specialist services. It also carries out investigative work and treatment on a number of diseases.

The second Halton-based unit is the Institute of Pathology and Tropical Medicine, which carries out pathological and medical investigations into all fatal air accidents in the UK, both civil and military. It also provides all three Services with pathological support. Third is the Institute of Health and Medical Training; predecessors of this unit were first established at RAF Halton in 1919, and the current institute consists of three elements: the Training Division conducts initial and continuation training for medical officers, together with airmen and airwomen who are members of the medical trade group; the Public Health Medicine Division is responsible for health promotion, controlling disease outbreaks, and for monitoring data and statistics relating to health matters; and the Environmental and Occupational Medicine Division monitors working practices throughout the RAF to ensure that current health and safety regulations are complied with.

The fourth unit at Halton is the Institute of Dental Health and Training, responsible for all dental health matters in the RAF. This includes the training of all personnel in the Dental Branch and TG 16, and the institute also contains the Central Dental Laboratory.

Doctors and physicians in the RAF Medical Branch are commissioned officers, and apart from serving at the main RAF hospitals, they are also posted to station medical centres throughout the RAF, each initially as a Junior Medical Officer with the rank of Flight Lieutenant. With experience, further positions in the RAF Medical Branch can include appointments as Senior Medical Officer on an RAF station, a specialist or consultant position in one of the RAF hospitals, or a research posting to the RAF Institute of Aviation Medicine at Farnborough.

The Royal Air Force Aeromedical Evacuation Service is responsible for the carriage by air of personnel who need to be moved for medical reasons. This covers personnel from all British Services, their dependants and MoD employees. In exceptional circumstances, the service may be extended to civilians, for which a charge may be made. The RAF operates a number of regular aeromedical flights to and from its major overseas operating locations. Medical evacuation is also carried out on the more regular transport services of No 38 Group, along with other passengers and/or cargo. In urgent cases, special aeromedical evacuation flights are mounted, and chartered civilian aircraft are also employed.

Training for this task is carried out by the Aeromedical Evacuation Training Centre (AETC), which is located at RAF Brize Norton. The service comprises three aeromedical evacuation squadrons (AESs). No 1 AES operates from RAF Lyneham, with No 2 AES located at RAF Brize Norton. No 3 AES is connected with units that undertake field operations, such as the Harriers and support helicopters. This trio of squadrons operate as small teams of trained personnel, who act as escorts for the patient. These teams consist of personnel with appropriate skills to suit the nature of the aeromedical task in hand.

RAF Music Services

In addition to display teams such as the 'Red Arrows' and the 'Falcons', other elements of the RAF that come into widespread contact with the general public are the various bands and other similar organizations that comprise the RAF Music Services. Currently, there are five main bands in the RAF, and they are located as follows:

The Central Band of the RAF
RAF Uxbridge
The Band of the RAF College
RAF Cranwell
The Western Band of the RAF
RAF Locking
The Band of the RAF Regiment
RAF Catterick
The Band of the RAF in Germany
Rheindahlen

It is possible that the Band of the RAF Regiment may move to RAF Honington in 1994 along with the other elements of the RAF Regiment.

These bands undertake a wide range of musical support for ceremonial parades and other similar functions throughout the UK and at many locations in Europe. This includes parades for visiting dignitaries, guards of honour, State visits, Freedom parades for RAF stations in local towns, the Royal Tournament, the Lord Mayor's Show, and many other similar functions, often alongside the Queen's Colour Squadron of the RAF Regiment. Further tasks include public concerts, radio and television appearances, and sessions in recording studios.

The Central Band is the largest unit, comprising some 80 musicians. It can operate either as the full Symphonic Concert Band, or the slightly smaller Concert Band. The Central Band can also provide Fanfare Teams, the Salon Orchestra or the RAF Squadronaires, for events requiring particular types of music presentation. Apart from the Central Band, the other RAF bands usually consist of some 40 musicians, plus administrative staff.

Training for RAF musicians is carried out at RAF Uxbridge by the RAF School of Music. The management of engagements for the bands based in the UK is carried out from a central control at this station, and requests for appearances usually far exceed the available opportunities. The Band of the RAF in Germany usually covers events in Europe, supported by the UK-based bands as and when required.

In time of war, personnel from the RAF bands would operate as assistants for medical services or casualty evacuation. Training for these emergency tasks is provided on courses run by the medical facilities at RAF Halton.

In addition to the bands listed above, there are several voluntary brass and pipe bands, located at RAF stations throughout the UK.

This chapter contains descriptions covering the majority of the training elements that have been transferred from the former Support Command to the new Personnel and Training Command. The changes in all elements of RAF training will continue for some while, and thus the size and format of the new command will also alter. Several other RAF units have also moved from Support Command to Personnel and Training Command. These include the RAF Provost and Security Service, the RAF Police and the Police Dog Training Squadron, amongst others.

FLYING UNITS OF THE RAF

Chapters One and Two of this book include descriptive details of all the flying units of the RAF, from the front-line and operational training units of Strike Command to the various training elements of Personnel and Training Command. All of these units are listed here in a tabular form, for ease of reference.

The first part of this listing indicates in numerical order all the active squadrons of the RAF. The second part of the list includes the remaining RAF flights, units and schools that carry out flying duties. It includes known changes to represent the situation that should exist in the spring of 1994. The addition of (R) following the squadron number indicates that the particular unit is known as a reserve squadron, and operates as an OCU or as part of an Advanced Flying Training School. At times of war some of the reserve squadrons may undertake operations, flown by instructor pilots.

Sqn	Command/Group	Aircraft Type(s)	Base
1	Strike/1	Harrier GR.7/T.4	RAF Wittering
2	Strike/1	Tornado GR.1/.1A	RAF Marham
3	Strike/2	Harrier GR.7	RAF Laarbruch
4	Strike/2	Harrier GR.7	RAF Laarbruch
5	Strike/11	Tornado F.3	RAF Coningsby
6	Strike/1	Jaguar GR.1A/T.2A	RAF Coltishall
7	Strike/1	Chinook HC.1/.2 Gazelle HT.3	RAF Odiham
8	Strike/11	Sentry AEW.1	RAF Waddington
9	Strike/2	Tornado GR.1	RAF Bruggen
10	Strike/38	VC-10 C.1/.1K	RAF Brize Norton
11	Strike/11	Tornado F.3	RAF Leeming
12	Strike/18	Tornado GR.1B	RAF Lossiemouth
13	Strike/1	Tornado GR.1/.1A	RAF Marham
14	Strike/2	Tornado GR.1	RAF Bruggen
15(R)	Strike/1	Tornado GR.1	RAF Lossiemouth
16(R)	Strike/1	Jaguar GR.1A/T.2A	RAF Lossiemouth
17	Strike/2	Tornado GR.1	RAF Bruggen

Sqn	Command/ Group	Aircraft Type(s)	Base
18	Strike/2	Chinook HC.1/.2 Puma HC.1	RAF Laarbruch
19(R)	P & T	Hawk T.1/.1A	RAF Chivenor
20(R)	Strike/1	Harrier GR.7/T.4	RAF Wittering
22(HQ)	Strike/18		RAF St Mawgan
22/'A' Flt		Wessex HC.2 Sea King HAR.3	RAF Chivenor
22/'C' Flt		Wessex HC.2	RAF Valley
22/'E' Flt		Wessex HC.2	RAF Coltishall
24	Strike/38	Hercules C.1K/.1P/.3P	RAF Lyneham
25	Strike/11	Tornado F.3	RAF Leeming
27(R)	Strike/1	Chinook HC.2 Puma HC.1	RAF Odiham
28	Strike	Wessex HC.2	Sek Kong
29	Strike/11	Tornado F.3	RAF Coningsby
30	Strike/38	Hercules C.1K/.1P/.3P	RAF Lyneham
31	Strike/2	Tornado GR.1	RAF Bruggen
32	Strike/38	BAe 125 CC.2/.3 Gazelle HT.3/HCC.4	RAF Northolt
33	Strike/1	Puma HC.1	RAF Odiham
39	Strike/18	Canberra PR.9	RAF Marham
41	Strike/1	Jaguar GR.1A/T.2A	RAF Coltishall
42(R)	Strike/18	Nimrod MR.2P	RAF Kinloss
43	Strike/11	Tornado F.3	RAF Leuchars
45(R)	P & T	Jetstream T.1	RAF Finningley
47	Strike/38	Hercules C.1P/.3P	RAF Lyneham
51	Strike/18	Nimrod R.1P	RAF Wyton
54	Strike/1	Jaguar GR.1A/T.2A	RAF Coltishall
55(R)	Strike/38	VC-10 C.1/.1K/K.2/.3/.4 TriStar K.1/KC.1/C.2/.2A	RAF Brize Norton
56(R)	Strike/11	Tornado F.3	RAF Coningsby
57(R)	Strike/38	Hercules C.1K/.1P/.3P	RAF Lyneham
60	Strike/1	Wessex HC.2	RAF Benson
70	Strike/38	Hercules C.1P/.3P	RAF Lyneham
72	Strike/1	Wessex HC.2	RAF Aldergrove
74(R)	P & T	Hawk T.1/.1A	RAF Valley
78	Strike	Sea King HAR.3 Chinook HC.1/.2	RAF Mt Pleasant
84	Strike	Wessex HC.5C	RAF Akrotiri
92(R)	P & T	Hawk T.1/.1A	RAF Chivenor
100	Strike/18	Hawk T.1/.1A	RAF Finningley
101	Strike/38	VC-10 K.2/.3/.4	RAF Brize Norton
111	Strike/11	Tornado F.3	RAF Leuchars
120	Strike/18	Nimrod MR.2P	RAF Kinloss
201	Strike/18	Nimrod MR.2P	RAF Kinloss
202 (HQ)	Strike/18		RAF Boulmer
202/'A' Flt		Sea King HAR.3	RAF Boulmer
202/'C' Flt		Sea King HAR.3	RAF Wattisham
202/'D' Flt		Sea King HAR.3	RAF Lossiemouth
202/'E' Flt		Sea King HAR.3	RAF Leconfield
206	Strike/18	Nimrod MR.2P	RAF Kinloss
208(R)	P & T	Hawk T.1/.1A	RAF Valley
216	Strike/38	TriStar K.1/KC.1, TriStar C.2/.2A	RAF Brize Norton
230	Strike/1	Puma HC.1	RAF Aldergrove
360	Strike/18	Canberra T.17/.17A	RAF Wyton
617	Strike/1	Tornado GR.1B	RAF Lossiemouth

List of RAF units (except numbered squadrons) that operate aircraft, i.e flights, schools and units.

Unit	Command/ Group	Aircraft Type(s)	Base
1312 Flt	Strike	Hercules C.1K	RAF Mount Pleasant
1435 Flt	Strike	Tornado F.3	RAF Mount Pleasant
1563 Flt	Strike	Puma HC.1	Belize IAP
CFS	P & T	Bulldog T.1	RAF Scampton
		Tucano T.1	RAF Scampton
		Hawk T.1/.1A	RAF Valley
		Gazelle HT.3	RAF Shawbury
No 1 FTS	P & T	Tucano T.1	RAF Linton-on-Ouse
No 2 FTS	P & T	Wessex HC.2	RAF Shawbury
		Gazelle HT.3	
No 3 FTS	P & T	Tucano T.1	RAF Cranwell
No 4 FTS	P & T	Hawk T.1/.1A	RAF Valley
No 6 FTS	P & T	Bulldog T.1	RAF Finningley
		Tucano T.1	
		Hawk T.1	
		Dominie T.1	
No 7 FTS	P & T	Hawk T.1/.1A	RAF Chivenor
RAFC Air Sqn	P & T	Bulldog T.1	RAF Cranwell
SKTU	Strike/18	Sea King HAR.3	RAF St Mawgan
SARTU	Strike/18	Wessex HC.2	RAF Valley
TTTE	Strike/1	Tornado GR.1	RAF Cottesmore
Queen's Flt	Strike/38	BAe 146 CC.2	RAF Benson
		Wessex HCC.4	
F.3OEU	Strike	Tornado F.3	RAF Coningsby
SAOEU	Strike	Tornado GR.1	A&AEE Boscombe Down
		Harrier GR.7/T.4	
Berlin Stn Flt	Strike/2	Chipmunk T.10	RAF Gatow
Northolt Stn Flt	Strike/38	Islander CC.2	RAF Northolt
St Athan Stn Flt		Hawk T.1	RAF St Athan
'Red Arrows'	P & T	Hawk T.1/.1A	RAF Scampton
BBMF	Strike/11	Lancaster B.1,	RAF Coningsby
		Spitfire lla/Vb/XIX/PR.XIX,	
		Hurricane IIc, Devon C.2,	
		C-47 Dakota, Chipmunk T.10	

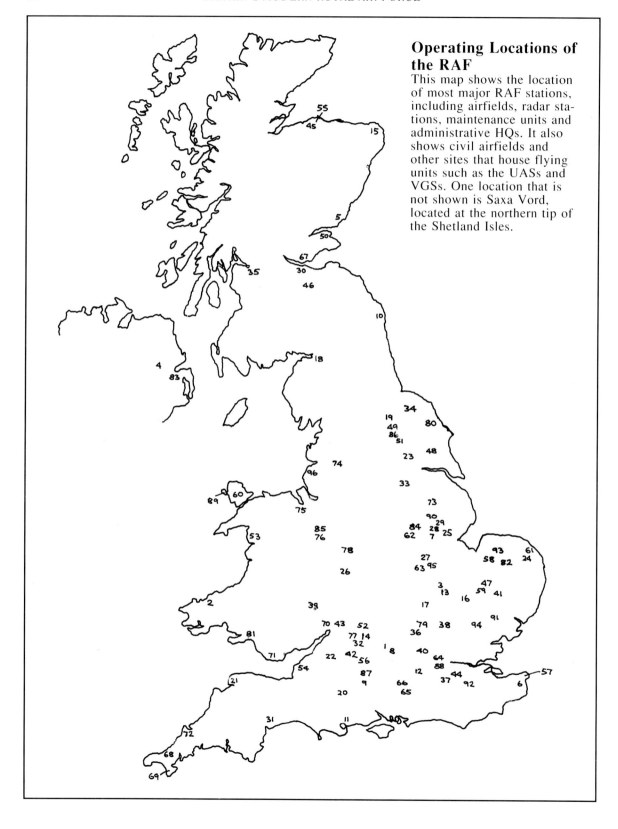

Operating Locations of the RAF

This map shows the location of most major RAF stations, including airfields, radar stations, maintenance units and administrative HQs. It also shows civil airfields and other sites that house flying units such as the UASs and VGSs. One location that is not shown is Saxa Vord, located at the northern tip of the Shetland Isles.

1	Abingdon, Oxon	50	RAF Leuchars, Fife
2	Aberporth, Dyfed (DRA)	51	RAF Linton-on-Ouse, N. Yorks
3	RAF Alconbury, Cambs (USAF)	52	Little Rissington, Glos
4	RAF Aldergrove, N.I.	53	Llanbedr, Gwynedd (DRA)
5	Arbroath, Tayside	54	RAF Locking, Avon
6	Ash, Kent	55	RAF Lossiemouth, Grampian
7	RAF Barkston Heath, Lincs	56	RAF Lyneham, Wilts
8	RAF Benson, Oxon	57	RAF Manston, Kent
9	Boscombe Down, Wilts (A&AEE)	58	RAF Marham, Norfolk
10	RAF Boulmer, N'thumb	59	RAF Mildenhall, Suffolk (USAF)
11	Bournemouth, Dorset	60	RAF Mona, Gwynedd
12	RAF Bracknell, Berks	61	RAF Neatishead, Norfolk
13	RAF Brampton, Cambs	62	RAF Newton, Notts
14	RAF Brize Norton, Oxon	63	RAF North Luffenham, Leics
15	RAF Buchan, Grampian	64	RAF Northolt, Greater London
16	Cambridge, Cambs	65	RAF Oakhanger, Hants
17	RAF Cardington, Beds	66	RAF Odiham, Hants
18	RAF Carlisle, Cumbria	67	Pitreavie, Fife
19	RAF Catterick, N. Yorks	68	Portreath, Cornwall
20	RAF Chilmark, Wilts	69	RNAS Predannack, Cornwall
21	RAF Chivenor, Devon	70	Quedgeley, Glos
22	Colerne, Wilts	71	RAF St Athan, South Glam
23	RAF Church Fenton, N. Yorks	72	RAF St Mawgan, Cornwall
24	RAF Coltishall, Norfolk	73	RAF Scampton, Lincs
25	RAF Coningsby, Lincs	74	Samlesbury, Lancs
26	RAF Cosford, Salop	75	RAF Sealand, Clwyd
27	RAF Cottesmore, Leics	76	RAF Shawbury, Salop
28	RAF Cranwell, Lincs	77	South Cerney, Glos
29	RAF Digby, Lincs	78	RAF Stafford, Staffs
30	Edinburgh/Turnhouse, Lothian	79	RAF Stanbridge, Beds
31	Exeter, Devon	80	RAF Staxton Wold, N. Yorks
32	RAF Fairford, Glos (USAF)	81	Swansea, West Glam
33	RAF Finningley, S. Yorks	82	RAF Swanton Morley, Norfolk
34	RAF Fylingdales, N. Yorks	83	Sydenham, N.I.
35	Glasgow, Strathclyde	84	RAF Syerston, Notts
36	RAF Halton, Bucks	85	Ternhill, Salop
37	RAF Headley Court, Surrey	86	RAF Topcliffe, N. Yorks
38	RAF Henlow, Beds	87	Upavon, Wilts
39	RAF Hereford, H & W	88	RAF Uxbridge, Greater London
40	RAF High Wycombe, Bucks	89	RAF Valley, Gwynedd
41	RAF Honington, Suffolk	90	RAF Waddington, Lincs
42	Hullavington, Wilts	91	Wattisham, Suffolk
43	RAF Innsworth, Glos	92	West Malling, Kent
44	Kenley, Greater London	93	RAF West Raynham, Norfolk
45	RAF Kinloss, Grampian	94	Wethersfield, Essex
46	Kirknewton, Lothian	95	RAF Wittering, Cambs
47	RAF Lakenheath, Suffolk (USAF)	96	RAF Woodvale, Mersey
48	RAF Leconfield, Humberside	97	RAF Wyton, Cambs
49	RAF Leeming, N. Yorks		

CHAPTER THREE

Logistics Command

THE BIRTH OF Logistics Command, which was officially inaugurated on 1 April 1994, followed a similar path to that of the arrival of Personnel and Training Command, in being a further product of the recommendations of the 'Prospect' report. This has resulted in the division of the former Support Command into these two new commands. The HQ staff for Logistics Command are housed mainly in the former HQ Support Command complex at RAF Brampton, but with the arrival of staff from other locations, additional accommodation has had to be provided at the former flying station of RAF Wyton, which is only a few miles from Brampton. The extra staff have come from the offices of the Air Member for Supply and Organization, based in London, and from RAF facilities at Harrogate, Swanton Morley and Stanbridge, which will all be reduced in size or closed in due course.

Logistics Command consists of three major functional groupings: the Maintenance Group, which is a Defence Support Agency; the Communications and Information Systems Group; and the Support Management Group. The process of creating this new command will continue through to 1997 and, whilst the actual composition of these various groups is not clear at the time of writing, the major elements and responsibilities of Logistics Command are described in the following sections.

AIRCRAFT MAINTENANCE

With the closure of the maintenance facilities at RAF Abingdon in 1992, the main task of overhauling many of the RAF's aircraft is now concentrated on the sprawling complex of RAF St Athan in South Wales. Aircraft maintenance and painting was also carried out at RAF Kemble, in Gloucestershire, but this facility has now closed and its tasks transferred to St Athan.

The maintenance effort at St Athan is controlled by the Engineering Division, which is responsible for a workforce of over 3,000, a quarter of whom are civilians. This division is split into four wings: Aircraft Engineering Wing, Aircraft Engineering Support Wing, Mechanical Repair and Overhaul Wing, and Supply and Support Engineering Wing. Each of the wings is further divided into a number of squadrons, some of which specialize on a particular aircraft type, whilst others concentrate on various sub-assemblies or equipment.

The Aircraft Engineering Wing consists of an HQ Flight and five squadrons (Nos 1, 2, 3, 4 and 10), which are responsible for the major overhauls of many of the RAF's front-line aircraft. (These squadrons should not be confused with the front-line units of Strike Command with similar numbers.) This wing has a personnel strength of some 1,100.

No 1 Squadron: A large new hangar, with two servicing bays, was erected at St Athan in 1992 for the purpose of carrying out major overhauls of the RAF's fleet of VC-10 tanker/transports, the work being carried out by this unit. This task was transferred from RAF Brize Norton in the winter of 1992/93.

No 2 Squadron: This unit is currently involved in fatigue-related modifications to the Tornado F.3 fighter. Following some well-publicized problems with the standard of work carried out by a civilian contractor, this operation is now being undertaken by St Athan personnel.

No 3 Squadron: The RAF's Harrier GR.7s, together with the Royal Navy's Sea Harriers, are overhauled by this unit, along with the two-seat Harrier T.4s of both Services. This unit undertook modifications to the Harrier GR.7 to provide an added reconnaissance capability for the type's deployment to Turkey in April 1993. Another task is the incorporation of various post-delivery modifications to the GR.7, and the squadron is also involved in the programme to convert the Royal Navy's Sea Harrier FRS.1s to FRS.2 standard. To carry out these tasks, the squadron has a personnel strength of about 140, the majority of whom are members of the RAF.

No 4 Squadron: Divided into two sections, this unit deals with work formerly carried out at RAF Abingdon. This is undertaken in two hangars that were used until the early 1990s for the overhaul of the RAF's fleet of Phantoms. The Jaguar Maintenance Flight deals with the aircraft of that name, carrying out major overhauls and various modifications. Hawk T.1/.1As are given similar treatment in the second hangar by the other half of this squadron, namely the Hawk Maintenance Flight. The interval between major overhauls for the RAF's Hawks is 2,000 flying hours. Following an aircraft's arrival at St Athan, items of equipment such as flying controls and the engine are removed, and paint is stripped off down to bare metal; this initial process taking five to six days. Then follows the major servicing, for which a period of 56 working days is allotted, this being carried out by a team consisting of a Sergeant and usually four Technicians. This is followed by reassembly, repainting and flight testing.

No 10 Squadron: The task of providing major servicing and overhauls of the Tornado GR.1/.1A fleet is the responsibility of this unit, together

Major servicing being carried out on a Harrier GR.7 at RAF St Athan. Note the sturdy cover to protect the cockpit windscreen. (Corporal K. Jones, RAF PR)

This Hawk has been stripped of all paint as part of its major servicing programme. (Corporal K. Jones, RAF PR)

with the incorporation of modifications. As the Tornado was produced in a number of batches over several years, there are minor detail variations between the batches, thus No 10 Squadron has a constant programme of updating earlier machines. Some 26 Tornados are dealt with in this programme of minor modifications each year, the work on each aircraft taking about one month to complete, and three bays are allocated in the squadron's hangar for this work.

The original number of hours that a Tornado flew before it required a major overhaul was 1,200, but this was increased to 1,600 and the current interval between 'majors' is 2,000 hours. Some of the earliest Tornados delivered to the RAF have seen intensive use in the training role with the Tri-national Tornado Training Establishment at RAF Cottesmore, and some of these aircraft have now received two major overhauls. No 10 Squadron aims to deal with 80 GR.1/.1As a year, on six servicing tracks, with each major service tasked to take 82 working days. On arrival for a major overhaul, each Tornado is stripped of many components such as cockpit canopies, ejection seats and engines, for specialist maintenance by other units at St Athan. Avionics are removed and sent to RAF Sealand for overhaul. The aircraft is then stripped of its paint and thoroughly cleaned and degreased, before being repainted in primer. The main task of inspection, maintenance, repair and replacement of defective or life-expired parts is then car-

ried out. This is followed by reassembly and functional testing of the many and varied systems to be found in the Tornado, after which the aircraft is repainted. An air test, lasting for between one-and-a-half and two hours, is scheduled for day 74, followed by any rectifications and further air tests if required. The aircraft is then delivered to its front-line unit on day 82.

Recent and current modifications of Tornados involve the fitting of the Thermal Imaging Airborne Laser Designator (TIALD) system, and alterations to adapt the aircraft for the maritime strike role and the carriage of the Sea Eagle anti-ship missile. More than 200 personnel, half of whom are civilians, are involved in Tornado maintenance.

The Aircraft Engineering Support Wing is comprised of four squadrons and a Design Authority, as follows:

No 5 Squadron: The production of components, particularly one-off items, is covered by this unit in its manufacturing workshops. This includes items for both aircraft and ground equipment, and the squadron has built up considerable experience and expertise in reclaiming and renovating used components, with considerable savings in cost when compared with new items. Items are produced to support other elements at St Athan, and for use throughout the RAF.

Bay Support Squadron: This unit is responsible for supporting the many tasks carried out by the Engineering Division, with workshops dealing in

Beneath this mountain of scaffolding is a Tornado GR.1 undergoing a major overhaul with No 10 Squadron, an element of the Aircraft Engineering Wing at RAF St Athan.

Aircraft of the RAF

Top *This No 9 Squadron Tornado GR.1 is based in Germany with No 2 Group of Strike Command. The aircraft is carrying ALARM anti-radar missiles under the fuselage.* (BAe)

Above *A spectacular view of a No 31 Squadron Tornado GR.1, one of four Tornado-equipped squadrons based at RAF Bruggen in Germany.* (Ken Delve)

Below *With 'burners cut in, a Tornado GR.1A of No 13 Squadron prepares to roll. The squadron is one of two front-line RAF units that operate the reconnaissance variant of the Tornado.* (Bob Munro)

Top *Grey-painted Harrier GR.7s of Nos 3 and 4 Squadrons deployed to Turkey during 1993 as part of Operation 'Warden', flying armed reconnaissance patrols over northern Iraq. (BAe)*

Above *In preparation for deployment to Italy in support of UN operations over Bosnia, this No 6 Squadron Jaguar GR.1A was repainted in an overall light grey scheme, nicknamed 'Baby Blue'. (Bob Munro)*

Below *No 41 Squadron operate the Jaguar GR.1A in the reconnaissance role, utilizing the large BAe camera pod fitted on a centreline station beneath the fuselage.*

Top *A Tornado F.3 of RAF Leeming-based No 11 Squadron 'cleans-up' after take-off.*

Above *This Tornado F.3 wears the markings of RAF Coningsby-based No 29 Squadron. Note the BAe Sky Flash AAMs under the fuselage. (BAe)*

Below *Arguably the most distinctive aircraft in RAF service in terms of appearance, the Sentry AEW.1 equips No 8 Squadron at RAF Waddington. (Bob Munro)*

Above *Nimrod MR.2Ps such as this example are operated by Nos 42 (Reserve), 120, 201 and 206 Squadrons, all based at RAF Kinloss in north-east Scotland.* (Bob Munro)

Below *The Canberra PR.9s of No 39 (1 PRU) Squadron will very likely be the last examples of the famous English Electric design to serve with the RAF.*

Bottom *A VC-10 K.2 tanker of No 101 Squadron from RAF Brize Norton, viewed from a sister-ship while flying in support of RAF fighters.*

Above *A Hercules C.3P of the Lyneham Transport Wing, caught on a test flight following overhaul and repainting by Marshalls of Cambridge. Note the feathered outboard propeller.* (Bob Munro)

Below *A low-visibility light grey and powder blue colour scheme is now worn by the BAe 125s of No 32 Squadron at RAF Northolt.* (Bob Munro)

Bottom *The light blue band around the rear fuselage of this Tucano T.1 identifies it as an aircraft of No 3 FTS at RAF Cranwell.*

Above *No 100 Squadron operates this Hawk T.1 from RAF Finningley on various target facilities training duties.* (BAe)

Below *A Jetstream T.1 of No 45 (Reserve) Squadron touches down at RAF Finningley after a training sortie. These aircraft are used for the advanced training of Group Two multi-engine pilots.*

Bottom *Wearing the markings of the Central Flying School at RAF Scampton, this Bulldog T.1 is used in the instructor training role.* (Bob Munro)

Above *Unique in having a tailwheel undercarriage, the Chipmunk T.10 is still widely used by the Air Experience Flights, such as No 6 AEF, shown here.*

Below *The bulbous nose and underwing antennae identify this as a Canberra T.17A ECM trainer of No 360 Squadron. (Bob Munro)*

Bottom *Touching down on its 'hind legs', this Chinook HC.1 serves with No 7 Squadron at RAF Odiham. (Bob Munro)*

Left *No 202 Squadron operates a number of Sea King HAR.3s from various locations around the UK. They are to be complemented in due course by a batch of six Sea King HAR.3As.* (Westland)

Below *The venerable Wessex HC.2 is used by No 2 FTS at RAF Shawbury for advanced flying training of future helicopter pilots.*

Bottom *Still wearing a smart VIP colour scheme, this Gazelle HCC.4 is operated by No 32 Squadron at RAF Northolt.* (Bob Munro)

hydraulics, wheels, tyres, avionics and armaments, amongst other items. This element is also responsible for the many aspects of painting, both of whole aircraft and of individual components, and new facilities have recently been provided for this task.

Three sections comprise the RAF Repair and Design Authority. The Aircraft Design Section prepares schemes for the repair of airframe components and mechanical items. This involves design studies into using metal to repair composite material structures, and the use of new composite materials for the repair of conventional metal structures and assemblies. The Mechanical Design Section covers design applications connected with equipment used for ground support, lifting devices, test rigs, jigs and fixtures. The Repair Design Liaison Office prepares and maintains histories of individual aircraft, organizes libraries containing drawings and standards, and co-ordinates any design and drawing requirements with outside industry.

The Aircraft Storage and Transportation Squadron, which moved from RAF Abingdon in 1992, is responsible for the safe storage of various numbers of different aircraft types which the RAF holds in reserve or for which there is no current task. This involves the aircraft being sealed against humidity and maintained in a condition that would enable them to be used by front-line units with a reasonable amount of notice. A further task for this squadron is the transportation of non-airworthy aircraft from site to site, together with the recovery of wreckage and material from the scenes of aircraft accidents, both civil and military. The squadron also carries out major servicing on Dominie T.1s and Jetstream T.1s.

The Repair Support Squadron is tasked to assist with the repair of RAF and Royal Navy aircraft that have been damaged in some way but are considered to be repairable at their current location or home base, this level of damage being classified as Category 3.

The Mechanical Repair and Overhaul Wing comprises an HQ Squadron, which is responsible for the planning and administration of the wing's tasks. Three production squadrons carry out the following functions:

No 7 Squadron: The repair and renovation of aircraft fuel tanks, radomes, flying control components, undercarriages and cockpit canopies are just some of the many tasks carried out. Techniques have been developed by this unit for the renovation of cockpit canopies which have resulted in existing items being reused at a far lower cost when compared with replacement by new components.

No 8 Squadron: Specializing in engine overhaul, this unit mainly deals with the RB.199

engines from the Tornado and the Adour turbofan engine that powers both the Jaguar and the Hawk. Both of these engines are of modular design, and the squadron is tasked with handling some 1,200 modules annually. Much of the work is shared in a partnership with Rolls-Royce, and several techniques have been developed to renovate and reuse components that were formerly scrapped.

No 9 Squadron: This unit is tasked with the production of various mechanical components, often in co-ordination with civilian industries, together with renovation of components from hydraulic systems on various aircraft.

The Supply and Support Engineering Wing is tasked to support the work of the other wings within the Engineering Division, and the station as a whole. It consists of three squadrons, who, between them, provide supply services covering over 100,000 items, apart from whole aircraft, engines and vehicles. Forward Stockholding Flights are maintained to support the various servicing and repair elements, and maintenance is carried out on St Athan's large fleet of vehicles, ground equipment, and communications and airfield aids.

The operation and administration of RAF St Athan is carried out by four units who, along with the Engineering Division, report to the Station Commander. One of these units is the Operations Squadron, which is responsible for many of the aspects connected with the flying operations of the airfield. The Officer Commanding, who is also the Senior Test Pilot, has a staff of two pilots and two navigators, who are tasked with the flight testing of all marks of Jaguar, Hawk, Harrier, Sea Harrier and Tornado following maintenance, overhaul, or modification. The St Athan Station Flight operates two Hawk T.1s as crew ferries in support of inward and return delivery flights.

In addition to the aircraft storage facility at RAF St Athan, further RAF and other aircraft are stored at RAF Shawbury.

SERVICING SUPPORT

The Central Servicing Development Establishment (CSDE) has been based at RAF Swanton Morley in Norfolk since 1958, but is due to transfer to Logistic Command's HQ complex of RAF Wyton/Brampton in the mid-1990s. The CSDE is responsible for providing the RAF with the suitable engineering information and support arrangements to ensure that aircraft and equipment are correctly maintained throughout their service lives. This task involves studies of how to improve reliability, maintenance procedures and techniques, balanced with the constant need to promote efficiency and cost-effectiveness.

The CSDE is organized into a number of wings,

covering Projects, Electrical Engineering and Mechanical Engineering, amongst other tasks. These wings are further divided into squadrons and flights, who between them cover a range of specialist responsibilities covering many RAF requirements. These elements are involved with most RAF aircraft types, weapons systems and other items of equipment from the time that the initial contracts are signed with the suppliers or manufacturers, through to entry into service. Studies for support continue during the items' service life and this includes establishing periods between overhauls, not only of the complete airframe, but also of all the many items of mechanical and electrical equipment on aircraft and on ground-based machinery.

Project Teams are formed for all new aircraft types or major weapons and other significant items of equipment. These teams operate at the manufacturers' plants at the initial stages of such projects and follow the development through to service entry. Smaller teams are also constituted to oversee modifications to existing aircraft, weapons or other equipment.

Teams from the Projects Wing are currently, or recently have been, involved with such aircraft as the Sentry AEW.1, Harrier GR.7 and the Eurofighter 2000, together with Mid-Life Update (MLU) programmes for the Tornado and the Chinook. In connection with aircraft purchased from the USA, teams from the CSDE are based in that country, at the Boeing plants located at Seattle (for the Sentry) and Philadelphia (covering the Chinook MLU).

Three squadrons and several flights of the Electrical Engineering Wing are tasked with pro-viding advice, support and information to the MoD and the British Services in matters relating to the introduction and in-service maintenance of electrical and avionic equipment, including some of the sophisticated items that are now fitted in the cockpits of modern combat aircraft. Amongst a wide range of items covered are support for the many flight simulators that the RAF operates.

The Mechanical Engineering Wing deals with service entry and operational maintenance support for aircraft, armaments, weapons and engines. Amongst its activities, the wing is involved in non-destructive testing of airframe structures and other related items.

Due to its importance as a major aircraft type for the RAF in the next century, the CSDE has recently formed the European Fighter Aircraft Wing, to cover the support and maintenance of the Eurofighter 2000 project from the outset.

RAF Swanton Morley is also the home of the Maintenance Analysis and Computing Division (MACD), which is the centre of computing expertise within the RAF's Engineer Branch. The MACD's role is to support maintenance and logistics operations with related information transfer, documentation and computing techniques. This unit will also move to RAF Wyton/Brampton in the mid-1990s.

EQUIPMENT SUPPLY AND DISTRIBUTION

An organization such as the RAF, with its many units scattered the length and breadth of the country, together with other elements at overseas loca-

The Eurofighter 2000, subject of much work on the part of the Central Servicing Development Establishment's Project Wing at RAF Swanton Morley. It is seen here in mock-up form.

tions, can only function effectively with an efficient back-up support system that will provide equipment and spares when required. To this end, a number of Equipment Supply Depots (ESDs) are in use, mainly in the north and west of the UK. Their locations were decided upon during the expansion of the RAF in the late 1930s, in order to keep them as far away as possible from any air attacks launched from the Continent. Seven ESDs were established prior to the Second World War, but under current plans these will be reduced to two or three, in line with similar reductions throughout the RAF.

The heart of the spares and equipment distribution system is at RAF Stanbridge, near Leighton Buzzard, home of the RAF Supply Control Centre (SCC). This unit utilizes one of the most powerful computers in the country, and maintains a central record of nearly all of the 1.5 million items of equipment that the RAF requires, with information on location and quantity. The ESDs and most major RAF stations, both in the UK and overseas, are linked via the computer at the SCC. Thus, information is readily available regarding the most suitable means of obtaining an urgently required item, be it from one of the ESDs or possibly from another RAF station, if that source would be more expeditious. Another major element in this organization is the Priority Freight Distribution System. This is a network of routes over which large transport vehicles link the ESDs and other storage facilities with a number of Major Distribution Centres and RAF stations. To give some idea of the activity at the ESDs, approximately 20,000 to 25,000 consignments are received each month, some of these being batches of spares and equipment arriving from manufacturers. In the opposite direction the ESDs issue about 60,000 to 65,000 items each month, or over 3,000 each working day.

Turning to the ESDs, the most northerly of these is located at RAF Carlisle, home of No 14 Maintenance Unit (MU). The ESDs were constructed to a standard pattern, which consisted of an HQ complex and six dispersed sites, covering a total area of some 330 acres (133 hectares). The site at Carlisle contains 40 major buildings, 27 of which are large storage sheds. No 14 MU is responsible for the warehouse storage of over 810,000 items of equipment and spares, which represents some 58 per cent of the RAF's total inventory. This includes such items as airframe parts, electrical, radio and instrumentation spares, together with tyres, hazardous materials, photographic equipment and hand tools. The aircraft spares are mainly connected with machines obtained from, or built in co-operation with, the USA, covering such types as the Hercules, Chinook, and later models of the Harrier. No 14

MU also holds the entire range of 'blue' uniforms for the RAF. Spares support is also provided for the Royal Navy, the Army Air Corps, contractors and foreign governments, in addition to the principal task of supporting the RAF.

RAF Carlisle has further responsibilities, covering engineering, accounting and distribution. The engineering task includes repairing stock, handling equipment within the ESD, ground support equipment and the large fleet of vehicles required for the distribution process. The stock at the MU is accounted for with the use of computers, linked to RAF Stanbridge, and through this network flows the constant stream of requests for spares issue, combined with listings for new stock received. Once the required item has been located, the key element in getting it speedily to the 'customer' is the distribution network run by the MU. This task is undertaken with the use of over 230 vehicles and trailers, and these cover an average of 3 million miles (4.8 million kilometres) per year.

RAF Carlisle is the largest civilian-manned unit in the RAF, with over 950 civilian personnel, and 14 RAF officers. The MU is organized into five wings, these being responsible for Supply, Support, Administration, Plans and Budget, and Depot Quality. However its days are numbered, following an announcement by the MoD in December 1993 that the ESD at RAF Carlisle is to close in 1997 as part of further rationalization measures.

Further south, at RAF Stafford, is another ESD, operated by No 16 MU. Fulfilling a similar role to that of RAF Carlisle, this MU also has a vast warehousing task, being responsible for over 600,000 different items of equipment or spares, representing some 41 per cent of the RAF's total inventory. Items held at RAF Stafford include spares for airframes and aero-engines, complete aircraft engines, ground and safety equipment, as well as spares for guided missiles, together with more mundane but essential items such as nuts, bolts and other fasteners. Regular deliveries by container are undertaken to various locations in Europe, whilst urgent requirements are dealt with by using RAF or civilian aircraft. There are some 1,500 personnel attached to the MU, half of whom are members of the RAF.

Another unit based at RAF Stafford is the Tactical Supply Wing (TSW), whose role is to provide fuel facilities and supply support for aircraft units that operate in the field, covering the Harrier squadrons and the Support Helicopter Force, the latter operating mainly Pumas and Chinooks. The fuel supply task can involve the deployment of tanker vehicles and flexible fuel bags, together with their associated pipework and valves and combined with adequate fire precautions, to remote locations with little or no facili-

While the crew of this Chinook HC.1 wait, the helicopter is refuelled in the field during an exercise in support of army units. Fuel facilities for such operations are provided by the RAF's Tactical Supply Wing. (Bob Munro)

ties. The TSW was fully involved in both the Falklands conflict and the Gulf War, and it has a permanent strength of more than 100 personnel.

Also at RAF Stafford is No 2 Mechanical Transport Flight (MTF), whose function is to provide transport for the movement of squadrons or units, and which is now part of the Engineering Wing. Additional tasks cover the movement of abnormal and special loads, sometimes over long distances, and the provision of transport support for the movement of equipment that is beyond the capability of a particular unit. No 2 MTF also undertakes the training and testing of heavy goods vehicle Class I drivers for the RAF.

The most southerly of the ESDs is located at RAF Quedgeley, near Gloucester, home of No 7 MU, whose main responsibility is for all the furniture and fittings that are required in the vast numbers of married quarters, barrack blocks and Messes, used by all three Services. This task covers the repair, replacement and renovation of such items as tables, chairs, cupboards, wardrobes and beds, and other related items that are required in any domestic or living accommodation, together with items used in offices, classrooms and other workplaces. Items that are slightly damaged or used are repaired for storage or redistribution, whilst life-expired items and those considered beyond economical repair are sold off in lots by auction. RAF Quedgeley has recently received much domestic equipment from the bases that

have closed in the UK and Germany.

Amongst a number of other tasks, RAF Quedgeley also stores all the trophies, silverware, pictures, memorabilia and other artefacts from the numerous disbanded squadrons of the RAF, which represents a fascinating insight into the history of the Service. To handle the various activities at No 7 MU, the unit employs some 300 civilians, with just eight RAF officers; but as with the ESD at RAF Carlisle, operations at Quedgeley are to be run-down following the announcement of its planned closure in 1998.

RAF Sealand, near Chester, fulfils a significant task in supporting the front-line units of the RAF and the other armed Services. The main resident unit, No 30 MU, is responsible for the third-line repair of the vast range of airborne avionic equipment that today's RAF requires. The distribution of avionic equipment, both before and after repair, is achieved through a system known as the Avionic Direct Exchange Scheme, in which items are received and issued on a one-for-one exchange basis. A fleet of vehicles is based at RAF Sealand, and these operate a variety of routes on a weekly schedule, visiting military bases throughout the UK and Germany to exchange, deliver and collect avionic equipment.

The repair task is undertaken by two Production Wings, one of which is concerned with work on communications equipment, whilst the other is responsible for repairs to electrical items and instruments. This work is carried out in an extensive new maintenance workshop complex, which includes dust-free clean rooms, erected in the early-1990s at a cost of over £10m. Many hundreds of individual items are dealt with each week, and the MU has composed its own work and servicing schedules. A further element, the Task Development and Support Wing, is responsible for devising test procedures, both manual and automatic, and many items of specialized test equipment have been built to assist in the servicing task.

In early 1990 a team was formed at RAF Sealand to develop a facility for the repair of Microwave Integrated Circuits (MICs), which are high-technology, micro-miniature electronic devices found in much of the current avionic equipment. Until recently, the RAF had no facilities to repair these items, and was incurring considerable costs in their replacement with new MICs. However, the repair facility is now operational, and will shortly recover the costs involved in its establishment when the savings from the reuse of repaired items are compared with the costs of new replacements.

The Supply Wing at Sealand carries out the task of receiving and issuing avionic equipment and draws, if possible, from existing stock. Should particular items not be available, the Supply Wing then tasks the Production Wings to produce the required equipment and to replenish back-up stocks, using computers to assist in stock control.

A number of supporting units exist within No 30 MU, consisting of an Engineering Support Squadron, a Management and Budgetary Services Wing, and a Unit Task Audit Team, amongst others, and these are mainly staffed by civilians at all levels. An Administrative Wing is responsible for the RAF personnel element of the station, whilst the civilian workforce, which amounts to some 40 per cent of the total personnel at RAF Sealand, is administered by the Civilian Management Wing.

Two other MUs exist within Logistics Command. No 11 MU, located at RAF Chilmark in Wiltshire, is responsible for the storage of munitions; however, this facility is being run-down for eventual closure. RAF Cardington, near Bedford, is the home of No 217 MU, which is tasked with the storage of various gases. The site at Cardington is dominated by two huge airship sheds, relics from the 1930s when there were high hopes for this form of aerial transport.

SIGNALS

RAF Henlow in Bedfordshire is the home of the RAF Signals Staff, which comprises nine units responsible for support tasks relating to telecommunications, signals engineering and ground radio repair. The operation of the RAF element of the Defence Communications Network is a further responsibility of the Signals Staff, who also act as consultants on various aspects of communications. This consultancy is used by the MoD, Strike Command, and Commonwealth and Allied Air Forces, amongst others. Also at Henlow is the Communications-Electronic Multi-Disciplinary Group, manned by the Signals Staff, who are responsible to the MoD for support functions relating to the Telegraphic Automatic Routing Equipment, together with ground radio and radar equipment used by the RAF, the Royal Navy, the Army and other organizations.

The operating responsibilities relating to signals within Logistics Command can be divided into four categories. The first of these is the operation of a large and complex network of high frequency transmitters and receivers, located throughout the UK, these installations including communications centres with automatic message-routeing equipment. These facilities conduct operations on behalf of NATO, Strike Command, the Military Air Traffic Organization and the Meteorological Office. The second category covers the operation of message relay centres, some of which are fully automatic, whilst others are controlled manually. Also in this category is the management of the RAF's General-Purpose Telephone Network. The RAF has obtained a fixed telecommunications network, known as 'Boxer', which will save the ever-increasing costs of line rentals from private companies. All Logistics Command signals networks are monitored to ensure that operating standards are maintained, and to ensure that security and classified information is not compromised.

The third operating responsibility of Logistics Command Signals covers the control and operation of the Skynet Military Satellite Communications System. This system provides secure data and speech communications with British Forces, including ships at sea, on a worldwide basis via the dish-aerial at RAF Oakhanger in Hampshire. This is operated by No 1001 Signals Unit, who are responsible for the management of the Skynet system. Further ground stations are located at Colerne in Wiltshire and at Defford in Hereford and Worcester, and two mobile ground terminals are available for deployment to other sites.

A number of Skynet 4 satellites are in orbit, having been launched by both French and US rockets in the late 1980s. These satellites, which have a design life of seven years, are of a modular design with a multi-frequency capacity. They are hardened against electromagnetic pulses and are resistant to jamming and ECM. Additionally, a management service is provided for the NATO-4 series of satellites, which are similar to the Skynet models.

The fourth category covers the repair and maintenance of ground radio, radar and communication equipment, which together with navigational aids is undertaken by the Ground Radio Servicing Centre, based at RAF North Luffenham. The command is also responsible for the erection and maintenance of aerials and antennae on a worldwide basis, covering the whole field of communications, radar and navigational aids. This is a highly specialized and skilled task, and training for this work is undertaken at the Aerial Erector School at RAF Digby in Lincolnshire.

The Signals Staff is responsible for electrical engineering covering almost the entire range of defence-related communications equipment, including radios, air traffic control and defence radar systems, together with ground-based navigational aids. This covers studies into feasibility, management of the particular project, design, development, construction, installation, commissioning, maintenance and refurbishing of most of the communications equipment in use by the British Services. The HQ of the Signals element has a design staff of draughtsmen, engineers and technicians, with general engineering and calibration capacity, and is situated at RAF Henlow.

DISPOSAL OF EXPLOSIVES

RAF Wittering, near Peterborough, is the home of the RAF Explosive Ordnance Disposal (EOD) Squadron, which is part of the RAF Armament Support Unit. Along with similar units from the Army and the Royal Navy, the EOD Squadron, through its subordinate EOD Operations Flight, is responsible for the location and disposal of unexploded devices and explosive material that may emanate from a number of sources. This can include bombs planted by terrorists, ammunition and weapons remaining from the Second World War, and devices that may exist on range areas throughout the UK.

The EOD Operations Flight comprises a number of two-man Improvised Explosive Device Disposal (IEDD) teams, who are on constant stand-by to respond to tasking from the civil police in co-ordination with the Joint Services EOD Operations Centre. To carry out their disposal tasks, IEDD teams have a range of suitable equipment which is transported in specially adapted vehicles. One such item of special equipment is the Mark 8 'Wheelbarrow', a remote-controlled tracked vehicle that can travel across uneven ground and can even climb steps. This vehicle can carry such items as a closed-circuit TV camera, portable X-ray equipment, and devices to handle, move and penetrate suspect devices.

One of the main tasks of the EOD Squadron is the clearance of area sites of possible unexploded hazards. This can include the location and disposal of ammunition and bombs from wartime aircraft crash sites (which are still being discovered), disused and currently active range areas, and the clearance of wartime mines which are still in place on a number of airfield sites. In recent years this unit has been responsible for the clearance of facilities used in the wartime handling of mustard gas weapons. Equipment in use with the EOD Squadron can detect a 1,000 lb (454 kg) bomb at a depth of 21 ft (6.4 m).

Further functions of the EOD Squadron include all aspects of RAF training relative to ordnance disposal, with instruction being carried out by the Airfield EOD Training Flight. Their main task is to instruct armament personnel on flying stations in the procedures and techniques involved in the rapid clearance of explosive ordnance on active airfields, in order to facilitate a speedy return to operational capability following an air attack. Much of this training is carried out at a specially prepared training area at RAF North Luffenham. Here, an area has been created to represent an airfield damaged in an air raid, with numerous items distributed throughout to simulate unexploded ordnance.

EOD personnel at many major RAF airfields have available two types of tracked armoured vehicles to assist in the clearance of unexploded ordnance. Under their official titles of combat vehicle reconnaissance tracked (CVRT), these two types are the Spartan armoured personnel carrier, which is fitted with a 7.62 mm general-purpose machine gun, and the Scimitar CVRT, which carries the much heavier 30 mm Rarden cannon. The CVRTs are used to patrol and reconnoitre airfields following an air attack in order that EOD personnel, protected in such vehicles, can assess the extent of damage inflicted and locate any unexploded bombs, mines, or similar devices, particularly those with time-delay fuses. The guns fitted to the CVRTs are intended to be used to detonate or disable any unexploded ordnance, with the vehicle being withdrawn to a safe distance. The intention is not always to detonate the unexploded device, as this may well cause further damage; instead, some ordnance can be broken open and the contents burnt out harmlessly. The training of personnel in the operation of these armoured vehicles and their weapons is also carried out by the EOD Training Flight.

Due to the significant changes in East-West relations, the chances of air attacks on RAF airfields in the UK and Germany are greatly reduced. However, the threat of terrorist action remains a stronger possibility and EOD skills

The Spartan APC is used for reconnaissance duties in connection with explosive ordnance disposal.

need to be maintained. With the withdrawal of armoured vehicles from the units of the RAF Regiment, the Spartan and Scimitar CVRTs of the EOD units are now the only such equipment used by the RAF.

USAF BASES IN THE UK

Throughout the Cold War, the United States Air Force (USAF) maintained significant elements at several airfields and other supporting bases in the UK, together with many more in what was then West Germany. However, with the remarkable changes in the international situation, there have been marked reductions in the levels of these forces recently, and this 'draw down' is expected to continue.

The bases from which the USAF operates in the UK have always remained as RAF stations, used under various agreements by the US Forces. A small RAF element, within the responsibility of RAF Logistics Command, exists on each of these bases to liaise with the USAF units. Currently, the USAF operates from three RAF airfields, all in East Anglia, plus a number of other locations. RAF Alconbury, near Huntingdon, is being run down, and the Special Forces units based there, equipped with HC-130N/P Hercules, MC-130H Combat Talon II and MH-53J Pave Low III transports, are due to move to RAF Mildenhall by 1995. RAF Mildenhall, near Newmarket in Suffolk, operates a squadron of KC-135R

Stratotankers for air-to-air refuelling tasks, and also acts as a cargo and passenger terminal for USAF services to and from the USA and Europe. Close to RAF Mildenhall is RAF Lakenheath, which is home to a squadron of F-15C Eagles and two squadrons of F-15E Strike Eagles. RAF Fairford, in Gloucestershire, although normally empty of aircraft, is maintained as a large stand-by base, and is used for occasional deployments of types such as the B-52 Stratofortress.

As already mentioned, the USAF has 'drawn down' the scale of its forces on this side of the Atlantic recently. Thus the large bases at RAF Woodbridge and RAF Bentwaters, both in Suffolk, and RAF Upper Heyford, in Oxfordshire, all with extensive facilities, are now empty of aircraft, and it is difficult to foresee a future military use for these locations. Further bases, such as Sculthorpe and Greenham Common, have been completely closed. Many other facilities used by the USAF in the UK, such as communications sites and storage units, have been reduced in size or closed.

There are a number of other units, not described in this chapter, that support the tasks of the three main groups within Logistics Command. As with any new organization, the structure of this new command may well change as the operation settles down. Under current plans, the division of the former Support Command, together with the relocation of units and personnel, is expected to take three to four years.

CHAPTER FOUR

The Organization of the RAF

THE FIRST THREE chapters in this book have examined the composition of the three commands within the Royal Air Force, together with the functions of their many subordinate units. This section outlines the RAF structure above Command HQ level, and also deals with the organization of a typical RAF station.

An important principle of the Armed Forces of the United Kingdom is that the three Services are subordinate to the Civil Authority as reflected in the elected government of the day. The vast amount of money that is required to equip, maintain and operate the Army, the Royal Navy and the Royal Air Force is voted through the Parliamentary system, and all three Services are governed by laws and regulations laid down in Acts of Parliament.

The supreme responsibility for national defence is held by the Prime Minister and the Cabinet. Control of the armed forces by the government is carried out through the Defence Council, the Chairman of which is the Secretary of State for Defence who is appointed by the Prime Minister. The Defence Council co-ordinates the elements and activities of the three Services in relation to the domestic and foreign policies of the government.

The three Services are controlled by staffs of senior officers; the Army Board, the Admiralty Board and the Air Force Board each control their respective Services. The Defence Council is composed of the heads of these Boards, along with other senior officers, senior civil servants, specialist advisors and government ministers connected with aspects of defence.

The Air Force Board comprises a number of senior officers and civil servants, each of whom is the head of a branch that specializes in a particular area of RAF operations. Collectively, these branches are known as the Air Force Department within the Ministry of Defence. Items dealt with by these branches include policy and planning, personnel, training, supply, logistics, air traffic control, legal matters and chaplaincy, amongst many others. Many of the branches are further sub-divided into directorates that specialize in various elements of the RAF, and together these bodies organize many aspects that contribute to the day-to-day running of the Service.

Most of these elements are located in the London area, although a number of them are in the process of moving away from the capital. The next feature in the RAF's chain of command are the three commands, already covered in detail.

RAF STATIONS

The location at which individual RAF units operate is known as a Royal Air Force Station, and these carry the name of the nearest village or town. Usually, the station and all the various squadrons and units based therein are controlled by one of the groups within a command. However, with the steady reduction in the numbers of RAF stations in recent years, units that report to a particular group or command may be a 'tenant' on a station of a different group or command.

There was a major expansion of RAF stations in the late-1930s, and most current operations are carried out from these locations. The dominant feature on flying stations are the hangars, and between three to five of these are arranged in an arc on one side of the airfield. The hangars built during the 1930s expansion programme are known as the 'C' type, and are substantial brick and steel structures. Behind the hangars, away from the airfield, are all the functional buildings

Hardened Aircraft Shelters, such as this example at RAF Coningsby, are now to be found on many RAF airfields. (Bob Munro)

from which the operational and administrative activities of the station are organized. Some of the accommodation and catering facilities are also in this area. These buildings have mellowed over the past 55-odd years, and trees are now fully-grown throughout the domestic areas of such stations.

In the early-1980s, the concept of protecting aircraft and their crews in enclaves of shelters was introduced. This was designed to enable operations to be conducted in the face of possible NBC warfare. A massive programme of construction resulted in numerous Hardened Aircraft Shelters (HASs) being installed at many RAF stations. These enclaves, located well away from the original hangar areas, are surrounded by secure fencing with one or two controlled access points. Squadrons now operate fully from their allotted enclave, which includes an Operations Room and facilities for air and ground crews. Most Tornado units operate from HAS areas; however, some RAF units still utilize the older hangars and the offices that are incorporated along the sides of these structures.

The Commanding Officer of an RAF station is known by the title of Station Commander, and on large establishments such as airfields and supporting depots this appointment would be held by an officer with the rank of Group Captain. On smaller stations the rank for this appointment may be a Wing Commander or a Squadron Leader.

A No 11 Squadron Tornado F.3 at readiness inside a Hardened Aircraft Shelter. Exhaust vents at the rear of each shelter enable the aircraft's engines to be started while still inside. (BAe)

The administration of most RAF stations is divided amongst three wings: Operations, Engineering and Supply, and Administration. The combined efforts of these wings is aimed at supporting the based flying squadrons in their specified roles and missions. Each of the wings has an officer of Wing Commander rank as its Officer Commanding, who reports directly to the Station Commander.

Operations Wing

Operations Wing (Ops Wg) is the first of the three elements, and is responsible for controlling and

These diagrams illustrate the organizational 'tree' of a typical RAF station. Only the major features are shown, as these would be common to many stations. As no two RAF stations are exactly alike, there would be variations in the system of organization, particularly amongst the smaller flights.

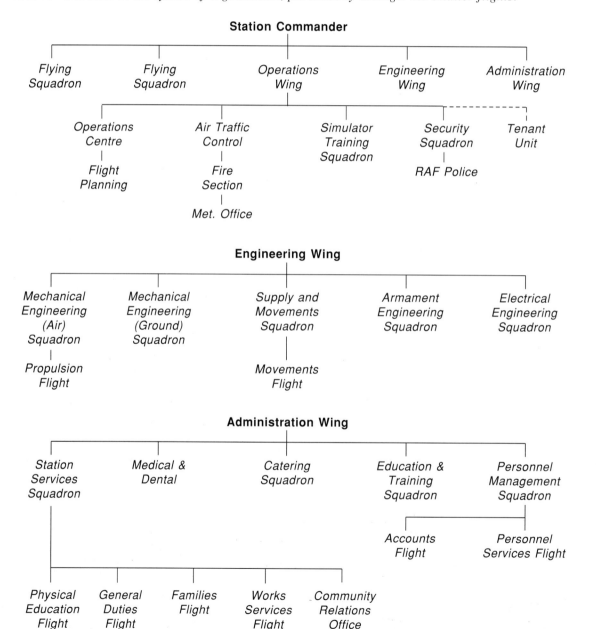

co-ordinating the day-to-day tasks of the active squadrons. Within the control of Ops Wg comes the Operations Centre. This is located in an area of enhanced security, and is the nerve centre of the base operations, with sophisticated communications facilities and displays detailing information relevant to the flying activities of the based squadrons. Within Operations Centre is the Flight Planning Cell, which contains supplies of maps and other documentation required for operations in the currently congested airspace over the UK and Europe.

A number of smaller units are also controlled by Ops Wg, covering such activities as Air Traffic Control, the Fire and Rescue Section and the Meteorological Office. If the station has a simulator, the Simulator Training Squadron would also form part of Ops Wg. Further responsibilities include operating procedures in war and peace, and security aspects, via the Security Squadron. This includes elements of the RAF Regiment who are responsible for ground defence training, and sections of the RAF Police, supported by police dogs. Any tenant units of other groups or commands liaise with the Station Commander through Ops Wg.

Engineering and Supply Wing

The second of the three wings is Engineering and Supply Wing (Eng Wg), again being divided into specialist squadrons for particular tasks. The main concern is aircraft maintenance, with the station being responsible for all servicing except major overhauls. Pre-flight checks are carried out by the pilot prior to take-off, and day-to-day servicing is undertaken by the operating squadron; this is known as 'first-line' servicing.

More involved ('second-line') servicing is in the hands of the Mechanical Engineering (Air) Squadron (ME(A)S). Aircraft of the RAF are serviced at intervals determined by the numbers of hours flown, which differs between types. The extent of each service varies according to the time flown since new, or since the last major overhaul. As an example, servicing on the Jaguar is carried out at intervals of 125 hours flown. Assuming the aircraft had been subjected to a major overhaul, the next time it would receive routine attention would be after 125 flying hours, with a short service being known as a 'primary', and taking about one day to complete. After 250 hours, the aircraft will undergo a 'primary star' servicing programme, involving a greater depth of inspection and maintenance, lasting for several days. A further 'primary' occurs after 375 hours, and then, 500 hours after the previous major, the aircraft receives a 'minor' service. This is a significant programme, occupying some 25 working days. Then, at the regular intervals of 125 hours, the Jaguar would respectively receive primary, primary star, and primary programmes of servicing.

After 1,000 hours airborne comes the 'minor star' inspection, with maintenance lasting for about 35 working days. Following this, the servicing cycle would recommence, with the above levels of maintenance every 125 hours, until the aircraft has logged 2,000 hours, at which stage it would be flown to RAF St Athan for an extensive major overhaul. The servicing carried out by ME(A)S is usually carried out in one or two of the large 'C' type hangars, with suitable access gantries, tools and lifting equipment. The Eng Wg is also responsible, via its subordinate Electrical Engineering Squadron and the Armament Engineering Squadron, for the maintenance and support of many items of equipment, including avionics and weapons systems. The servicing of aircraft engines is tasked to the Propulsion Flight, an element within the ME(A)S. Modern engines,

Second-line servicing being carried out on a Jaguar T.2A of No 6 Squadron at RAF Coltishall.

such as the Adour and the RB.199, are constructed on a modular basis, and thus defective sections can be removed and replaced with comparative ease. On a base with two or three flying squadrons, the Propulsion Flight can be an extensive operation, with its own workshop complex and facilities for ground running of engines under test, and with suitable noise suppression!

Eng Wg is also responsible, through the Mechanical Engineering (Ground) Squadron (ME(G)S), for the supply and maintenance of all the many and varied vehicles required by the station, as well as all items of ground equipment, such as generators, cranes, towbars, gantries, snowploughs, etc.

A further squadron within Eng Wg is Supply and Movements, this again being divided into a number of flights. These deal with the vast array of stores and equipment required for the day-to-day functioning of the station and its units. This involves several tens of thousands of different items, with computers being employed to assist in stock control and management. A Movements Flight has responsibilities that cover the specialist clothing and equipment deemed necessary should the flying squadrons be deployed to locations overseas where extremes of climate may be encountered.

Administration Wing

The third of the station's wings, Administration Wing (Admin Wg) is also divided into a number of squadrons. The Personnel Management Squadron, through subordinate flights, covers items such as accommodation, accounts, and administration of both service and civilian men and women who are assigned to the station. The Station Services Squadron (SSS) also comprises a number of flights, each responsible for such activities as catering, families, medical, chaplaincy, general duties and buildings. On larger stations, the catering and medical functions are often the responsibility of separate squadrons within the wing.

The Community Relations Office (CRO) is part of the SSS, this being a busy section on most RAF stations, with visits from school parties, local dignitaries, politicians, aviation enthusiast societies and members of the press to be arranged and escorted. The CRO is responsible for keeping the media advised of station activities, such as fundraising events for local and national charities, and is also on the receiving end of the inevitable complaints regarding aircraft noise and low flying.

A further element of Admin Wg is the Education and Training Squadron, with flights covering various relevant aspects. With recent reductions in the personnel strength of the RAF,

staff from this squadron will have been busy of late in offering resettlement advice to those who have been leaving the Service for future civilian careers.

The format of a three-wing organization is the usual system of administration on most RAF stations. However, in recent years there has been a steady growth in the number of tasks that have been contracted out to private companies, as part of government policy. This is particularly noticeable on flying training stations, where all the first- and second-line servicing, aircraft handling, towing, fuelling and flight-line preparation is undertaken by civilians, many of whom are ex-RAF personnel. They are employed by the company that successfully tendered for the aircraft handling contract. This has resulted in a marked reduction in the size and activities of the Eng Wg on such stations, and in certain areas on some stations, very few personnel in RAF uniform are to be seen.

Of course, the many and varied aspects of RAF activities means that the three-wing structure of station organization is not suitable for all tasks. For example, RAF Lyneham has a separate Supply and Motor Transport Wing, to reflect the particular role that this station performs. It also has a very large Eng Wg, to cater for the first- and second-line servicing of the RAF's Hercules fleet. This is in contrast to the small Eng Wgs to be found on training bases.

Stations that have a major training role include a Training Wing as part of their organizational structure. This wing comprises several subordinate squadrons and flights, all of whom are responsible for various aspects of the training task. Bases that contain Maintenance Units also differ from flying stations in their administrative structure. As an example, RAF St Athan has a Civilian Management Wing, to cover the large number of civilians employed. St Athan also has a Task, Budget and Plans Wing to organize the functions indicated in its title.

The Officer Commanding of a flying squadron is usually an officer of Wing Commander rank, and he reports directly to the Station Commander. Most squadrons consist of two or more flights, the commanders of which are officers of Squadron Leader rank.

This chapter has dealt with, in outline form, the significant aspects of RAF organization. It has not attempted to describe all the many elements that can be found on RAF stations. Many of these are unique to the particular task, aircraft type and role that the station or unit undertakes. In addition, small units are occasionally formed for a limited period of time to carry out a specific assignment, and are then disbanded upon completion of that task.

CHAPTER FIVE

The Royal Air Force Regiment

OVER 50 YEARS have now passed since a Royal Warrant was issued to form the Royal Air Force Regiment, as an answer to a perceived threat against RAF aircraft and equipment on unprotected airfields. This threat could come from strikes by enemy air action, and also from infiltration and sabotage by hostile ground forces, the Regiment being equipped to counter both eventualities. The RAF Regiment is a Corps within the RAF, with the same uniform regulations and rank system, and it continues with the same tasks, i.e. the protection and security in depth of RAF installations. It is additionally responsible for the training of other RAF personnel in the tactics, procedures and weapons that would enable them to defend their units and bases against possible ground attack. Further tasks include policies concerning procedures and training to cover NBC warfare.

For the role of defence against air attack, the RAF Regiment has a number of short-range air defence (SHORAD) squadrons, equipped with the Rapier surface-to-air missile (SAM) system. To meet the task of ground defence, Regiment field squadrons are equipped with a variety of weapons, and both of these types of squadrons are deployed to various bases in the UK and overseas.

Armed and watchful, a member of the RAF Regiment provides cover as a No 5 Squadron Tornado F.3 emerges from its HAS. (Aviation Photographs International)

Until recently, the field squadrons were known as light armoured squadrons, equipped with light armoured vehicles such as the Scorpion, Spartan, and Sultan, but these were withdrawn in the early 1990s. A number of SHORAD and field squadrons were disbanded under the 'Options for Change' programme. Both types of squadrons are provided with a variety of vehicles to enable them to carry out their tasks.

Since the late 1980s, the RAF Regiment has had an additional and increasing commitment to the concept of 'Survive to Operate' (STO). In the event of an attack on an RAF installation, it is most likely that a senior RAF Regiment officer would become the focal point in advising the Station Commander on defence, and organizing the various aspects of security and survival, both during and after any incident. A wide range of items need to be organized in an emergency situation, such as fire cover and prevention, rescue, first aid, shelter arrangements, awareness of NBC hazards, restoring communications, bomb disposal, and organizing secondary defence tasks for RAF personnel. Officers of the RAF Regiment are trained to act as STO co-ordinators in the Ground Combat Centre on RAF stations. This training was put into practice during the Gulf War in 1991, which provided a classic scenario for preparations to cover a possible STO situation.

The Directorate of the RAF Regiment has, since 1993, been combined with command staff at HQ Strike Command to provide a dual function: a command structure for the active squadrons, together with policy and planning to cover personnel, equipment and the structure of the Regiment. This involves studies into current and future requirements that are relative to the roles for which the Regiment is responsible. This information is conveyed to the Regiment's units through the relevant groups in Strike Command, who provide a day-to-day command function for their Regiment units. The head of the RAF Regiment is known by the title of Commandant-General, and, in addition to this appointment, he is also responsible for the Defence Fire Services, as well as being a Senior Staff Officer within HQ Strike Command.

The principal location of the RAF Regiment in the UK is the Regiment Depot, currently located at RAF Catterick, but due to move south to RAF Honington in 1994. The Depot undertakes the training required for all Regiment personnel, covering both officers and airmen. Unusually, this includes Initial Service training for airmen. All types of training are carried out at the Depot, including continuation training for officers and NCOs, together with post-graduate instruction courses. This training is supported in the field by the Training Support Flight, based at the Regiment Depot, a unit that also provides specialist personnel for other tasks.

The Regiment is now closely integrated within Strike Command, with its chain of command established through three groups. The RAF Regiment's unit distribution is as follows:

No 1 Group:

No 2 Squadron	RAF Catterick (to RAF Honington in 1994)	
No 3 Squadron	RAF Aldergrove	

Both of these units are field squadrons, and in the event of war would be deployed to Germany. In addition, No 2 Squadron is fully trained for a parachute role, to similar standards as those of the Parachute Regiment of the British Army. The squadron's parachute capability is provided to cater for any such requirements on the part of the RAF, including possible non-NATO operations at any location worldwide. The principal task of No 3 Squadron is internal security.

No 2 Group:

No 1 Squadron	RAF Laarbruch	Field unit
No 26 Squadron	RAF Laarbruch	Rapier unit
No 37 Squadron	RAF Bruggen	Rapier unit

No 11 Group:

No 15 Squadron	RAF Leeming	Rapier unit
No 27 Squadron	RAF Leuchars	Rapier unit
No 48 Squadron	RAF Lossiemouth	Rapier unit

Also within No 11 Group is the Rapier Training Unit, which, since the spring of 1993, has adopted the identity of No 16 (Reserve) Squadron; this squadron is due to move from RAF West Raynham to RAF Honington in 1994. In the event of an emergency, No 16(R) Squadron would adopt an active wartime role.

Whilst most RAF Regiment units are controlled by Strike Command, RAF Personnel and Training Command is also involved, in that it is responsible for the Queen's Colour Squadron (QCS), which is based at RAF Uxbridge, to the west of London. The QCS has a peacetime role to represent the RAF as a ceremonial drill unit, and to function as an escort for the Queen's Colour of the RAF at various ceremonial events. This unit acts as custodian of the Queen's Colour for the RAF, a new version of which was presented to the RAF by Her Majesty The Queen at a ceremony held at RAF Marham in April 1993, to mark the 75th anniversary of the formation of the RAF.

The QCS participates in numerous parades, such as the annual Service of Remembrance at the Cenotaph in London in early November, as well as mounting guard at Buckingham Palace, Windsor Castle, Edinburgh Castle, or the Tower

Protection for the Harrier GR.7s at RAF Laarbruch is provided by No 1 Squadron, RAF Regiment, one of whose members is seen manning a GPMG mounted on a Land Rover. (Aviation Photographs International)

of London on various occasions. The QCS often provides a Guard of Honour for the Royal Family at various events, and for visits by Royalty and Heads of State. Each year, the QCS performs its unique displays of continuity drill demonstrations at a wide range of events throughout the country, including the Royal Tournament in London. However, the QCS also has a wartime role, and between the events already mentioned, and through the winter months, it trains as a field squadron for possible deployment to Germany or some other overseas location, adopting the identity of No 63 Squadron.

There is a further element of the RAF Regiment that does not fall directly within the responsibility of Strike Command. This is No 34 Squadron, which is a field unit that comes under the control of HQ British Forces, Cyprus, and is based at RAF Akrotiri. Its primary task is the internal security of the British sovereign base area on that island.

The Regiment units mentioned so far are dedicated to the protection of the RAF, through the control of their parent groups or command. There are, however, three further Rapier-equipped squadrons committed to the protection of United States Air Force (USAF) bases located in the UK:

No 6 Wing:
No 19 Squadron   RAF Brize Norton
No 20 Squadron   RAF Honington
No 66 Squadron   RAF West Raynham

These squadrons were formed between 1983 and 1985, and are fully financed by the USAF. They are based on suitably located RAF airfields, and would move out to defend various USAF bases in the time of an emergency. No 6 Wing is the only Wing HQ remaining in the RAF Regiment; although it is in No 11 Group, Strike Command, its operational control is in the hands of the USAF. With the planned closure of RAF West Raynham, the units there will move to RAF Honington in 1994.

The RAF Regiment has further commitments overseas, and for these tasks it must draw upon the men and equipment already listed. The main obligation is to the air defence of the Falkland Islands, with the deployment of a full squadron-sized element comprising eight Rapier fire units, together with supporting radar, to provide cover by both day and night. All five Rapier squadrons within Nos 2 and 11 Groups are involved in supporting this duty on a rotational basis. Until recently, the RAF Regiment provided a flight of four Rapier fire units in Belize, for daylight air defence cover, and this commitment was also drawn from the SHORAD units in the UK and Germany. However, this deployment was withdrawn in early 1994 as part of the run-down of British forces in Belize.

Until a few years ago, RAF Regiment units on the UK mainland and in Germany had to provide detachments for internal security duties in Northern Ireland. However, the permanent provi-

The RAF Regiment provides detachments for the air defence of the Falkland Islands. One of the Regiment's Rapier units is seen here, tracking an RAF Hercules out of RAF Mount Pleasant. (Aviation Photographs International)

Members of No 1 Squadron's Mortar Flight load an L16A2 81 mm mortar. The L16A2 can fire shells at a rate of 15 per minute. (Aviation Photographs International)

sion of No 3 Squadron at Aldergrove has proved most beneficial to the Regiment as a whole, providing stability within the various units and professional continuity in the Province.

The principal task for a field squadron is to deny the area around any RAF station, airhead, radar site or other RAF asset to any potential enemy at any location in the world where the RAF is operating. Each of the squadrons (Nos 1, 2, 3 and 34, together with No 63 (QCS) Squadron in time of war) consists of three Field Flights, a Mortar Flight, and an HQ Flight. Total personnel strength of a field squadron is 164, while the Field Flights each comprise 31 personnel. These flights can operate as fire-teams, each consisting of four personnel, with support from the remainder as required. The Mortar Flight also consists of 31 personnel, and is divided into two sections, each with two mortars. These mortar sections can be detached to support a Field Flight to suit the situation. The HQ Flight is in overall command of the other four flights, with command post and control capability. Supporting these functions are technicians specializing in transport, weapons, radios and other relevant equipment, together with supply, administrative and catering personnel.

One of the key elements of the Regiment's field squadrons is self-sufficiency, and each unit has enough supplies and equipment to be able to operate for seven days without external resupply or support. A further major feature is flexible mobility, and each squadron is equipped with more than 40 Land Rovers, plus around a dozen large trucks, refuelling tankers, etc.

Turning to the SHORAD squadrons equipped with Rapier, these are controlled by an HQ Flight, and also include an Engineering Flight. The latter has the use of container box-bodies, which are fitted out as mobile workshops and carried on four-tonne trucks. The Rapier-equipped flights are responsible for eight Rapier fire units, each towed by Land Rovers. With each fire unit is an optical tracker, which can be backed-up by a DN 181 Blindfire radar scanner when required.

To be effective, any air defence missile system must aim to destroy an attacking aircraft, which may have a stand-off capability, before it reaches the defended area or has released its weapons. Thus, the Rapier fire units would endeavour to deploy away from the airfield or RAF asset that they are defending, moving out to preselected sites at a distance of about two to three miles (three to five kilometres). In addition to defending the main area from aerial attack, the SHORAD units must be capable of defending themselves from ground attack, and maintain the ability to continue to operate under full NBC conditions. A high standard of aircraft recognition is required of

SHORAD personnel, with an initial identification of 'friend or foe', prior to the actual aircraft type being determined.

Having been deployed away from the main base, the Rapier fire units need to be resupplied and supported, and this task was well tested and accomplished successfully in the Falkland Islands during the conflict in 1982. All SHORAD units currently deploy the Rapier Field Standard B1(M) variant, but some squadrons will re-equip with the improved Rapier Field Standard C (or Rapier 2000) in the mid-1990s.

All members of the RAF are expected to be able to assist in the defence of the installation at which they are carrying out their duties, and are thus required to undergo regular periods of training. This is called Ground Defence Training (GDT), and tuition is carried out by RAF Regiment instructors who are on the establishment of most RAF stations. Training in live-arm guarding, to counter any terrorist threat, is also provided to RAF personnel by Regiment instructors, together with tuition in NBC hazards and warfare. Regiment officers work closely with RAF Station Commanders to provide advice on security and defence aspects.

Further locations where members of the RAF Regiment may be found are with RAF flying squadrons that are required to operate in the field, with aircraft types such as the Harrier, together with Chinook, Puma and Wessex support helicopters; these elements can include RAF Regiment specialists in advisory roles.

As already mentioned, RAF Regiment instructors undertake training in ground defence tasks for RAF personnel at most RAF stations. In the past, this training was carried out on an individual basis to suit the local conditions. However, during the Gulf War, elements were drawn from many units of the RAF, and it was found that there were differing levels of skill in terms of ground defence capability amongst the personnel involved. Therefore, the Regiment is introducing a co-ordinated training package, with the aim of producing a common programme. Much of the training has been computerized, and use will be made of simulators. This even covers the use of small arms, which can be fired in a simulated form instead of on a traditional outdoor range.

Looking to the future, from 1994 RAF Honington will become the main focal point for the RAF Regiment for training (both basic and continuation), field units and Rapier systems subjects, with the aim of establishing a centre of excellence. RAF Honington will also become the home of an STO Training Unit, which will co-ordinate the skills required for ground defence, covering instruction, command post operations, and specialist advice to RAF Station Commanders on survival and security aspects. The RAF

The RAF Regiment's primary individual weapon for security patrols and base defence is the 5.56 mm L85A1. (Aviation Photographs International)

Regiment will also provide additional forces for the role of enhanced ground defence and security at certain key RAF airfields.

Since the withdrawal of the Bloodhound SAM in 1991, the RAF has had no medium-to-long-range ground-launched air defence weapons. However, there are proposals for the RAF to once again operate such a system, under the title (at present) of the Medium Surface-to-Air Missile (MSAM). A principal feature of any new system is that it should be fully mobile, unlike the Bloodhound which operated from fixed launch sites. If a new system is purchased it will be operated by the RAF Regiment, whose current expertise with the Rapier air defence missile, combined with techniques in tactical mobility, would make them well-suited to operate a larger weapon. Such an operation by the RAF Regiment would be co-ordinated with air defence elements of Strike Command. Various SAM systems are being studied, against possible threats from sea level up to high altitude. One such weapon that may be considered is the American Patriot air defence missile, which achieved a great deal of publicity in the Gulf War as a result of its use to intercept 'Scud' missiles fired by the Iraqi forces. No in-service date for an MSAM system is known.

The men of the RAF Regiment regard themselves as unique, and specially trained for their tasks. They have a very high *esprit de corps*; they train and work hard; and their year is often full of exercises and detachments that take them to some remote locations. The task of airfield defence is critical and essential, and so the RAF Regiment is set to remain an integral and operational part of the RAF for many years to come.

SURFACE-TO-AIR GUIDED MISSILES

Following the withdrawal of the Bloodhound SAM system in the early 1990s, variants of the Rapier system are the only ground-based missile weapons in current and foreseeable service with the RAF, and these are operated by the RAF Regiment.

Rapier Field Standard Model B1(M)

(Mk 2 Missile dimensions): Length 7 ft 4 in (2.24 m); **Body diameter** 5 in (0.13 m); **Fin span** 1 ft 5in (0.43m); **Weight** 94 lb (43 kg); **Missile speed** Mach 2+; **Missile power** Two-stage solid rocket motor.

The origins of this SAM system go back some 30 years, when the then British Aircraft Corporation (BAC) promoted, as a private venture, a project known as ET-316. From this was to emerge the Rapier system, and BAC was subsequently awarded a design and development contract. BAC was eventually to become British Aerospace (BAe), Dynamics Division, which has continued to develop what has proved to be a highly successful system. The Rapier was first fired against a target in mid-1967 and a production contract was announced in the same year. It first entered service in 1974 and various versions are also in use with units of the British Army. The system has also achieved a number of export orders.

The initial version, known as the Field Standard Model A, was optically-guided, and its use was thus limited to daylight and fair weather conditions. To counter a possible threat of air attacks in poor visibility or at night the Rapier system was improved by the addition of the Marconi DN181 Blindfire tracking radar, which gives a round-the-clock operational capability in marginal weather conditions. Thus modified, the Rapier was redesignated as the Field Standard Model B1 (FSB1), and the SHORAD units of the RAF Regiment were re-equipped with this variant between 1978 and 1981.

In the late 1980s, the Rapier FSB1 was further enhanced by a mid-life update programme, with improvements to its electrical systems and its resistance to possible countermeasures; this version is known as Field Standard Model B1(M). A further refinement to the system was the introduction of the Mk 2 version of the missile, which incorporates enhanced electronics, and improvements to the warhead and the rocket motor.

Rapier Field Standard Model C

Commercially promoted as the Rapier 2000 by BAe, this system is not simply a variant of the existing Rapier models but should be regarded as a completely new design. It has been designed to incorporate the latest technology into a weapons system to counter low-level air attack, and to be effective in all weather conditions against aircraft, helicopters, surveillance drones and even cruise missiles. The system is able to engage a range of targets around the full compass of 360°, at ranges of up to five miles (eight kilometres), and up to altitudes of 9,800 ft (3,000 m). It has to be able to operate in the face of ECM, and in an NBC environment.

The complete system comprises three main elements: the fire unit, a new three-dimensional digital surveillance radar, and the differential tracker radar. These are supported by a manual acquisition facility (MAF) and control units for commander and operator.

The fire unit carries eight ready-to-fire Rapier Mk 2 missiles, and includes a missile command

The Fire Unit of Rapier Field Standard Model C, fitted with eight Mk 2 missile drill rounds.

guidance transmitter, together with missile- and target-tracking facilities suitable for use in most conditions. The MAF can be used for passive target designation when transmissions from the system's radars are not available or may be undesirable, due to a possible threat from anti-radar systems. An effective air defence system can be set up with just an MAF and a fire unit. Of the two control units, one is used by the operator of the fire unit for the control of engagements, with the other being used by the unit commander, who has an overall picture of the air battle. Both control units provide information on the readiness and serviceability of the whole system, through built-in test facilities.

The Rapier 2000 is designed to operate as follows: the surveillance radar will detect and interrogate multiple targets, this information being presented to the operator as a set of priorities according to predefined criteria. Once the targets have been allocated, the operator can select tracking either by radar or electro-optical methods. In the former case, the tracker radar is used to acquire the target with the highest priority, which is then automatically tracked. A missile would then be launched and guided into the tracker radar

A Rapier Field Standard Model C SAM blasts away from its Fire Unit. (BAe Dynamics)

beam, where commands for guidance are transmitted from the tracker radar until impact. In the electro-optical mode, the operator views a visual display unit, aligning a sight on the target. The missile is guided by commands related to a line-of-sight path, assisted by flares in the missile's tail.

Once the first Rapier missile has been fired, attention can be switched to the next highest priority target. When this has been acquired, another missile is launched and guided with commands from the transmitter fitted on the fire unit. With this system, two targets can be engaged simultaneously.

The three main elements of the system (the fire unit and the two radars) are each transportable on two-axle trailers of the same basic design. The radars are linked to the control units and to the fire unit by fibre-optic cables that transmit digital data. The increased number of missiles carried by the fire unit means that RAF Regiment squadrons who re-equip with this version will consist of just six fire units, as opposed to eight previously. However, these squadrons will possess a far greater capability in the SHORAD role. A complete system, with three trailers, can be transported within one Hercules aircraft.

Current plans envisage the Rapier Field Standard Model C entering service with the RAF Regiment in the mid-1990s.

SMALL-ARMS WEAPONS

Most members of the RAF are trained in the use of one or more of a variety of small arms, primarily for the ground defence of the station or facility at which they are based. The weapons described in this section are used by various elements in the RAF, whose personnel are trained by members of the RAF Regiment, hence their inclusion in this chapter. Within the context of this book, the use of these weapons is defined between the RAF and/or the RAF Regiment. However, it should be remembered that most of these weapons are also widely used by many other elements within the British Services.

9 mm Pistol Automatic L9A1

Calibre 0.354 in (9 mm); **Length** 7.86 in (198 mm); **Length of barrel** 4.45 in (112 mm); **Weight empty** 1.94 lb (0.88 kg); **Weight loaded** 2.23 lb (1.01 kg); **Muzzle velocity** 1,230 ft/sec (375 m/sec); **Magazine capacity** 13 rounds; **Rate of fire** Single-shot; **Max effective range** 130 to 165 ft (40 to 50 m).

Incredible though it may seem, the initial versions of this weapon first entered production, by the FN

company in Belgium, almost 60 years ago. Since then, it has been produced in vast numbers by a number of concerns. In the early 1960s it became the standard service pistol for use throughout the UK Armed Forces. In the RAF it is used by certain personnel for security purposes, and is also carried by non fast-jet aircrew when operating in high-risk areas, in order to provide a degree of self-defence should they force-land or parachute into a hostile location.

The Browning is a robust and generally reliable weapon, capable of withstanding rough handling. It is a rather bulky item, with a noticeable recoil 'kick' on firing, and accuracy at distances of over 65 ft (20 m) requires sustained training. Despite its longevity, no replacement weapon of a similar type has been announced.

7.65 mm Pistol Automatic Walther PPK L47A1

Calibre 0.301 in (7.65 mm); **Length** 6.81 in (173 mm); **Length of barrel** 3.90 in (99 mm); **Weight empty** 1.5 lb (0.68 kg); **Weight loaded** 2.2 lb (1.0 kg); **Muzzle velocity** 951 ft/sec (290 m/sec); **Magazine capacity** 8 rounds; **Rate of fire** Single-shot; **Max effective range** 130 ft (40 m).

This small weapon is carried by fast-jet aircrew of the RAF, for similar self-defence purposes to the larger Browning pistol. It has been in production in Germany for many years, and originated as a weapon to be used and concealed by plain-clothed police, hence its small size.

5.56 mm Rifle Individual Weapon L85A1 (IW)

Calibre 0.219 in (5.56 mm); **Length overall** 2 ft 6.9 in (785 mm); **Length of barrel** 1 ft 8.4 in (518 mm); **Weight (complete)** 10.98 lb (4.98 kg); **Weight (rifle only)** 8.38 lb (3.8 kg); **Muzzle velocity** 3,084 ft/sec (940 m/sec); **Magazine capacity** 30 rounds; **Rate of fire (cyclic)** 610 to 775 rpm; **Combat range** Up to 1,310 ft (400 m)

This weapon, which is now the standard service rifle for the British Forces, has evolved after a great deal of protracted studies and development over many years. This has involved the need to produce a standard NATO weapon suitable for small-calibre ammunition, which has a number of advantages over larger sizes, including performance and logistics. A variety of small-calibre cartridges were evaluated, and these eventually led to the SA-80 family of compatible weapons. The development and early service use of the

L85A1 has been marked by a number of problems, necessitating several programmes to rectify these shortcomings.

The L85A1 is operated by gas, and its short, compact design makes for ease of use in confined spaces. An adaptor can be fitted to the muzzle to suppress flash, to fire rifle grenades, or to hold a bayonet. An optical sight can be fitted, which provides a magnified image under poor lighting conditions. The weapon is used throughout the RAF and the RAF Regiment, by both men and women, as a primary individual weapon for use in security patrols and unit/base defence.

5.56 mm Light Support Weapon L86A1

Calibre 0.219 in (5.56 mm); **Length overall** 2 ft 11.7 in (900 mm); **Length of barrel** 2 ft 1.4 in (646 mm); **Weight (complete)** 14.5 lb (6.58 kg); **Weight (rifle only)** 11.9 lb (5.4 kg); **Muzzle velocity** 3,183 ft/sec (970 m/sec); **Magazine capacity** 30 rounds; **Rate of fire (cyclic)** 610 to 775 rpm; **Combat range** Up to 2,625 ft (800 m).

A further member of the SA-80 family, the L86A1 Light Support Weapon (LSW) was developed along similar lines to that of the L85A1, and the two weapons share some 80 per cent commonality of parts. It is intended to provide fire-support for a squad, and is thus used by field squadrons of the RAF Regiment and by certain other personnel in the RAF.

The LSW differs from the IW in a number of respects. The folding support bipod was moved forward to be fitted on an extension, just under the muzzle, and an additional hand grip was provided behind the magazine. These changes were required to add stability to the LSW while firing bursts. It was also fitted with a longer and heavier barrel, and there were other internal alterations when compared with the IW. A bayonet cannot be fitted to the LSW.

7.62 mm Rifle L96A1

Calibre 0.300 in (7.62 mm); **Length** 3 ft 8.3 in/3 ft 11 in (1.124 m/1.194 m); **Length of barrel** 2 ft 1.8 in (655 mm); **Weight** 14.33 lb (6.5 kg); **Muzzle velocity** 2,750 ft/sec (838 m/sec); **Magazine capacity** 10 rounds; **Rate of fire** Single-shot; **Max effective range** 3,280 ft (1,000 m).

The L96A1 is used in small numbers by the RAF Regiment as a sniper rifle. It dates from the mid-1980s, and was produced to a very exacting specification, with early teething troubles now

The 5.56 mm Rifle – the Individual Weapon used in large numbers by the RAF, the RAF Regiment and throughout the British Services.

resolved. Various sights can be fitted to suit specific tasks and conditions, and the weapon uses carefully selected ammunition from specially produced batches. There are different types of cases in which the weapon can be stored, transported or protected.

7.62 mm General-Purpose Machine Gun L7A2

Calibre 0.300 in (7.62 mm); **Length** 3 ft 5.3 in (1.049 m); **Length of barrel** 2 ft 0.76 in (629 mm); **Weight (gun only)** 24 lb (10.9 kg); **Muzzle velocity** 2,750 ft/sec (838 m/sec); **Type of feed** 100-round belt; **Rate of fire (cyclic)** 25 to 750 rpm; **Rate of fire (practical)** 200 rpm; **Max effective range** 5,900 ft (1,800 m).

This weapon dates from the late 1950s, when trials were carried out to define a future general-purpose machine gun (GPMG) for use by the British Services. In 1958, the Belgian FN 7.62 mm was selected, but modifications to suit British requirements delayed production in the UK until 1963. The initial production version, the L7A1, was modified to become the L7A2, the basic variant in current use. Sustained fire is limited by the air-cooled barrel, which has to be changed after prolonged use. The GPMG is used only by the RAF Regiment.

51 mm Light Mortar L9A1

Calibre 2.035 in (51.25 mm); **Length overall** 2 ft 5.53 in (750 mm); **Length of barrel** 1 ft 9.38 in (543 mm); **Weight complete** 13.84 lb (6.275 kg); **Max range** 2,625 ft (800 m); **Rate of fire (normal)** 3 bombs/min for 5 min; **Bomb weight (HE)** 2.03 lb (0.92 kg).

The development life of this weapon, known as the Light Mortar, extended for some 10 years. It is deployed and carried by one man, although a second is usually employed to carry additional ammunition. The Light Mortar consists of the barrel, a breech-plate, a sling and a sight. When firing at short ranges, an insert is added to the bottom of the barrel.

The Light Mortar can fire a variety of bombs: high explosive, with impact or delay fuses; smoke; or illuminating. This mortar is used only by field squadrons of the RAF Regiment.

81 mm Mortar L16A2

Calibre 3.19 in (81 mm); **Length of barrel** 4 ft 2.4 in (1.28 m); **Weight complete** 83.64 lb (37.94 kg); **Max range** 18,537 ft (5,650 m); **Rate of fire** 15 bombs/min; **Bomb weight** 9.26 lb (4.2 kg).

Although having now been in service for more than 30 years, the 81 mm mortar proved to be an effective weapon in both the Falklands and Gulf conflicts. It was jointly developed by the UK and Canada, and is in service with the US Army.

It is normally carried on Land Rover vehicles, in a dismantled form. It can be broken down into three main sections for carrying as back-packs, with additional personnel being required to carry ammunition. A variety of projectiles can be fired, covering high explosive, smoke, illumination and practice rounds. As with the 51 mm mortar, its

The Hunting LAW 80 Anti-Armour Weapon, shown in its shoulder-mounted ready-to-fire position. (Hunting Engineering Ltd)

RAF use is restricted to the field squadrons of the RAF Regiment.

LAW 80 Anti-Armour Weapon L1A1

Tube bore 4.055 in (103 mm); **Length (extended)** 5 ft 1 in (1.55 m); **Shoulder weight** 19.8 lb (9 kg); **Projectile diameter** 3.7 in (94 mm); **Max effective range** 1,640 ft (500 m).

The Light Attack Weapon (LAW) 80, developed by Hunting Engineering, is in service with the field squadrons of the RAF Regiment. It is fired by one man from the shoulder position, and the tube-like launcher is aimed with the built-in optical sight. A spotting rifle capable of use in low-light conditions is also fitted, and this can be used to establish aiming accuracy prior to firing the anti-armour rocket projectile. The spotting rifle is preloaded with five 9 mm rounds, which are ballistically matched to the main rocket projectile. Once fired, the round from the rifle can be monitored by virtue of its tracer path, and a flash that the round's tip produces on impact. If this flash is on the required target, the anti-armour rocket is then fired. The rocket's shaped charge is claimed to be capable of penetrating most known types of armour.

The weapon can be supplied in a unit container which comprises 24 launchers, each containing a preloaded projectile, or as a two-weapon pack. The launcher is discarded after use. However, should the weapon not be fired, the container can be resealed for possible later use. The LAW 80 is supported by a training package, which utilizes an indoor training simulator, and a drill round for use in handling and deployment tuition.

CHAPTER SIX

The Reserve Units of the RAF

WITH THE PLANNED reductions in regular forces, it is possible that greater use may be made of reserve and volunteer personnel in various elements of the British Services. The administration of these forces saw some changes in the spring of 1993 and all reservists, both volunteer and ex-regular, are now the responsibility of the Controller Reserve Forces (RAF). This is based at RAF Innsworth, as part of the Personnel Management Centre, which in turn is an element within the new Personnel and Training Command.

Officers who have served with Short Service Commissions in the RAF have a mandatory reserve liability of four years. This figure also applies to officers who have served with the Princess Mary's Royal Air Force Nursing Service. Similarly, the liability for reserve service for Class 'E' airmen and airwomen is six years.

One aspect of the use of reservists is to tap the skills these personnel may have acquired through previous full-time service with the military, or in civilian employment. However, the RAF (along

Realistic training of medical staff serving with No 4626 (County of Wiltshire) Aeromedical Evacuation Squadron. (Aviation Photographs International)

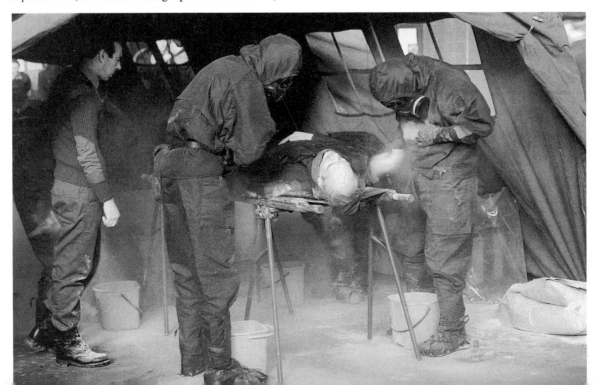

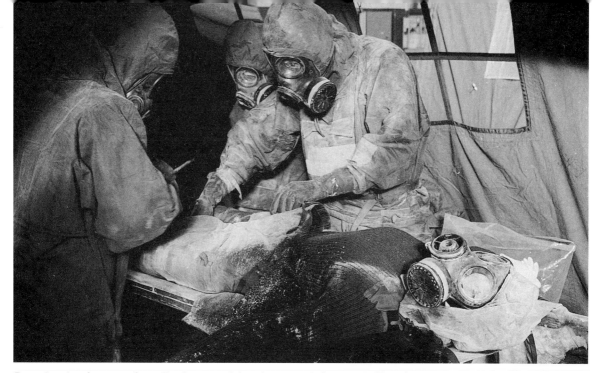

Practice in the art of medical supervision is essential, especially when it comes to dealing with the restrictions imposed by the wearing of NBC protection equipment. (Aviation Photographs International)

with the Army and Royal Navy) may not be in a position to employ such personnel on a full-time basis, but can make use of their skills through their enrolment as part-time volunteers.

There are a number of units that employ part-time volunteers, who receive training for operations in a variety of roles and tasks, with the purpose of assisting and supplementing the full-time members of the RAF. These tasks cover a wide spectrum of activities, ranging from administration, through logistical and medical tasks, to local ground defence. Following a period of expansion in the 1980s, these elements have been subject to a small reduction in size in recent months, due to the altered military situation.

ROYAL AUXILIARY AIR FORCE

Members of the Royal Auxiliary Air Force (RAuxAF) serve at three Maritime Headquarters Units (MHUs), with the task of augmenting the HQ staffs in times of an emergency. They are trained to participate in operations, communications and intelligence tasks, amongst others, supplementing the existing full-time personnel. The MHUs are located as follows:

No 1 (County of Hertford) MHU RAF Northwood
No 2 (City of Edinburgh) MHU RAF Turnhouse
No 3 (County of Devon) MHU   RAF St Mawgan

The titles in brackets indicate the areas from

which the members of these RAuxAF units are largely drawn. No 3 MHU was, until recently, based near Plymouth in Devon.

Two further units of the RAuxAF are involved in specialist tasks, with part-time volunteers supplementing regular RAF personnel in times of an emergency. No 4624 (County of Oxford) Movements Squadron is based at RAF Brize Norton, and carries out similar tasks to those undertaken by UK MAMS (see Chapter One). This involves the organizing and handling of cargo and passenger movements through air transport bases and other locations in the UK and overseas, in support of the British Services. This squadron consists of a number of flights that can be deployed as required.

With the closure of RAF Hullavington, No 4626 (County of Wiltshire) Aeromedical Evacuation Squadron moved to RAF Lyneham in 1993. The members of this unit are trained to provide medical supervision and escorts for casualties that require evacuation from locations in north-west Europe back to the UK.

ROYAL AUXILIARY AIR FORCE REGIMENT

Men and women from all walks of life are enrolled as members of the Royal Auxiliary Air Force Regiment (RAuxAF Regt) to provide local defence at a number of bases in the UK. During an emergency situation, members of field squadrons would undertake the bulk of ground defence and guard duties at various RAF stations, thus allowing the full-time trained personnel of the RAF to carry out their intended tasks. The RAuxAF Regt field squadrons are provided with vehicles and equipment (to a slightly reduced standard compared with the full-time RAF Regiment squadrons) to enable them to carry out their ground defence tasks. This includes Land Rovers and four-tonne trucks for local transport, together with rifles, general-purpose machine guns, light mortars and anti-tank weapons. Each field squadron is divided into a number of field flights, controlled by an HQ Flight. These field flights would undertake patrols in the local area and guard the base installations. Although the main task of the field squadrons is to defend the station at which they are based, they are capable of being deployed to other RAF stations, as required.

The principal field element within the RAuxAF Regt is No 1310 Wing, the HQ of which is currently located at RAF Catterick, although it will shortly move to RAF Honington. This wing is responsible for the five RAuxAF Regt field squadrons, which again are named to indicate the general areas from which their volunteer members are recruited, and which are currently deployed as follows:

No 2503 (County of Lincoln) Field Squadron
RAF Scampton
No 2620 (County of Norfolk) Field Squadron
RAF Marham
No 2622 (Highland) Field Squadron
RAF Lossiemouth
No 2624 (Cotswold) Field Squadron
RAF Brize Norton
No 2625 (County of Cornwall) Field Squadron
RAF St Mawgan

A further field unit, No 2623 (East Anglian) Field Squadron, based at RAF Honington, was disbanded recently as part of a number of reductions in defence assets in response to the declining threat of attack.

In addition to the above five squadrons, there is a further element called the Royal Auxiliary Air Force Defence Force, which is administered by the RAF Regiment. Its members are tasked with the local defence of a number of RAF stations, but they have a reduced commitment in terms of hours of training and duty, and their training is to a basic standard when compared with that of the five RAuxAF Regt field squadrons. Units of the Defence Force are based at RAF Brampton, RAF High Wycombe, RAF Lyneham and RAF St Athan. Their principal role is to supplement the existing resources in guarding these bases, and it is unlikely that they would deploy away from

Acquired during the Falklands conflict, the Oerlikon anti-aircraft guns (right) *and Contraves Skyguard fire control radar units* (left) *serve with two RAuxAF Regiment squadrons. (Aviation Photographs International)*

their parent stations, unlike the field squadrons. There were plans to expand the number of Defence Force units, but with the changed international situation and the reduction in the possible threat, these plans have been put into abeyance.

There are two further squadrons within the RAuxAF Regt, No 2729 (City of Lincoln) Squadron and No 2890 Squadron, operating in the short-range air defence role, both of which are based at RAF Waddington, near Lincoln, under the control of No 1339 Wing. The equipment that these two units operate in the air defence role is of particular interest, being Oerlikon 35 mm radar-controlled anti-aircraft guns captured from the Argentinian forces during the Falkland conflict of 1982. A large number of these weapons, together with their associated Contraves Skyguard fire control radars and ammunition, were shipped back to the UK, and refurbished prior to the formation of No 2729 Squadron in April 1985. This unit was later split to form No 2890 Squadron. There has been some discussion of late regarding the future of these units, and it seems unlikely that the Oerlikon/Skyguard equipment will remain in service. However, there is a possibility that these two squadrons may convert to the Rapier Field Standard B1(M) system when Rapier Field Standard C is introduced to the regular units of the RAF Regiment.

ROYAL AIR FORCE VOLUNTEER RESERVE

The Royal Air Force Volunteer Reserve (RAFVR) consists of approximately 200 part-time members, who have a number of specialist skills that are utilized by the RAF in times of war or a similar emergency, or to supplement regular elements on special occasions. These personnel are organized into four flights, as follows:

No 7006 Flight: Based at RAF High Wycombe, this flight is involved in various aspects of intelligence support.

No 7010 Flight: The members of this flight are skilled in the unique task of photographic interpretation and are based at RAF Wyton, although this unit may move due to the change in role of this station.

No 7630 Flight: This unit is also involved in duties connected with intelligence activities.

No 7644 Flight: Public relations (PR) is an important element in the current era of mass communications, with events being subject to minute scrutiny by the media organizations of TV, radio and the press. This flight's personnel are skilled in the field of PR and are tasked with presenting the activities of the RAF to the media in time of war, or at special events.

A further small element of the RAFVR is the Airmen Aircrew Augmentation system. In this, former full-time members of the RAF who are skilled in the role of AEOps, train with the Nimrod squadrons at RAF Kinloss on a part-time basis, and would be called upon to serve full-time on maritime patrol operations in time of war.

In mid-1993, proposals were announced which would amalgamate the RAFVR elements that have a war role with the RAuxAF, but the exact details and timing of these changes have yet to be defined.

CHAPTER SEVEN

Air Cadets

THE MAIN ELEMENT within the term of Air Cadets is the Air Training Corps (ATC), a national voluntary youth organization, which was established by Royal Warrant in February 1941, although its foundations can be traced back to 1928. Alongside the ATC there are a number of Combined Cadet Force units, based in certain schools, who also offer their members similar facilities of an aviation-related nature.

The main aims of the ATC are to promote and encourage a practical interest and knowledge of aviation and air-mindedness, particularly relating to the RAF, as well as providing a stimulus for adventure and sporting activities. Other objectives are to train members of the ATC in various skills, and to promote a sense of leadership and good citizenship. The RAF provides support for the ATC in many ways, ranging from flights in various types of aircraft to gain air experience, to facilities on stations for cadet activities. Although no pressure is put on ATC cadets to join the RAF, it is hoped that the interests gained whilst a member of the ATC will encourage young people of both sexes to consider a career in the Service.

HQ ATC is situated at RAF Newton, near Nottingham, and the Commandant is a full-time RAF officer, with the rank of Air Commodore, supported by Regular and Reserve officers, and civilian staff. For administrative purposes, the UK is divided into seven regions, each with a Group Captain (RAF Retired) as its Regional Commandant. The regional HQs are located as follows:

Scotland and Northern Ireland Region
RAF Turnhouse
North and East Region
RAF Linton-on-Ouse

Central and East Region
RAF Henlow
London and South-East Region
RAF Northolt
South-West Region
RAF Locking
Wales Region
RAF St Athan
North and West Region
RAF Sealand

These regions are further sub-divided, normally into six wings, with a total of 40 located throughout the UK. Wings are administered by a Squadron Leader (Retired), together with clerical staff, and organized by part-time officers in the Training Branch of the Royal Air Force Volunteer Reserve (RAFVR(T)). The wings are responsible for approximately 1,000 squadrons and detached flights located throughout the UK, these being the units in which cadets are enrolled as members. The majority of ATC squadrons have a membership of some 30 to 50 cadets; detached flights are elements that have less than 30 members, these being administered by a nearby ATC squadron.

Units are identified by a number and a geographical place name; the letter 'F' following the number designates the unit as one of the first 50 'Founder' squadrons. Squadrons and flights are managed by local civilian committees, and are organized by volunteer RAFVR(T) officers, ATC Adult Warrant Officers and civilian instructors. A number of ATC squadrons are located overseas, mainly at RAF stations in Germany and also in Cyprus and Gibraltar.

The ATC employs a graded system of classifications and ranks for its members. The basic classification on enrolment is Second Class Cadet, but training and success in examinations can progress ATC personnel to First Class Cadet, Leading Cadet, Senior Cadet and Staff Cadet gradings. Once enrolled into the ATC, cadets are trained in a variety of subjects, including first aid, target-shooting, the history of the ATC and the RAF, and aircraft recognition. Training for Leading Cadets deals with such items as map-reading, the principles of flight, and aeronautical knowledge, with Senior and Staff Cadets undertaking further specialist tuition. Promotion through the ranks of Cadet Corporal, Cadet Sergeant, Cadet Flight Sergeant and Cadet Warrant Officer is the result of selection by the squadron commander.

Most ATC squadrons and flights attend an annual camp which is held on an RAF station in the summer months. This is designed to provide cadets with an insight into the day-to-day activities of the RAF. Various courses are provided with the aim of promoting leadership potential and qualities. A variety of sports form part of the Corps' activities, and the ATC also undertakes adventure training, being a major participant in the Duke of Edinburgh's Award Scheme.

One of the main attractions of membership of the ATC is the opportunity to fly in either powered aircraft or gliders. For powered flying, a number of Air Experience Flights (AEFs) were formed in 1958, equipped with the de Havilland Chipmunk T.10 two-seat trainer, and these units continue as such to this day. In order to fly with an AEF, the cadet must have achieved a 'First Class' classification within his or her unit. The aim of the AEFs is to provide instructional aviation for Air Cadets and to promote their aeronautical interest. The staff pilots of the AEFs are all RAFVR officers, with experience as pilots in one of the three British Services; currently some 250 serve with the 13 AEFs now active. No 13 AEF operates Bulldog T.1 aircraft borrowed from the co-located Queens University Air Squadron; the remaining 12 AEFs all still fly the Chipmunk T.10. The designations and locations of the AEFs are as follows:

No 1 AEF   RAF Manston
No 2 AEF   Bournemouth (Hurn) Airport
No 3 AEF   Colerne, Wilts
No 4 AEF   Exeter Airport
No 5 AEF   Cambridge (Teversham) Airport
No 6 AEF   RAF Benson
No 7 AEF   RAF Newton
No 8 AEF   RAF Shawbury
No 9 AEF   RAF Finningley
No 10 AEF   RAF Woodvale
No 11 AEF   RAF Leeming
No 12 AEF   RAF Turnhouse
No 13 AEF   RAF Aldergrove

The ATC also operates a large number of gliders and motor-gliders, giving cadets the opportunity to attain a solo standard, and between 1,500 and

The mainstay of the Air Experience Flights is the venerable Chipmunk T.10; these examples belong to No 6 AEF at RAF Benson.

Nearly 100 Grob Viking T.1s are in service to provide training in glider flying for members of the Air Training Corps.

1,800 cadets achieve their gliding 'wings' each year. The Air Cadet Gliding Organization consists of the Air Cadet Central Gliding School (ACCGS), based at RAF Syerston, in Nottinghamshire, which provides training for glider instructors, together with 27 Volunteer Gliding Schools (VGSs) located throughout the UK. The instructors on these units are officers of the RAFVR(T), together with civilian gliding staff. Also based at RAF Syerston is the Mobile Glider Servicing Party (MGSP), a unit that is responsible for the servicing and maintenance of gliders in use at the VGSs.

The VGSs fall into two categories, being equipped with either the Grob 103 glider, which is known as the Viking T.1 by the RAF, and is launched by a static ground winch, or the Grob 109B motor-glider, named the Vigilant T.1 for service with the RAF. These are both high-performance machines built in Germany and constructed largely of glass-reinforced plastic. One hundred Vikings were obtained as replacements

A number of Volunteer Gliding Schools operate the Grob Vigilant T.1 powered glider.

The elegant Grob Viking T.1 glider.

for the elderly Sedburgh and Cadet T.3 gliders, and the type entered service with the ATC in 1983. In 1989 an order for 53 Vigilants was announced, with the first examples entering service in early 1990, replacing the Venture T.2 motor-glider then in operation. The ACCGS, as well as flying both of these types, also operates three Valiant T.1 single-seat and two Janus C two-seat gliders for advanced training in soaring techniques.

The VGSs have a number of tasks: to provide air experience flights for cadets; to give basic flying training; to offer more advanced flying training; and to give standards training for instructors in order to maintain their currency on type. In order to reach solo standard, a cadet will average between 40 to 60 launches in the Viking, whilst a student flying in the Vigilant will take some eight to 12 hours airborne to reach solo status. The 27 VGSs and their principal equipment are currently deployed as follows:

No 611 VGS   RAF Swanton Morley   Viking
No 612 VGS   Abingdon   Vigilant

A Viking T.1 glider commences its steep climb from take-off under the power of a static winch.

The front cockpit of a Viking T.1 glider. The switches under the instrument dials are for the radio.

No 613 VGS	RAF Halton	Vigilant
No 614 VGS	RAF Wethersfield	Viking
No 615 VGS	RAF Kenley	Viking
No 616 VGS	RAF Henlow	Vigilant
No 617 VGS	RAF Manston	Viking
No 618 VGS	West Malling	Viking
No 621 VGS	Hullavington	Viking
No 622 VGS	Upavon	Viking
No 624 VGS	RAF Chivenor	Vigilant
No 625 VGS	Hullavington	Viking
No 626 VGS	RNAS Predannack	Viking
No 631 VGS	RAF Sealand	Viking
No 632 VGS	RAF Ternhill	Vigilant
No 633 VGS	RAF Cosford	Vigilant
No 634 VGS	RAF St Athan	Viking
No 635 VGS	Samlesbury	Vigilant
No 636 VGS	Swansea	Viking
No 637 VGS	Little Rissington	Vigilant
No 642 VGS	RAF Linton-on-Ouse	Vigilant
No 643 VGS	RAF Syerston	Vigilant
No 644 VGS	RAF Syerston	Vigilant
No 645 VGS	RAF Catterick	Viking
No 661 VGS	Kirknewton	Viking
No 662 VGS	Arbroath	Viking
No.663 VGS	RAF Kinloss	Vigilant

The ATC currently has a cadet membership of some 47,000 and is one of the largest youth organizations in the country. The wide range of activities available to cadets reflects the dedication of the numerous Service and civilian instructors and staff, who provide many hours of voluntary effort.

Specifications of the two principal aircraft types in service with the ACCGS and the VGSs are as follows:

Viking T.1

Wing span 57 ft 5 in (17.5 m); **Length** 26 ft 10 in (8.18 m); **Height** 5 ft 1 in (1.55 m); **Max take-off weight** 1,278 lb (580 kg); **Max speed (smooth air)** 155 mph (250 km/h).

Vigilant T.1

Powerplant One 90 hp (67 kw) Grob 2500 piston engine; **Wing span** 57 ft 1 in (17.4 m); **Length** 26 ft 7 in (8.1 m); **Height** 5 ft 11 in (1.8 m); **Max take-off weight** 1,874 lb (850 kg); **Max speed** 149 mph (240 km/h); **Service ceiling** 19,675 ft (6,000 m).

For their size, the variants of the Tornado that serve with the RAF are arguably the most sophisticated aircraft that have been procured by the Service. The initial model, the GR.1, has now been in front-line service with the RAF for over 10 years, during which time Tornados were used in anger in the Gulf War. Indeed, the name of this aircraft became a household word thanks to frequent TV reports of the sorties undertaken against Iraqi forces as part of Operation 'Desert Storm'.

The fact that the Tornado has proved to be a highly successful aircraft is all the more remarkable when consideration is given to the potential problems that can arise with multi-national collaborative projects. The ever-increasing costs and lengthening timescales in developing and producing sophisticated military aircraft have and will continue to force national self-interest and pride to give way to co-operation and compromise, in order to achieve an affordable product.

The origins of the Tornado go back to the 1960s, when the Cold War between NATO and the Warsaw Pact was the dominant factor in military planning. Several NATO countries perceived the need to collaborate in the design and production of a common military design, which became known as the Multi-Role Combat Aircraft (MRCA), to replace existing types. Panavia Aircraft GmbH, based in Munich, was formed to oversee and co-ordinate development of the MRCA. Some of the original countries withdrew from the project, leaving just three participating nations: the United Kingdom, West Germany and Italy. Panavia comprised three major aerospace companies: British Aerospace (BAe) in the UK, Messerschmitt-Bolkow-Blohm in West Germany, and Aeritalia in Italy. Also, a joint company, Turbo-Union, was set up by Rolls-Royce, Motoren und Turbinen of Germany, and Fiat of Italy, to produce the RB.199 three-spool turbofan engines; whilst a further tri-national company was formed to cover the avionics.

The title MRCA was most apt, as no less than six operational roles were defined as tasks that were to be fulfilled by the new aircraft. These were: close air support/battlefield interdiction, long-range strike, maritime strike, reconnaissance, air superiority, and interception/air defence. A variant of the original Interdictor Strike Version (IDS) was to be developed to cater for the final two of these tasks, this being known as the Air Defence Version (ADV), with the RAF being the (then) sole customer (this variant is described elsewhere in this chapter). For these various tasks, the MRCA was to be capable of carrying most of the current and projected missiles, bombs and other weapons systems in the arsenals of the three customer nations. The ability to operate from semi-prepared airstrips some

3,000 ft (914 m) in length was also stipulated.

To combine these tasks into one design was an unprecedented and formidable challenge to the design teams involved. In the strike role, the MRCA was expected to be able to penetrate the sophisticated air defence systems of Warsaw Pact countries, in all the many and varied types of weather conditions that central Europe can muster. These missions were to be carried out at very low-level, and the target was to be reached and destroyed with pin-point accuracy.

The design that evolved into the Tornado is a variable-geometry, twin-engined aircraft, with a fly-by-wire flight control system, operated by a crew of two seated in tandem. Most versions are fitted with two Mauser 27 mm cannon, mounted within the lower forward section of the fuselage. All other weapons and stores are carried on external positions, with three stations under the fuselage, and two pylons under each wing. The underwing pylons swivel so as to remain aligned with the fuselage when the wings' angle of sweep is altered.

The sophisticated heart of the Tornado lies in its avionics systems, controlled by a central main digital computer. Information is fed to the computer from a wide range of sensors, via digital data links, the sensors including ground mapping radar, terrain-following radar (TFR), an inertial navigation system (INS), Doppler radar, an air data computer, twin gyroscopes, a radar altimeter, approach aids and the laser rangefinder and marked target seeker (LRMTS). Information from the sensors is presented by the computer to the pilot and navigator using a variety of methods. The pilot has available a head-up display (HUD), a horizontal situation indicator which provides heading and distance-to-go data, and a moving map display which gives current position and track. Also, there is the radar warning receiver (RWR) to alert the crew to any threat situation, and a terrain-following display.

The navigator has two TV display screens, on which mission data can be monitored or changed if required. There is also a combined display, incorporating both radar and moving map information, and displays providing data on distance and heading. The vast amount of information required for a typical mission is programmed into a computer at the aircraft's home base, this data then being transferred to the Tornado's computer by tape prior to take-off. Such data would include details of the proposed flight plan, with points en route, target location TACAN beacons, areas to be avoided, alternative points should a mission path need to be changed, and any other relevant details. Obviously, problems can occur with this vast amount of sophisticated avionics, so Tornados are fitted with an On-board Checkout

Tornado GR.1
1:72 scale

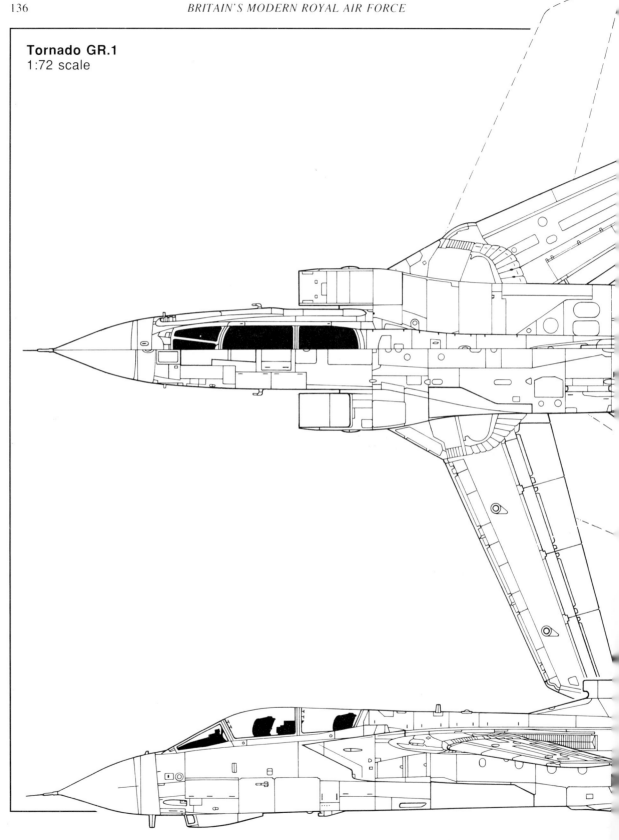

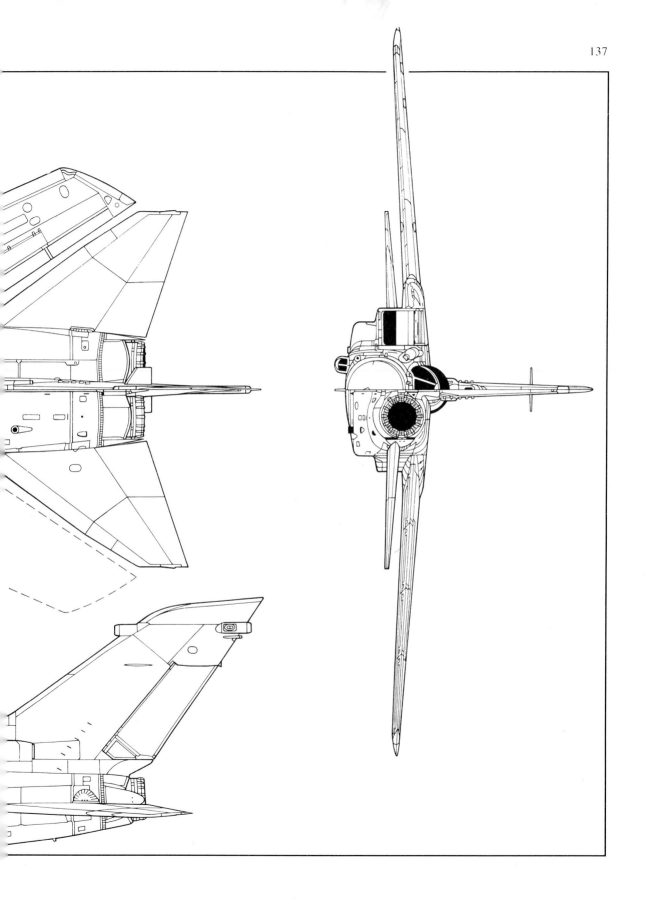

and Monitoring System which analyzes and indicates any faulty equipment. This equipment is mainly in the form of replaceable plug-in modules, accessible via a large number of removable panels on the aircraft's exterior.

A number of Tornados are configured with dual-controls, to act as conversion trainer aircraft, but retaining a full operational capability. A control column, foot pedals and engine throttles are provided in the rear cockpit, and basic flight instruments are also fitted; these extra items add to the existing mass of equipment in the rear cockpit of these 'twin stick' aircraft.

Separate production lines were set up in the UK, West Germany and Italy, each of which was responsible for the final assembly and flight testing of the aircraft ordered by the respective nations. Apart from these items, there was to be no duplication in production. Thus the UK was responsible for producing the nose and tail sections, representing 42.5 per cent of the project. A similar proportion of work was allocated to West Germany, which built the fuselage centre-sections, whilst Italy provided the wings as its 15 per cent contribution. The first IDS prototype flew (in West Germany) on 14 August 1974, and this was followed by eight further prototypes and six pre-production aircraft. Over a period of 12 years, starting in mid-1976, 805 Tornados were ordered, in six production batches. Of these, 220 were of the IDS attack version for the RAF, in whose service they carry the GR.1 designation, with a development of the basic model for reconnaissance purposes being designated the GR.1A.

The first unit to operate the Tornado was a true multi-national operation, comprising aircraft and personnel from the three producing countries. This was the Tri-national Tornado Training Establishment (TTTE), which received its first aircraft in mid-1980, and then commenced the immense task of converting aircrew of all three nations onto the new aircraft at RAF Cottesmore in early 1981.

To provide training in using the Tornado as a weapons system, the Tornado Weapons Conversion Unit (TWCU) was established at RAF Honington, and it started to receive aircraft in mid-1981. No 9 Squadron, also at Honington, became the first front-line RAF unit to equip with the Tornado, in June 1982. Nos 27 and 617 Squadrons, both at RAF Marham, re-equipped in 1983, following which it was the turn of RAF Germany to receive the new aircraft, with No 15 Squadron at RAF Laarbruch converting from Buccaneers in the same year. In 1984 the TWCU gained the 'shadow' identity of No 45 Squadron, whilst Nos 16, 20 and 31 Squadrons, all based in West Germany, reformed on the type. The following year saw Nos 14 and 17 Squadrons at RAF

Bruggen re-equipping with Tornados, these units being joined in 1986 by No 9 Squadron which had transferred from Marham.

In the strike role, the RAF's Tornados can carry a wide range of weapons on seven external positions. No doubt nuclear devices, in the form of WE177 free-fall bombs, were available for use should the Cold War have ever turned into an actual conflict. With the demise of Communism and the Warsaw Pact in the early 1990s, the current mission plans of the RAF in the strike role will probably have been revised, but these may well still involve the carriage of the WE177 bomb in what is known as the sub-strategic strike role.

RAF Tornados undertook some of the most dangerous aerial strike missions against Iraq during the Gulf War, involving low-level attacks on airfields which were often heavily defended. For these strikes, the RAF used the JP233 area denial weapon, two of which can be carried on the underfuselage mountings. A wide variety of conventional bombs can also be carried on the fuselage pylons, combined with fuel tanks. The accurate delivery of these weapons is aided by the LRMTS equipment housed in a fairing on the underside of the nose. The radius of action of the Tornado can be extended by AAR, via a detachable probe fitted on the starboard side of the nose, near the cockpit.

Large fuel tanks are normally carried on the innermost underwing pylons, the inner sides of which can carry a Sidewinder AAM to provide a degree of self-defence. Further self-defence is provided by equipment usually carried on the outermost underwing pylons: an ECM pod on the port pylon and a chaff and flare dispensing pod on the starboard pylon.

The RAF was the first air arm to introduce a dedicated reconnaissance variant of the Tornado, designated the GR.1A; initially, West Germany and Italy utilized standard IDS aircraft fitted with external recce pods for this task. The GR.1A is a modified version of the standard Tornado GR.1, the conversion work being carried out by BAe to produce an aircraft capable of providing all-weather, day and night reconnaissance at low-level. The two Mauser cannon were deleted to make room for the camera equipment, but in all other respects the GR.1A is fully capable of operating in the strike role, using the same external hardpoints as those of the GR.1 version.

The equipment for the reconnaissance role is fitted in the lower part of the forward fuselage, beneath the cockpits. The main sensor is the downward-looking infra-red line scanner (IRLS), mounted in a small bulge under the fuselage, and this provides a scanning 'window' of 80° either side of the aircraft's vertical centreline. Complementing the IRLS are two sideways-look-

Extended air-to-air refuelling probe on a Tornado GR.1A of No 13 Squadron.

ing infra-red (SLIR) sensors, one on each side of the lower forward fuselage. Together, these three devices provide 180°, horizon-to-horizon coverage beneath and to the sides of the aircraft.

With this reconnaissance equipment, the navigator is able to view on his left-hand TV display the images being obtained in 'real time' and can replay, magnify or freeze information on the screen in order to evaluate and report on the current situation. Unlike earlier systems, all the images obtained are recorded on video tape rather than 'wet' film that would require processing once the aircraft had returned to base after completing its mission. Standard three-hour VHS video cassette tapes are used to record information, the tapes being played at three times normal speed. Six video recorders are fitted in the Tornado GR.1A, three of which are dedicated to

recording new images from the IRLS and two SLIRs. The remaining three recorders act as back-ups and as a secondary recording system to allow editing or in-flight viewing. Thus data on the tapes can be analyzed immediately upon arrival back at base.

The first development Tornado GR.1A made its maiden flight in July 1985, and the first 15 production aircraft were converted from existing GR.1s. No 2 Squadron, based at Laarbruch, was the first unit to operate the new variant, from January 1989, having relinquished its Jaguars. A further 14 Tornado GR.1As were built as new, these forming the equipment of No 13 Squadron, which reformed at Honington in January 1990. Following the 'Options for Change' defence review, No 2 Squadron moved to Marham in December 1991, and No 13 Squadron moved to

The 'eyes' of the Tornado GR.1A reconnaissance aircraft. The bulge under the fuselage houses the IRLS, whilst the vertical windows (one on each side) *are for the SLIR sensors.*

the same base in early 1994.

To make room at the Norfolk base for the two reconnaissance-dedicated units, two Tornado GR.1-equipped units, Nos 12 (formerly No 27) and 617 Squadrons, have moved to RAF Lossiemouth. Their move to Scotland is to cover the retirement of the Buccaneer S.2B from front-line service in the maritime strike role. Thus yet another role has been added to the Tornado's repertoire, and these two squadrons' aircraft are now being equipped to carry the Sea Eagle anti-ship missile. Four of these weapons can be carried by the Tornado, with two under the central fuse-lage and one each on the innermost underwing pylons. Suitable wiring and other modifications have been introduced to a number of Tornados to enable them to carry the Sea Eagle, resulting in a a new designation of Tornado GR.1B.

Current plans call for the RAF's Tornado GR.1s to undergo a Mid-Life Update (MLU) pro-gramme in the early 1990s, following which they will be redesignated as GR.4s. However, this pro-gramme is running behind schedule due to bud-getary constraints, and it is not known at the time of writing whether all of the proposed MLU mod-ifications will actually be incorporated.

The MLU is designed to introduce and inte-grate advanced avionics, which will improve the Tornado's performance with regard to naviga-tion, weapons delivery, and survivability. One such advance will be the installation of terrain-referenced navigation, a major feature of which is a digital map generator (DMG). The DMG presents a topographical map area in a high-res-olution display, from digital data stored on a disc read by a laser. This information is com-bined with data from a radar altimeter and the INS to provide an advanced terrain-following capability. A further aspect of the MLU will be the addition of forward-looking infra-red (FLIR), from which a thermal image will be pre-sented on to the head-up/head-down displays. Combined with the use of night-vision goggles (NVGs), information from this system will enable missions to be flown in poor weather, by day and night. Images from the FLIR will be presented to the pilot's view, and combined with flight data and the actual scene. Both cockpits will have new, full-colour displays, presenting information on flight conditions, weapons sys-tems, maintenance status, and navigation data from the DMG.

Although designed to counter the perceived threat from the now-defunct Warsaw Pact forces in central Europe, the Tornado GR.1 was first used in anger in a much warmer climate, against the forces of Iraq. Only time will reveal the extent of any modifications made to improve the strike version of this aircraft, but it is certain to remain the mainstay of the RAF's attack capability for many years to come.

British Aerospace/McDonnell Douglas Harrier GR.5/.5A/.7/T.10

Powerplant One Rolls-Royce Pegasus 105 vectored-thrust turbofan, rated at 21,750 lb st (96.75 kN); **Wing span** 30 ft 4 in (9.25 m); **Length (GR.7)** 47 ft 1 in (14.36 m), **(T.10)** 51 ft 10 in (15.79 m); **Height** 11 ft 8 in (3.55 m); **Max take-off weight (STO)** 29,750 lb (13,495 kg); **Max speed (at sea level)** 661 mph (1,065 km/h). **Operating Units** Nos 1, 3, 4, 20(R) Squadrons; SAOEU.

Although there have been numerous attempts to develop and produce aircraft with vertical or short take-off and landing (V/STOL) capabilities, the Harrier, in its various forms, remains by far the most successful example, having now been in ser-vice with the RAF for some 25 years. Large num-bers of the initial variants have served with the Royal Air Force (as the Harrier GR.1 and .3), while the US Marine Corps (USMC) used a simi-lar model with the US designation of AV-8A. Most, if not all of these earlier models have now been withdrawn from service.

From the mid-1970s onwards, studies were undertaken on both sides of the Atlantic with the general aim of improving the payload and range of the Harrier. Following a licence agreement between Hawker Siddeley (later to form part of BAe) and the US manufacturer McDonnell Douglas (McDD), the latter company gained the rights to produce and market the Harrier and its subsequent derivatives in the USA and for export. Co-operation on future development of the Harrier also formed part of this agreement. The Harrier II, as it became known, was designed and produced within the framework of the licence agreement, with a great deal of the development work being carried out in the USA. The two com-panies joined forces in 1976 to develop the Harrier II, with the prospect of orders from the US Marine Corps (USMC) and the RAF, as replacements for the earlier models. With the new aircraft, McDD was designated as the prime con-tractor and BAe as the principal sub-contractor, a reversal of roles when compared with the devel-opment programme for the first generation of Harriers.

The first AV-8Bs (as the new aircraft was des-ignated in US military service) were, in fact, modified AV-8As, and these were used to conduct test flights in the USA during the late 1970s. The first of four full-scale development AV-8Bs took to the air in November 1981, and later in the same year authorization was given for the production of the Harrier II, with orders from the USMC for 257 aircraft, and the RAF, who required 60. Aircraft for the RAF were given the designation of GR.5.

In addition to the main Harrier II order for the RAF, two development aircraft were also acquired, the first of which made its maiden flight on 30 April 1985. Deliveries of production Harrier GR.5s commenced in mid-1987. In April 1988, a further order for 34 aircraft for the RAF was announced. With the availability of the night attack version of the Harrier II, again developed in the USA, the two development GR.5s were converted to this standard, adopting the GR.7 designation in the process. The first of these conversions took to the air in November 1988. The final 19 of the initial 60-aircraft order were built as GR.5As, this being an interim version between the GR.5 and the definitive night attack GR.7. The GR.5As were completed to a similar specification as the GR.7, but they lacked the latter's full avionics fit. Initially, the GR.5As were placed in storage, pending a conversion programme that called for 58 GR.5/.5As to be brought up to GR.7 standard. The first such converted GR.5 was redelivered to the RAF in December 1990, while the first converted GR.5A was redelivered in April 1991. Most of the GR.5 and all of the GR.5A conversions have now been carried out. All 34 aircraft in the follow-on order were built as GR.7s, with the last being delivered in early 1992.

The work in producing the Harrier II was shared between BAe and McDD, with the latter responsible for 60 per cent of the airframe on machines for the USMC. The GR.5/.5A/.7s for the RAF were produced on a 50:50 percentage split in the production effort between each company, and final assembly of aircraft for the USMC and RAF took place in the USA and the UK respectively. As with other international programmes, various sections of the airframe were 'single-sourced', being the responsibility of one or the other of the participating companies, as were the various systems contained within that section. Thus the wings, apart from small leading-edge extensions, were manufactured by McDD, whilst the tail fins and rudders were constructed by BAe. The fuselages were built by both companies, with McDD producing the forward section and BAe the centre and rear sections; fuselage assembly (and production of the horizontal tail surfaces) was undertaken in each country, against the numbers of aircraft ordered by the USMC and RAF respectively. The landing gear and cockpit canopies were the responsibility of McDD on all aircraft, whilst BAe provided the complete control system for all aircraft. The Pegasus 105 vectored-thrust turbofan engine was primarily the responsibility of Rolls-Royce, with Pratt & Whitney being responsible for some 25 per cent (in terms of value) of the engines in aircraft for the USMC.

In terms of weight, some 26 per cent of the aircraft's structure is made from graphite-eopxy composite materials, with significant savings in weight when compared with conventional metal assemblies. Main elements constructed from composite materials are the forward fuselage, the majority of the wing and the rear horizontal flying surfaces. The design of the wing is one of the major features of the new generation of Harriers, with an increased area and greater span, whilst its supercritical aerofoil section contains a larger fuel capacity.

Under each wing are four weapons-carrying pylons, with one of these (the second pylon outboard of the fuselage) specifically for the carriage of AAMs such as Sidewinder and ASRAAM. This particular weapons station is mid-way along the wing, in line with the undercarriage outrigger leg installation, and is unique to the RAF aircraft. A

The spread of eight stores-carrying pylons is clearly shown in this head-on view of a No 1 Squadron Harrier GR.7.

Harrrier GR.7
1:72 scale

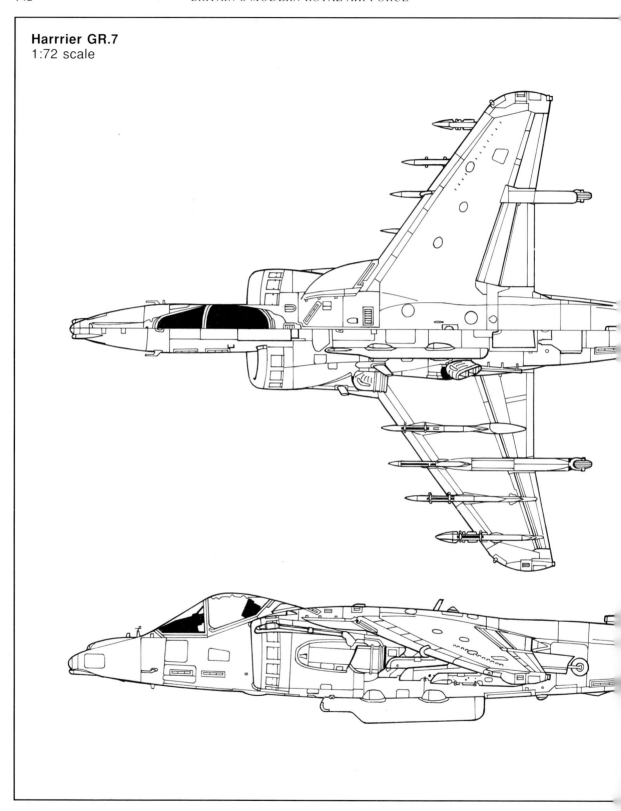

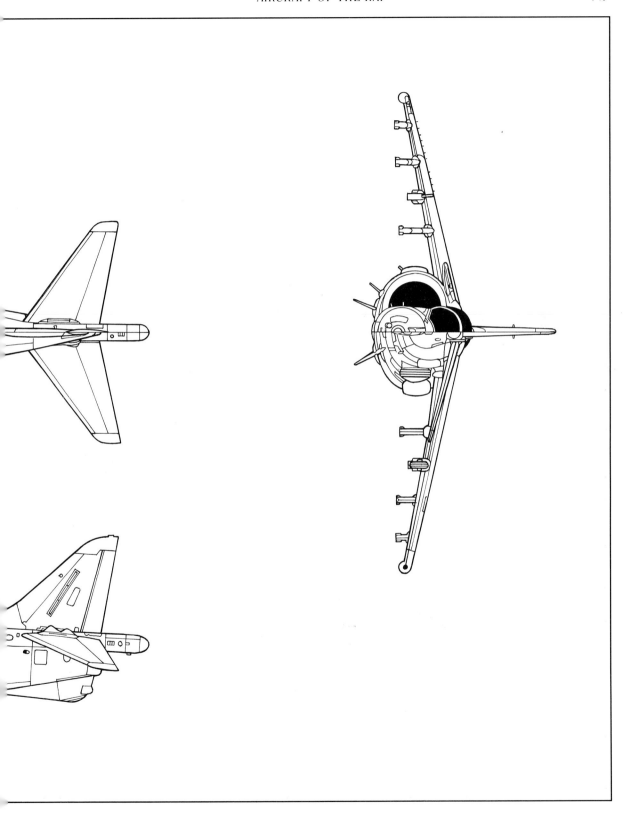

variety of stores can be carried on the other pylons, including additional AAMs, fuel tanks, free-fall, retarded or cluster bombs, and carriers for practice bombs. There is a further weapons-carrying position under the fuselage centreline, and RAF aircraft carry two 25 mm Aden gun pods, one either side of this centreline station.

As with many current military aircraft, the Harrier II's operational capability is based on a mission computer, from which information is presented to the pilot via a HUD, together with two identical Multi-Purpose Colour Display (MPCD) units. In addition to controls for the MPCDs, the pilot can utilize switches on the control column by means of the Hands-on-Throttle-and-Stick system. Weapons delivery is aided by various sophisticated systems, including the Angle Rate Bombing System, which locates the target by laser, monitors angles and distances, and supplies computed steering data to the pilot.

The HUD presents information covering flight conditions, navigation, weapons delivery, and threat warnings to the pilot whilst he looks ahead and out of the cockpit. With the GR.7, additional information from FLIR sensors is transmitted onto the HUD. Combined with the latter is a push-button panel, just below the windscreen, from which functions such as communications, navigation, identification and weapons control can be operated. Lower in the cockpit are the two MPCDs, presenting data covering engine conditions, systems testing, and stores details, together with information displayed on the HUD. Navigation is assisted by a Digital Electronic Map Unit, displayed on either MPCD, along with the other data outlined above. A major innovation

introduced with the GR.7 variant is the use of NVGs, and the cockpit lighting has been made compatible with this equipment.

The Harrier IIs for the RAF differ in many respects from the aircraft procured for the USMC, with several items of UK-sourced avionics and defensive equipment being fitted, together with Martin-Baker ejection seats. In a number of respects, the RAF aircraft are more capable than their USMC counterparts, but these changes resulted in increased costs and a two-year delay of entry into service. Initial training of the first RAF pilots destined to fly the Harrier GR.5 was carried out in the USA, utilizing USMC facilities. The first GR.5s arrived at RAF Wittering in early 1988, and No 233 OCU commenced conversion of pilots to the new model the following year. Late 1989 saw No 1 Squadron operational on the GR.5. Further deliveries were then made to RAF Germany's Harrier-equipped squadrons, with No 3 Squadron being fully-equipped with GR.5s by April 1990, and No 4 Squadron receiving new GR.7s later the same year. No 3 Squadron subsequently converted from the GR.5 to the GR.7 in late 1990, and GR.7s from both squadrons were deployed to Turkey in April 1993 in support of UN operations in northern Iraq.

As more Harrier GR.5/.5As were converted to GR.7 standard, aircraft became available to re-equip No 1 Squadron at Wittering, so that by the middle of 1993 this unit had fully converted to the new night attack variant. This leaves just No 20 (Reserve) Squadron (formerly No 233 OCU) operating the few remaining GR.5s.

In addition to the single-seat variants, McDD has designed and developed a two-seat trainer

Nose detail of a Harrier GR.7 of No 1 Squadron. Note the air-to-air refuelling probe by the port side of the cockpit.

version of the Harrier II, known in US service as the TAV-8B, with 28 having been ordered for the USMC. This variant flew for the first time in October 1986, with deliveries commencing the following year. In 1992, an order was announced for 13 two-seat Harrier IIs for the RAF, to be known as Harrier T.10s. These aircraft will be fitted with FLIR and be NVG-compatible, as per the GR.7s, as well as having a training function. The T.10 variant is due to enter service in 1995.

British Aerospace Harrier T.4

Powerplant One Rolls-Royce Pegasus 103 vectored-thrust turbofan, rated at 21,500 lb st (95.6 kN); **Wing span (combat)** 25 ft 3 in (7.70 m); **Length** 57 ft 5 in (17.50 m); **Height** 13 ft 8 in (4.17 m); **Max take-off weight** 26,200 lb (11,884 kg); **Max speed (at sea level)** 730 mph (1,176 km/h); **Max range** 2,070 miles (3,330 km); **Service ceiling** 51,200 ft (15,616 km). **Operating Units** Nos 1 and 20(R) Squadrons; SAOEU.

The RAF first commenced operations with the initial single-seat version of the revolutionary V/STOL Harrier in 1969, but it was not until the following year that a two-seat conversion trainer variant entered service. It was designated the T.2, and the characteristics of V/STOL performance meant that the modifications needed to provide an additional seat were far greater than would be required for other high-performance combat aircraft. Thus the two-seat Harriers have a rather odd appearance, with a large, sideways-opening cockpit canopy, under which the rear seat is mounted noticeably higher than the front seat. The Harrier T.2's fuselage had to be considerably lengthened, not only to accommodate the additional cockpit and seat but to maintain aerodynamic balance, with the tail fin being moved further aft. The two-seater's fuselage extends aft of the fin with a long tail cone that houses the rear reaction control valve. The tail fin's height was also increased, although this feature was subsequently altered along with later modifications.

The RAF required that the Harrier T.2 should be capable of operational use, in addition to its primary role as a conversion trainer, so stores-carrying hardpoints were retained, together with avionics and other features of the single-seat Harrier GR.1.

The first of two Harrier T.2 development prototypes took to the air in April 1969, this being followed in October of the same year by the first of an initial production batch of 12 aircraft. The final two aircraft from this batch were fitted with the uprated Pegasus 102 engine, being redesignated as T.2As; the earlier T.2s were later modified to this standard. Further development of the Pegasus vectored-thrust engine resulted in the Pegasus 103, with greater thrust than the earlier versions. Existing Harrier T.2As were again re-engined, this time with the Pegasus 103, which resulted in a change of designation to T.4. Further production of this variant resulted in 14 all-new aircraft, these being ordered in four batches (one batch of two followed by three batches of four aircraft each).

As with the Harrier GR.3 single-seat version, most of the early T.4s were modified by the addition of nose-mounted LRMTS equipment, which

The unique lines of the two-seat Harrier T.4 are revealed by this RAF Wittering-based example serving with No 1 Squadron.

resulted in an altered nose profile that did little to improve the two-seat trainer's appearance. A box-like antenna was added to the leading-edge of the tail fin, which, in conjuction with another antenna added to the fuselage tail cone, was a sensor for the Passive Warning Receiver. However, a number of T.4s had their LRMTS equipment removed, in order to save weight and improve performance. These aircraft, used solely for conversion training, and thus lacking the need for the LRMTS, have received yet another change of designation, now being known as T.4As.

Most, if not all, of the RAF's two-seat Harrier T.4/.4As have operated, at one time or another, with what was No 233 OCU at RAF Wittering. All of the current front-line Harrier squadrons (Nos 1, 3 and 4) have had one or two T.4s on strength, for conversion training and check-out flights. For a period, the T.4s based in West Germany were concentrated into the RAF Gutersloh Station Flight. However, with the introduction into service of the Harrier GR.5/.5A/.7 models, most of the surviving T.4/.4As are now at Wittering, apart from a couple with the SAOEU at Boscombe Down. No 1 Squadron also operates a two-seater, whilst the remaining trainers continue their task of conversion work with No 20 (Reserve) Squadron. With the impending introduction of the radically different Harrier T.10 two-seater, time may be running out for this earlier model.

SEPECAT Jaguar GR.1A/T.2A

Powerplant Two Rolls-Royce/Turbomeca Adour 104 turbofans, each rated at 8,040 lb (35.76 kN) with afterburning; **Wing span** 28 ft 6 in (8.69 m); **Length (GR.1)** 55 ft 3 in (16.83 m), **(T.2)** 57 ft 6 in (17.53 m); **Height** 16 ft 1 in (4.89 m); **Max take-off weight** 34,171 lb (15,500 kg); **Max speed (low-level)** 820 mph (1,320 km/h), **(high-level)** 1,057 mph (1,700 km/h); **Service ceiling** 45,000 ft (13,716 m). **Operating Units** Nos 6, 16(R), 41 & 54 Squadrons.

Various aspects of the history of the Jaguar combine to produce an interesting story. One such is the fact that the evolution of this close support and reconnaissance aircraft can be traced back to requirements on the part of the RAF and the French Air Force for an advanced jet trainer of high performance. Considering that it was one of the first major joint international co-production programmes, the result can be deemed a success. At one time Jaguars equipped several front-line RAF and French Air Force squadrons, and it has achieved reasonable export success over the years, notably to India. Although the French Air Force used its Jaguars in anger several years ago,

in various conflicts in North Africa, it was only recently that the RAF's Jaguars went to war, during the Gulf War of 1991.

It is over 30 years since the separate proposals for a trainer design were put forward by both air forces, although the French requirement also included a capability for use in the tactical strike role. Even then, the rising costs of the design and development of new combat aircraft led both France and the UK into studies aimed at combining their respective requirements, in order to reduce wasteful duplication of effort. Thus, in 1964, the defence ministries of both nations began to merge their needs into one design. However, due to differing requirements on the part of the two air forces, agreement was reached between France and the UK in early 1965 to produce not one, but two designs. One was a variable-geometry strike aircraft, for the RAF, but this project was cancelled in 1967. The other machine was a much simpler concept, and was based on a French-designed airframe, known as the Breguet 121, and this subsequently became the Jaguar. To produce the new aircraft the participating companies, British Aircraft Corporation (BAC) and Breguet, formed a joint company in May 1966 under the title of Societe Europeenne de Production de l'Avion d'Ecole de Combat et d'Appul Tactique – SEPECAT. Agreement was also reached in 1965 for the joint production of a new turbofan engine for the aircraft, with Rolls-Royce as project leader assisted by Turbomeca of France; this powerplant was subsequently given the name of Adour.

Under the 1965 agreement, the UK would buy 150 Jaguars for use by the RAF and the Royal Navy; all of these would be two-seat advanced trainers. However, with cancellation of the variable-geometry design, a new agreement was made in January 1968 whereby France and the UK would each purchase 200 Jaguars, with 90 of the RAF aircraft being of a new strike variant. The RAF order was revised again in October 1970, with the total of 200 aircraft being split between 165 Jaguar S single-seat strike aircraft and 35 Jaguar B two-seat conversion trainers. Thus the original requirement for a new advanced jet trainer for the RAF was not fulfilled by the Jaguar; later, the BAe Hawk was to undertake this role. The Jaguar S was given the GR.1 designation, whilst the Jaguar B emerged as the T.2.

Production of the Jaguar was split on a 50:50 basis between BAC and Breguet, with the latter undertaking design and manufacture of the nose section and centre fuselage, while BAC were responsible for the rear fuselage, tail unit, wings and air intakes. Production lines for final assembly of each customer's aircraft were set up in both countries, and a similar arrangement was established for the co-production of the Adour engines. Manufacture of the robust undercarriage was the responsibility of the French company Messier. In 1971 Breguet was taken over by Dassault, whilst in the UK, BAC was absorbed into the nationalized BAe in 1977.

Out of the eight Jaguar prototypes that were built, France was responsible for five of them. The first British-built prototype, a single-seater, took to the air on 12 October 1969, followed by a second single-seater in June 1970. The first British-built two-seater made its maiden flight on 30 August 1971.

The first production Jaguar GR.1 for the RAF was delivered to RAF Lossiemouth in May 1973, to be used initially for training groundcrews, and it was to be the following September before further examples arrived. These first machines formed the equipment of the Jaguar Conversion Team (JCT), tasked with the conversion of existing experienced pilots to the new aircraft. These pilots went on to form the first Jaguar-equipped squadron, No 54, which moved to RAF Coltishall in August 1974, with No 6 Squadron following a similar path in November of the same year. Meanwhile, the JCT had been reformed into No 226 OCU at Lossiemouth, and this unit (now known as No 16 (Reserve) Squadron) continues with the task of training pilots for the Jaguar force to this day.

As delivery of Jaguars to the RAF gathered pace, a number of RAF Germany units began to re-equip, and between 1975 and 1977, Nos 14, 17, 20 and 31 Squadrons, all based at RAF Bruggen, converted to the new type. All had previously flown the Phantom II, except for No 20 Squadron which had operated Harriers. No 2 Squadron, based at RAF Laarbruch, converted from the Phantom II to the Jaguar GR.1 in 1976 and continued to specialize in its traditional role of tactical reconnaissance. Another unit to operate in this role was formed at Coltishall in 1977, this being No 41 Squadron, who continue with their reconnaissance task to this day. For some nine years, the Jaguar units (along with two squadrons of Buccaneers) formed RAF Germany's principal strike/attack element, armed with both nuclear and conventional weapons. In 1984/85, the Tornado GR.1 began to replace the Jaguar GR.1 in the strike role, and Nos 14, 17, 20 and 31 Squadrons converted to the far more sophisticated variable-geometry aircraft. The Jaguar GR.1 continued to operate with the RAF in Germany until late 1988, when No 2 Squadron re-equipped with Tornado GR.1As for its reconnaissance role. Many of the Jaguars, now withdrawn from frontline service, have continued to serve the RAF as ground instructional aircraft at the Schools of Technical Training.

The Jaguar is of all-metal construction, and it has the ability to operate from semi-prepared airfields thanks to its sturdy undercarriage. Due to flaps occupying the entire trailing-edge of each wing, spoilers are fitted to the upper surfaces to provide control. RAF aircraft are fitted with zero-zero Martin-Baker ejection seats, these being of a

This Jaguar GR.1A is seen in the 'desert pink' livery worn by these aircraft for the Gulf War and the deployment to Turkey. It carries the combat configuration of ECM pod (port outer pylon), *PHIMAT pod* (starboard outer pylon), *fuel tanks* (both inner pylons) *and Sidewinder AAMs on overwing rails.*

Jaguar GR.1A
1:72 scale

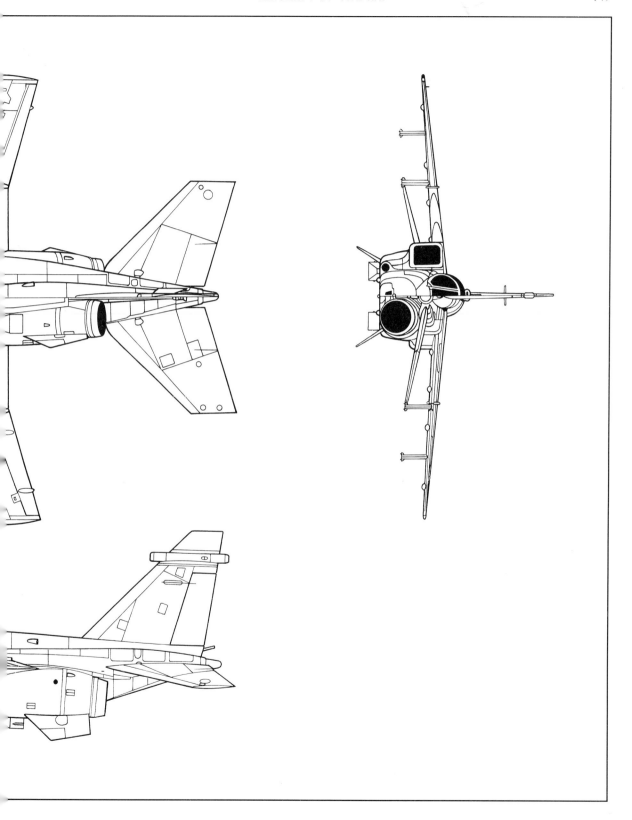

higher performance standard than the seats fitted in French Jaguars.

Built-in armament on RAF Jaguars consists of two 30 mm Aden cannon, fitted in the lower fuselage below the air intakes. There are four underwing stores positions, two per wing, and a further underfuselage centreline position. This last position, and the two innermost underwing points are 'wet', i.e. they are capable of carrying fuel tanks. Peacetime practice strike exercises are normally carried out using lightweight practice bombs fitted into Carrier Bomb, Light Stores units. More serious ordnance can include 1000 lb (454 kg) conventional or retarded bombs, or cluster bomb units, together with a variety of ECM pods and chaff dispensers. Flares can be dispensed from the ALE-40 equipment via twin outlets under the fuselage, just forward of the engine jetpipes.

A completely new navigation and attack system was developed for the RAF's Jaguars, and at one time was considered to be the most advanced avionics of its type. Known as the Navigation and Weapon-Aiming System (NAVWASS), it comprised the linking of a digital INS, a computer, a HUD and a projected map display. However, technological advances led to the NAVWASS being replaced by a new system in the mid-1980s.

This replacement system was the Ferranti FIN1064, in which a new computer and INS were integrated into the other existing features to provide a lighter, smaller and much more reliable arrangement, with significantly greater accuracy. Mission details can be entered into the computer in the squadron Operations Room, with the computer cursor and mouse being run over the map. This data is stored in a portable module, about the size of two cigarette packets, which is taken out to the aircraft and plugged into the onboard computer in the port side of the cockpit. Information is presented to the pilot via the HUD, the projected map display, and instrumentation on the port upper area of the instrument panel. With reference to preprogrammed positions on the planned route (known as waypoints), the last of these displays will indicate time and distance to go to the next waypoint, the actual speed being flown, any departure from the planned arrival time, and the true speed required to arrive at the next waypoint at the preplanned time. RAF Jaguars fitted with the FIN1064 system were redesignated as GR.1As (covering 75 aircraft) and T.2As (14 aircraft), as appropriate.

The Jaguar is fitted with the Sky Guardian RWR, which senses when the aircraft is being 'painted' by a possibly hostile radar, and alerts the pilot. It then compares and classifies the signal against a library of preprogrammed transmissions, and indicates to the pilot the angle and range from which the threat is coming, and when defensive measures, such as chaff and flares, should be deployed. The display equipment is mounted on the upper starboard side of the instrument panel.

The nose profile of RAF Jaguar GR.1/.1As differs from that of their French counterparts, with the unique chisel-shaped windows that house the Ferranti LRMTS. Also prominent on the RAF single-seat Jaguars is the horizontal housing that extends across the upper section of the tail fin; this housing contains the antennae for the RWR. Jaguar GR.1As are fitted with a retractable AAR probe, housed in the starboard side of the nose, in line with the front of the windscreen. The T.2As lack the LRMTS nose profile, the RWR tail fin housing and the AAR probe.

For the reconnaissance role, a large BAe pod is mounted under the fuselage on the centreline station. The pod is normally configured with five Vinten F95 cameras, with one facing forwards and the remainder arranged in a fan to cover a viewing area on both sides of the aircraft, as well as directly below. The cameras are fitted with lenses of varying focal lengths to cater for differing ranges of view, and are linked to the FIN1064 system, with such details as aircraft position, height, and direction of flight being marked on the film. The five cameras are mounted in the forward section of the BAe pod, and are contained in two rotatable drums, which turn to expose the lenses for the task in hand. The majority of reconnaissance tasks would be carried out at low-level, using the above cameras. However, missions can be carried out at medium- or high-level, for which tasks an F126 camera may be fitted in the rear of the rotary drums.

The rear section of the BAe pod contains the IRLS equipment, which compiles a picture from radiated heat and thus has a particular value for operations by night or in poor visibility. Targets such as underground installations and heavily camouflaged equipment are amongst the items that can be detected by the IRLS. The normal 'view' is vertical, but it can be tilted to give limited coverage to either side. The whole reconnaissance pod weighs 1,200 lb (545 kg).

The Gulf War of 1991 resulted in a number of modifications being made to RAF Jaguars. These included upgrading of the RWR capabilities with the Sky Guardian equipment, the incorporation of a video recording camera into the HUD and, most noticeably, the fitting of overwing mountings for AIM-9L Sidewinder AAMs. Additional weapons systems, such as the Canadian CRV-7 rocket pod and the American CBU-87 cluster bomb, were adapted and cleared for use by the Jaguar, and software for the weapons-aiming computer system was modified to suit. With the successful conclusion of the Gulf War, some of these modifications

The smooth lines of the Jaguar T.2A, here carrying the markings of No.16 (Reserve) Squadron, based at RAF Lossiemouth.

were removed from a number of the Jaguars involved. Other aircraft retained these new features for the subsequent deployment to Turkey, where they were used to cover the situation in northern Iraq, although the Jaguars were replaced by Harrier GR.7s in April 1993. However, Jaguars from Coltishall were again deployed overseas, in July 1993, when 12 aircraft were flown to a base on the east coast of Italy, to support UN operations over Bosnia. The actual weapons and avionics fit adopted is configured to suit the area of operations, be it over the UK, or, alternatively, for overseas deployments.

At the time of writing, it is envisaged that the Jaguar will continue in service until it is replaced by the Eurofighter 2000, some time after the year 2000. However, financial considerations may well lead to another round of cuts in defence spending, which could mark the demise of the Jaguar sooner rather than later.

AIR DEFENCE

Panavia Tornado F.3

Powerplant Two Turbo-Union RB.199-34R Mk 104 turbofans, each rated at 9,100 lb st (40.48 kN) dry, or 16,520 lb st (73.48 kN) with afterburning; **Wing span (fully swept)** 28 ft 2 in (8.60 m), **(fully spread)** 45 ft 8 in (13.91 m); **Length** 59 ft 4 in (18.08 m); **Height** 19 ft 6 in (5.95 m); **Max take-off weight** 61,700 lb (27,986 kg); **Max speed** Mach 2.2; **Range (ferry)** 2,650 miles (4,265 km); **Service ceiling** 70,000 ft (21,335 m). **Operating Units** Nos 5, 11, 25, 29, 43, 56(R) & 111 Squadrons; No 1435 Flight; F.3 OEU.

The design teams of the Panavia organization were faced with a daunting task in combining the required mission roles into one airframe, as outlined earlier in the Tornado GR.1 entry. The requirement issued by the UK MoD was for an air defence and air superiority fighter, this being adapted from the original IDS concept with minimal changes, and at the lowest possible cost. The then perceived threat was from cruise missiles, launched by long-range strike aircraft from the Soviet Union. In answer to this, the Tornado was to be capable of long-range air defence, assisted by AAR tankers and AEW aircraft. Thus was born the Air Defence Variant (ADV), to meet a requirement from the RAF that was not shared by West Germany or Italy. This was to be no local 'dogfighter'; what was envisaged was a beyond-visual-range bomber destroyer, fighting at considerable distance from the target, primarily with long-range AAMs.

The airframe and avionics system in the Tornado ADV share some 80 per cent commonality with that of the GR.1/.1A variants, with such items as TFR being deleted in favour of an airborne interception (AI) radar, known as Foxhunter. To accommodate this radar, the fuselage of the Tornado ADV is 4 ft 5 in (1.35 m) longer than that of the Tornado IDS. Also, the main computer software was reprogrammed to suit the air defence role. As in the IDS model, the Tornado ADV's central computer analyzes inputs from the various sensors, and then displays the information to the pilot and navigator. The pilot's main tasks are flying the aircraft, weapons control, and attack and weapons delivery; whilst the navigator is responsible for navigation and target detection, communication with the main computer, operation of the radar and other sensors, and tactical situation evaluation.

Tornado F.3
1:72 scale

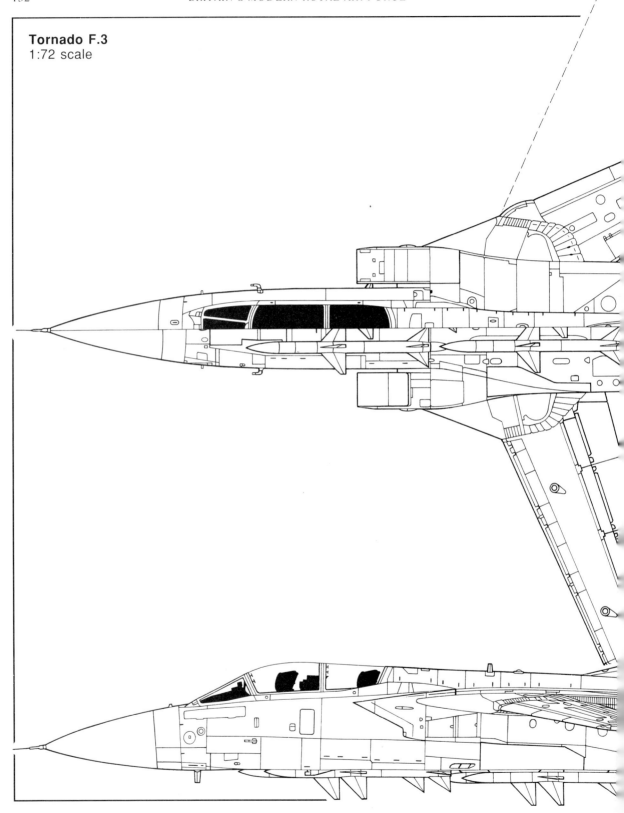

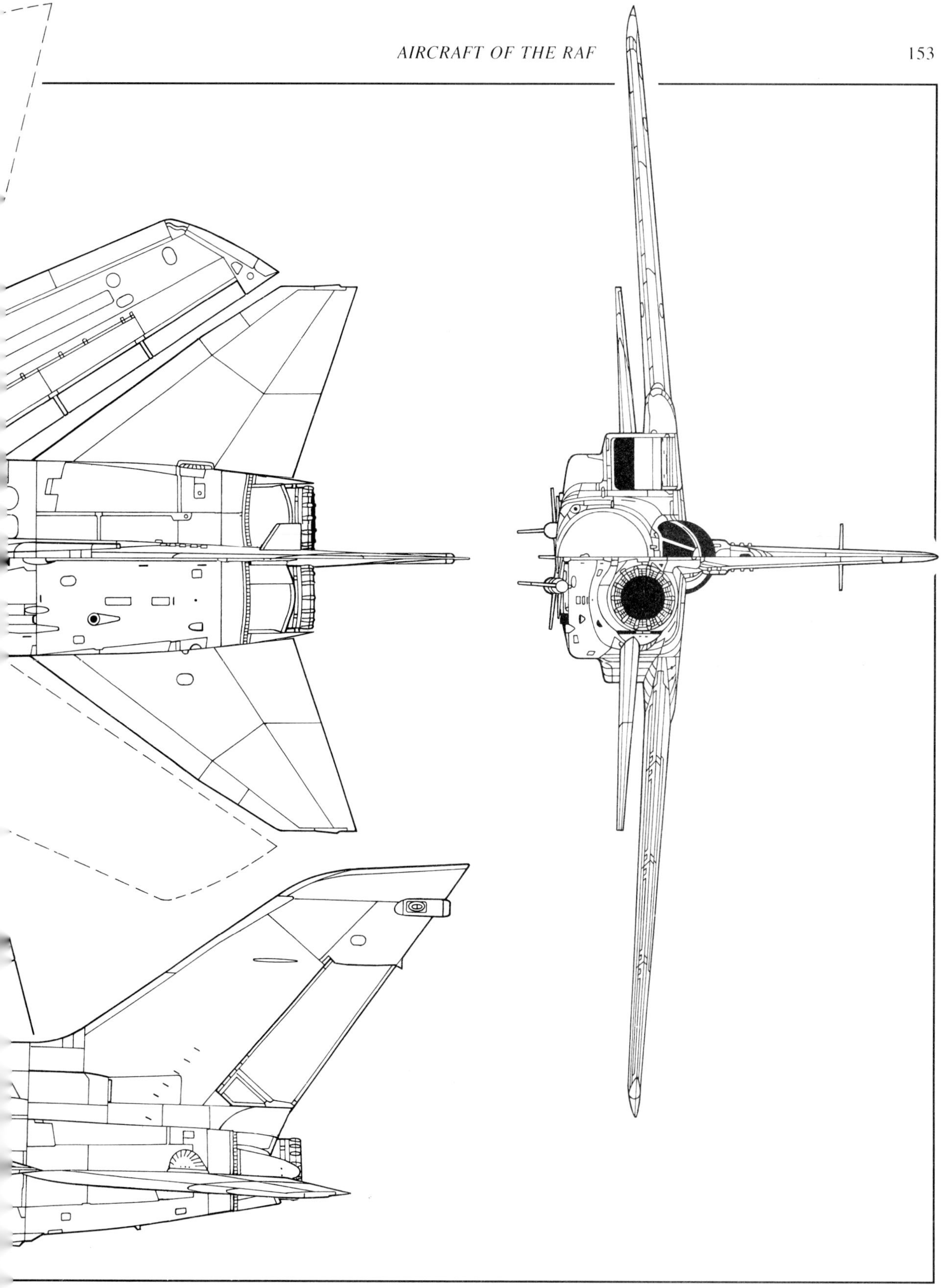

The ability of the Foxhunter radar system to detect and track airborne targets automatically is a significant feature of the Tornado ADV. The radar has an effective range in excess of 115 miles (185 km), and can track a number of targets simultaneously. Information on the tracks and positions of targets selected by the navigator is constantly updated, with data being presented to both crew and to the weapons systems. Details pertaining to the use of AAMs or gun-fire are displayed, with selection to suit the current situation available to both pilot and navigator. Although optimized for AI, the radar also has a ground mapping capability to aid navigation.

In addition to the Foxhunter radar, the Tornado ADV has a number of variations in the avionics fit when compared with the IDS model. One of these is the Data Link System, through which information can be exchanged with the Sentry AEW.1 aircraft and the IUKADGE ground-based air defence radars. The moving map displays in the Tornado IDS are not present in the ADV model; instead the pilot's display is capable of presenting full flight and technical data. The INS, combined with the main onboard computer are the principal aids to navigation, and information can be fed into the system via a preprogrammed tape cassette, or entered directly via the keyboards positioned below the cockpit TV displays.

Apart from the lengthened fuselage, the Tornado ADV airframe differs from the IDS version in other respects. The fixed leading-edges of the wing roots have increased sweep, and the AAR probe is fitted on the port side of the forward fuselage, near the front cockpit, and is fully retractable.

The Tornado ADV is fitted with one 27 mm Mauser cannon, buried in the lower starboard side of the forward fuselage, and can carry four BAe Sky Flash medium-range AAMs under the fuselage. These are arranged in staggered pairs, with the front two missiles being semi-recessed into the fuselage to help reduce drag. In addition, four AIM-9L Sidewinder AAMs can be carried, these being mounted on rails on either side

Two Tornado F.3s from No 29 Squadron, based at RAF Coningsby. (Denis J. Calvert)

of the inner underwing pylons.

The decision to proceed with development of the Tornado ADV was made in March 1976, with the prospect of orders for the RAF of 165 aircraft, these being in addition to orders for the IDS models. The first of three ADV prototypes took to the air in October 1979, followed by the second and third aircraft in 1980. The first production aircraft, known to the RAF as the Tornado F.2, were delivered to No 229 OCU at RAF Coningsby in late 1984, and delivery of the first production batch of 18 F.2s was completed by the end of 1985. Production then switched to the improved F.3 variant, this being ordered in a number of batches, along with IDS machines.

The Tornado F.2s were fitted with RB.199 Mk 103 turbofan engines, which were slightly less powerful than the current Mk 104s. There were a number of problems with the initial versions of the Foxhunter AI radar, and some F.2s flew for a period with ballast fitted in the nose radome in place of the radar equipment. However, the problems were all but rectified by the mid-1980s, and the F.2s carried out a number of service-entry trials, as well as undertaking crew conversion training with No 229 OCU at Coningsby. With the arrival of the Tornado F.3s, the F.2s were withdrawn from service by early 1988, and the majority placed in storage. It was intended that the F.2s would be modified to incorporate most of the features of the F.3, apart from the uprated engines, with the F.2s then being redesignated as F.2As, but this programme did not proceed. One or two F.2s have continued in service with trials organizations such as the A&AEE and the DRA.

The main production variant of the Tornado ADV for the RAF was the F.3, featuring a number of changes from the F.2. The tail jetpipes were extended by 14 in (0.36 m) to accommodate the improved afterburners of the RB.199 Mk 104 engines, each of which provides 450 lb st (2 kN) extra thrust over the Mk 103. This modification also changed the profile of the lower trailing-edge of the tail fin, this being cut-away on the F.2, but continuing down in a straight line on the F.3. Automatic wing-sweep equipment, with a number of preprogrammed settings, was introduced, and a second INS was added. Tornado F.2s could carry only two Sidewinder AAMs, whereas the F.3 is capable of carrying four. Larger fuel tanks, each of 495 gal (2,259 l) capacity, can be carried on the inner underwing pylons.

The first Tornado F.3s were delivered to No 229 OCU in mid-1986, and as further examples arrived, so the F.2s were withdrawn. The new F.3s became the first to carry RAF squadron markings, as No 65 Squadron was designated the 'shadow' unit within the OCU in early 1987, with a reserve role in the event of war. The first front-line Tornado F.3 squadron, No 29, reformed at Coningsby later in 1987. No 5 Squadron, one of the last two units to fly the English Electric Lightning, became the next Tornado F.3 operator, also based at Coningsby, and was declared operational in May 1988. A third unit at the Lincolnshire base was formed in 1987, this being the Tornado Operational Evaluation Unit, tasked with the operational work-up of the F.3 and its radar systems. This unit subsequently became the F.3 OEU.

Soon it was the turn of the three units based at the newly rebuilt RAF Leeming to receive the F.3. No 11 Squadron, the last unit to operate the Lightning, was reformed at Coningsby in the spring of 1988, and it subsequently transferred to Leeming with the first of its new aircraft, these being followed by further deliveries in due course. The squadron was declared operational on the F.3 in November 1988. The build-up of Tornado F.3s at Leeming continued, with No 23 Squadron reforming in November 1988 and No 25 Squadron being established in October 1989. Next, two air defence units based at RAF Leuchars, Nos 43 and 111 Squadrons, commenced their conversion from the Phantom II to the Tornado F.3, acquiring their new aircraft in 1990.

Up to mid-1992, all RAF Tornado F.2/.3s were based in the UK, but, in July of that year, four F.3s undertook the long journey south to the Falkland Islands, to replace the ageing Phantom IIs serving with No 1435 Flight, based at RAF Mount Pleasant. Here, they provide air defence cover for the British Services operating in the area, and for those living in this remote location in the South Atlantic.

Of the 165 Tornado F.2/.3s acquired by the RAF, 44 have dual controls. Production of Tornados for the three original customers ended in late 1992, with an F.3 for the RAF being the final machine to be delivered, although work continues on export aircraft for the Royal Saudi Air Force.

SURVEILLANCE/ RECONNAISSANCE/PATROL

Boeing Sentry AEW.1

Powerplant Four SNECMA-GEC CFM-56-2A-3 turbofans, each rated at 24,000 lb st (106.76 kN); **Wing span** 147 ft 7 in (44.89 m); **Length** 152 ft 11 in (46.61 m); **Height** 41 ft 9 in (12.73 m); **Max take-off weight** 332,500 lb (150,820 kg); **Max speed** 530 mph (853 km/h); **Service ceiling** 30,000 ft (9,145 m); **Endurance (unrefuelled)** Up to 12 hours. **Operating Unit** No 8 Squadron.

For many more years than originally intended, the RAF's Shackleton AEW.2s faithfully plodded their way around the area covered by the UK Air Defence Region, their obsolescent radar providing the AEW information required by the RAF's air defence forces. It had been intended that a number of BAe Nimrods would be converted to the AEW role to replace the Shackletons, but the sad saga of technical difficulties and escalating costs that led to the cancellation of the Nimrod AEW.3 project is now part of history. As a consequence, Boeing E-3A Sentry AWACS aircraft from the NATO AEW Force (NAEWF) based in West Germany were detached to the UK to provide airborne radar cover.

To fill the gap in radar cover, so vital for effective air defence, the RAF placed an order in December 1986 for six Sentries, with an option on a seventh machine being converted into a firm order 11 months later. These aircraft carry the US designation of E-3D, but are known to the RAF as Sentry AEW.1s.

The Sentry AEW.1 differs from earlier versions of the E-3 in being powered by CFM-56 turbofan engines, these being cleaner, quieter and more fuel-efficient than the powerplants fitted to USAF, NAEWF and Royal Saudi Air Force machines. Also, an AAR probe is mounted above the cockpit, offset to starboard, and is compatible with the HDU system used by the RAF. In addition, the Sentry AEW.1 can be refuelled by the USAF's 'flying boom' method, via a receptacle above the cockpit.

Other distinctive features on the RAF machines are the wing-tip pods, which house the 'Yellow Gate' ESM equipment. This passive equipment intercepts communications for analysis and information. The RAF aircraft are also fitted with rearward-facing High Frequency aerials, mounted above the wings, just inboard of the ESM pods. The addition of the pods and aerials necessitated strengthening of the wing structure.

The dominant feature of the Sentry is the 30-ft (9.14 m) diameter 'rotodome', mounted on two legs above the rear fuselage. This houses a Westinghouse AN/APY-2 radar, the principal 'eye' of the E-3 system. The mass of information gathered by the radar is fed to the onboard computers for analysis and further distribution. Data from the wing-tip ESM sensors, and other information-gathering systems, is combined with the main radar input and processed by the computers for presentation on colour radar consoles inside the main fuselage.

The new Sentries were delivered to the UK as virtually empty airframes, with ballast in place of the radar consoles and cabinets. They were then fitted out with equipment of British origin under the supervision of teams from Boeing, as part of

Sentry AEW.1
1:3000 scale

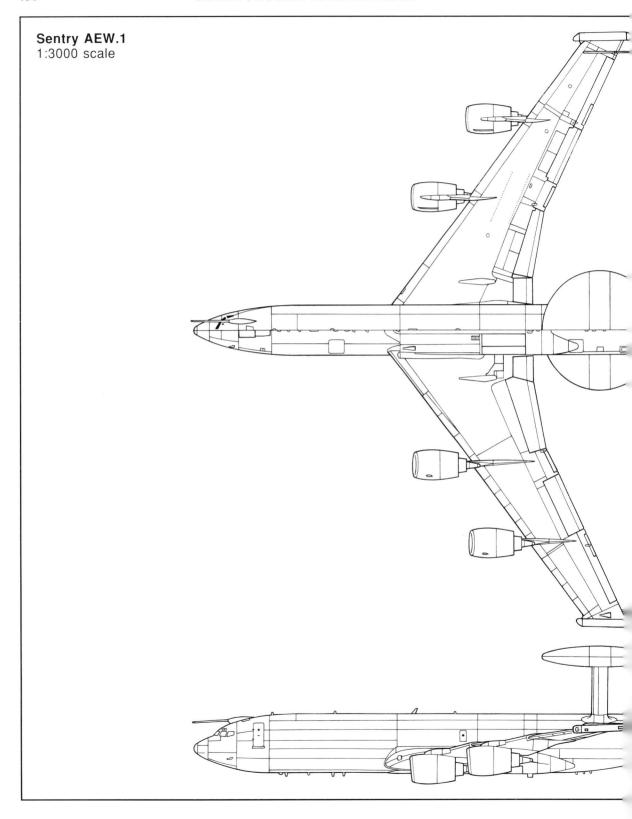

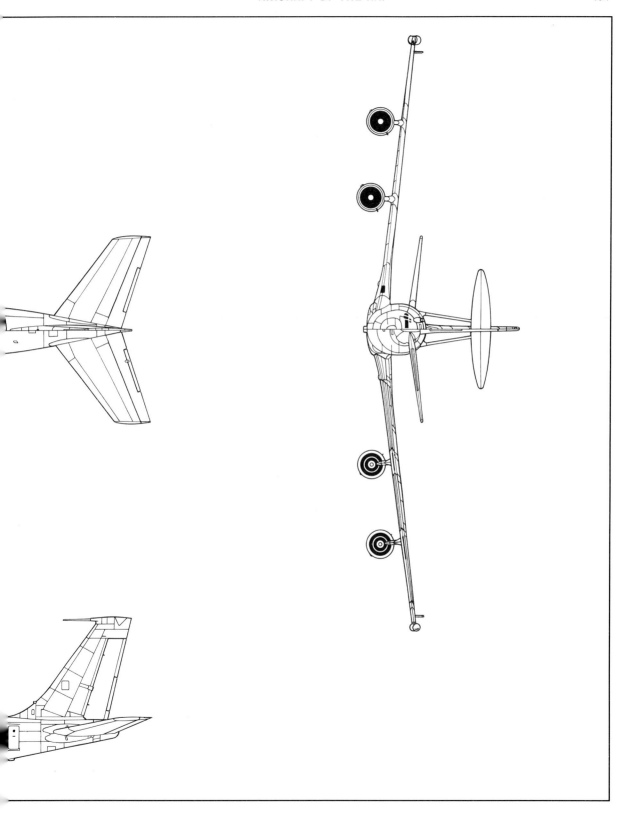

A Sentry AEW.1 of No 8 Squadron inside its servicing hangar at RAF Waddington. Note the rail-mounted gantry which provides access to the 'rotodome'.

the off-set contract. Computers of the latest type, with greater capacity than those fitted in earlier E-3 variants, together with sophisticated datalink information transmission equipment has been installed. The Sentry AEW.1 is also part of the Joint Tactical Information Distribution System, and is compatible with the IUKADGE and the Tornado F.3 air defence force.

The first Sentry AEW.1 for the RAF made its maiden flight from the Boeing plant in Seattle on 5 January 1990, with delivery taking place the following August. After fitting-out, it was formally handed over to the RAF in March 1991. The seventh and final aircraft was delivered to the UK in August 1991, being handed over to the RAF in May 1992. No 8 Squadron, previously equipped with the venerable Shackleton AEW.2s, was declared fully operational with the Sentry AEW.1 at a ceremony held at RAF Waddington in August 1992, and was subsequently integrated into the NAEWF, undertaking missions alongside the multi-national-crewed E-3As based in Germany. The NAEWF has been involved in monitoring the confused civil war that has torn apart various areas of the former Yugoslavia.

Considering the vast complexity of the Sentry AEW.1 and its onboard systems, its entry into service with the RAF has gone remarkably smoothly. The threat scenario has changed considerably from that when the aircraft were first ordered by the RAF, when it was probably envisaged that they would be deployed to provide AEW cover to the North and East of the UK. In today's changed

and very uncertain international situation, the fact that the Sentry AEW.1s have been considerably involved in monitoring the situation in what was Yugoslavia reflects the diverse tasks that No 8 Squadron, through NATO, will be required to perform in the years to come.

The Sentry AEW.1 was established in service with No 8 Squadron by the time the 75th anniversary of the formation of the RAF was celebrated in April 1993; it may well still be in service by the time the RAF marks its centenary in April 2018.

Nimrod MR.2P
1:168 scale

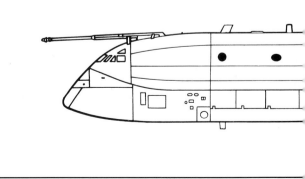

Hawker Siddeley (BAe) Nimrod R.1P/MR.2P

Powerplant Four Rolls-Royce RB168-20 Spey Mk 250 turbofans, rated at 12,140 lb st (54.0 kN) each; **Wing span** 114 ft 10 in (35.00 m); **Length (MR.2P)** 129 ft 1 in (39.35 m), **(R.1P)** 120 ft 1 in (36.60 m); **Height** 29 ft 9 in (9.08 m); **Max take-off weight** 177,500 lb (80,510 kg); **Max speed** 575 mph (926 km/h); **Typical low-level patrol speed (on two engines)** 230 mph (370 km/h); **Typical ferry range** 4,500 to 5000 nm (8,340 to 9,265 km); **Endurance** 12 hours; **Operating Units MR.2P:** Nos 42(R), 120, 201 & 206 Squadrons; **R.1P:** No 51 Squadron.

The UK is responsible for vast areas of ocean within the framework of its NATO commitments, and thus has maintained a significant force of maritime patrol aircraft since the Second World War. The Avro Lancaster equipped units of RAF Coastal Command up until the late 1950s, by which time its descendant, the Shackleton, was well-established in service. Even then, though, the Shackleton was considered to be nearing obsolescence, and a requirement was issued to the aircraft industry for a replacement long-range maritime patrol and anti-submarine aircraft. Meanwhile, various NATO member nations combined to design and produce the Atlantic twin-turboprop maritime patrol aircraft, which is still in service with France, Germany and Italy, among others. However, the RAF regarded the Atlantic's speed to be less than adequate for its own requirements.

Several years passed without a definite decision being taken on a Shackleton replacement.

Eventually, both cost and timescale ruled out a completely new design, so attention turned to the conversion of an existing airliner type to fulfil the required role. Various types were evaluated, and the de Havilland Comet 4 emerged as the best airframe upon which to base the desired aircraft. Under the title of Hawker Siddeley HS.801, design work began in mid-1964, and the order to proceed was given in June 1965, with the new type being christened the Nimrod MR.1.

Two newly-built but unsold Comet 4Cs were used as prototypes, being rebuilt to the configuration of the Nimrod MR.1. One was re-engined, the existing Avon turbojets giving way to the planned Spey turbofans, whilst the second aircraft was fitted with the Nimrod's avionics systems. Both Comet 4Cs made their first flights following conversion in the summer of 1967. The initial contract called for 38 aircraft, and the first true production Nimrod MR.1 took to the skies on 28 June 1968. These were new-build aircraft, and not, as is often thought, conversions of existing Comet airliners. A further eight Nimrod MR.1s were ordered in 1972.

Although based on the Comet design, the Nimrod differed in many respects. The pressurized main fuselage was shortened by 6 ft 6 in (1.98 m), and beneath this was added a large, unpressurized section which contains the weapons bay and other equipment. A large radome was added to the tip of the tail fin to house ESM equipment, while the magnetic anomaly detection (MAD) sensors were housed in an extended tailboom. A large dorsal fillet was added to the leading-edge of the tail fin, and the window area of the cockpit was increased. A powerful searchlight was fitted at the front of the starboard wing leading-edge fuel tank.

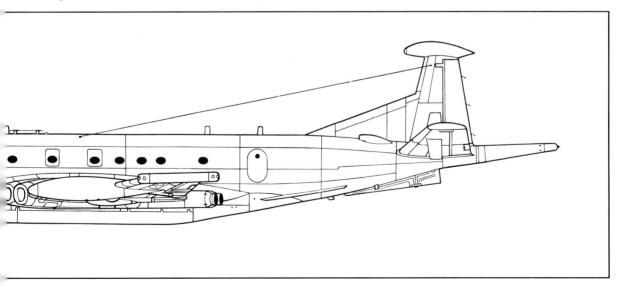

Nimrod MR.2P
1:168 scale

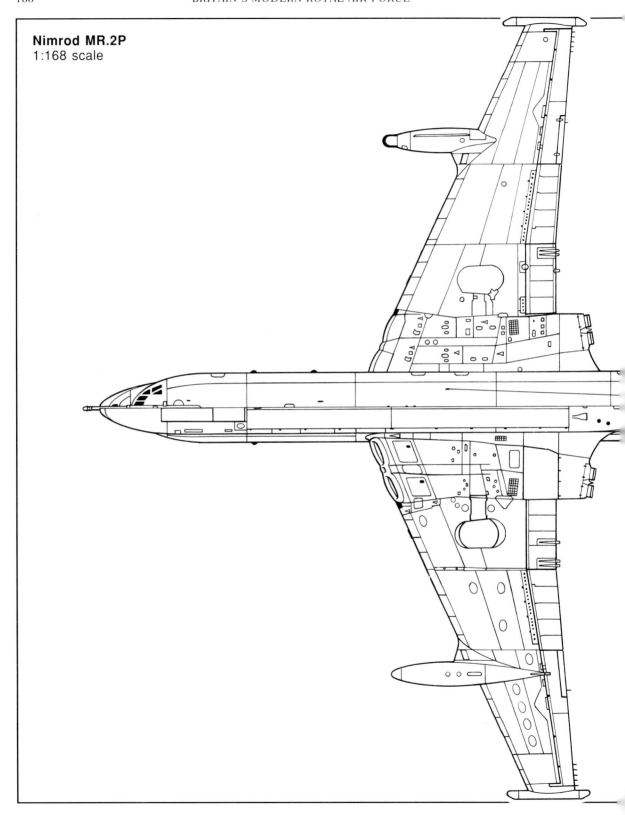

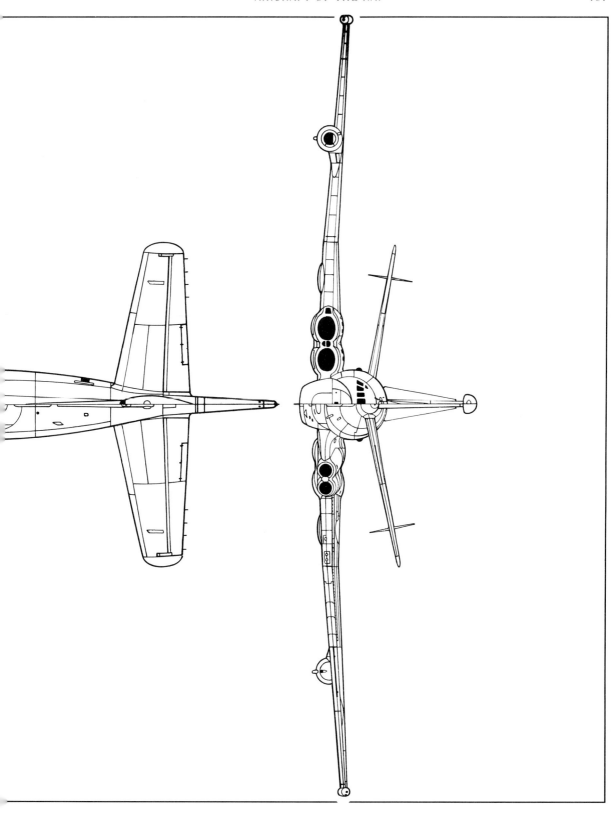

The first deliveries of this sophisticated new aircraft were made in October 1969 to No 236 OCU at RAF St Mawgan, in Cornwall. The first RAF squadron to operate the Nimrod MR.1 was No 201, who converted from Shackletons at RAF Kinloss in October 1970. No 206 Squadron received its first Nimrod MR.1s the following month, again at Kinloss. The following year saw Nos 42 and 120 Squadrons commence their use of the new type, and No 203 Squadron also subsequently re-equipped, this last squadron being based in Malta until disbandment in the mid-1970s.

Three further Nimrods, with the designation R.1, were ordered for use by No 51 Squadron at RAF Wyton in the electronic surveillance role. The first of the trio was delivered in mid-1971, and they differ from the maritime patrol variants by virtue of the absence of the MAD tailboom, a different profile to the wing leading-edge pods/fuel tanks, and the addition of many aerials. Each aircraft was later fitted with an AAR probe, above the cockpit, in which form they are now designated as Nimrod R.1Ps.

1975 saw the start of a programme to upgrade the Nimrod MR.1 fleet, with most of the internal equipment such as the search radar, communications suite and sensors being replaced with more advanced units. Externally, pods were added to the wing-tips to house Loral ESM equipment. The Falklands conflict of 1982 prompted further modifications, including the fitting of an AAR probe above the cockpit and the ability to carry Sidewinder AAMs for self-defence on underwing pylons. Aerodynamic modifications included a new ventral fin, located under the extreme rear fuselage, and the addition of finlets above and below the horizontal tailplanes. In this revised form, the aircraft were redesignated as Nimrod MR.2Ps.

The programme to utilize the Nimrod airframe in the AEW role was announced in 1977, with 11 existing airframes being converted to Nimrod AEW.3 standard. Three of the additional eight Nimrods ordered in 1972 were completed to an interim AEW.3 standard. However, as is now well known, the Nimrod AEW programme failed to materialize as planned, and ended with the project being cancelled, the AEW requirement being met in due course by seven Sentry AEW.1s. The 11 converted Nimrod airframes remained in store for some while, but most have since been scrapped.

The Nimrod MR.2P is operated by a crew of 13, comprising two pilots, a flight engineer, a tactical navigator (TN), a route navigator, an air electronics officer (AEO) and seven air electronic operators (AEOps). The AEOps are divided into two teams, with three of them forming the 'wet' team, which is responsible for dealing with sub-surface operations, covering sonars and anti-sub-

marine tasks. The remaining four AEOps form the 'dry' team, dealing with above-surface activities. The crew captain may or may not be the aircraft's pilot; at times this role is undertaken by another senior and experienced officer in the crew.

The inputs from the various AEOps are co-ordinated by the AEO, who transfers the data to the aircraft's Central Tactical System, which is the responsibility of the TN. An 18-in (45.5 cm)-diameter screen displays information from all of the various sensors carried by the aircraft, and the TN analyzes the situation to enable the mission to be carried out.

With the recent changes in international relations, the numbers of Nimrod MR.2Ps in active service have been reduced, and all are now based at Kinloss. The three Nimrod R.1Ps are due to move to RAF Waddington by 1995, following the announcement that Wyton is to close as an active flying station. Consideration is being given to a possible Nimrod replacement, but given the current financial situation and cuts in defence spending, this could be a long way off, and thus the Nimrod should continue to patrol the seas for some time to come.

English Electric (BAC) Canberra PR.9

Powerplant Two Rolls-Royce Avon 206 turbojets, each rated at 11,250 lb st (50.04 kN); **Wing span** 67 ft 10 in (20.68 m); **Length** 66 ft 8 in (20.32 m); **Height** 15 ft 7 in (4.75 m); **Max take-off weight** 55,000 lb (24,948 kg); **Max speed (high-level)** 550 mph (885 km/h); **Range (max fuel)** 3,790 miles (6,098 km); **Service ceiling** 48,000 ft (14,630 m). **Operating Unit** No 39 (1 PRU) Squadron.

Over 1,300 Canberras of all versions were built, and of these only a fraction remain in service, including a few PR.9s operated by No 39 (1 PRU) Squadron at RAF Marham. These are the survivors of 23 examples of this variant that were built by Short Brothers of Belfast, with the first PR.9 making its initial test flight in July 1955. The remaining 22 aircraft were delivered between late 1958 and October 1961.

The Canberra PR.9 differs from other variants of the Canberra family in a number of respects. The most obvious change is the enlarged wing, with extended span and broader chord inboard of the engines. The resulting increase in wing area, combined with more powerful engines, are features that enable the PR.9 to carry out high-level reconnaissance operations. The pilot is housed beneath a fighter-type cockpit canopy, offset to port, with the navigator buried in the nose, for-

Nose detail of the Canberra PR.9. The sideways-hinging nose allows access for the navigator, while the pilot gains entry to the offset cockpit via the substantial clip-on ladder.

ward of and below the pilot. The extreme nose of the aircraft opens to one side to allow access for the navigator.

The Canberra PR.9 is fitted with an array of cameras in the underside of the fuselage, with three F95 units providing low-level coverage for forward and side views. Behind these come five F96 cameras, fitted at various angles to give a spread of coverage from vertically downwards to oblique sideways; these cameras are used for high-level tasks. Survey work is undertaken with the F49 camera, housed in a temperature-controlled box, or the newer Zeiss survey camera. A further device is an IRLS, used for image recording in darkness or poor light conditions.

It is anticipated that the Canberra PR.9s of No 39 (1 PRU) Squadron will continue in service in their current role for the forseeable future, and will probably be the last variant of this famous British design to be operated by the RAF.

TANKER/TRANSPORTS

Vickers (BAe) VC-10 C.1/.1K

Powerplant Four Rolls-Royce Conway R.Co.43 Mk 301 turbofans, each rated at 21,800 lb st (97 kN); **Wing span** 146 ft 2 in (44.55 m); **Length** 158 ft 8 in (48.36 m); **Height** 39 ft 6 in (12.04 m); **Max take-off weight** 323,000 lb (146,510 kg); **Max cruising speed** 568 mph (914 km/h); **Range (maximum fuel)** 7,127 miles (11,470 km); **Service ceiling** 42,000 ft (12,800 m). **Operating Unit** No 10 Squadron.

1994 marks the 28th year of service for the mainstay of the RAF's transport fleet, the venerable VC-10 C.1. The version of the VC-10 that the RAF acquired was, in fact, a hybrid of the standard VC-10 and the larger Super VC-10, with the RAF machines featuring the shorter fuselage of the former, combined with the wings and more powerful engines of the latter. A large cargo door was added to the port side of the forward fuselage, together with a strengthened cabin floor, and an additional fuel tank was incorporated within the tail fin.

The first of the RAF's fleet of VC-10s made its maiden flight on 26 November 1965, and the type entered service the following July with No 10 Squadron, which had reformed at RAF Brize Norton. In all, 14 VC-10 C.1s were acquired, but one machine was withdrawn from service for use as a flying test-bed for the RB.211 turbofan engine; eventually this aircraft was scrapped.

The RAF's VC-10 C.1s were built with internal fittings to enable them to receive fuel in-flight, and an AAR probe was later fitted to the nose. In mid-1989 a decision was announced that involved modifying the VC-10 C.1s by adding a Mk 32 HDU pod under each wing to enable the aircraft to act as two-point tanker/transports. These pods are fed from the existing fuel system, and no extra tanks are fitted. The flight engineer's instrument panels have been altered to include controls for the AAR equipment, and for the provision of closed-circuit TV (CCTV) to monitor the AAR operation.

The first contract within this conversion programme involved the modification of eight VC-10 C.1s, with the work being carried out by Flight Refuelling Limited at their Bournemouth (Hurn)

Canberra PR.9
1:72 scale

VC-10 C.1K
1:192 scale

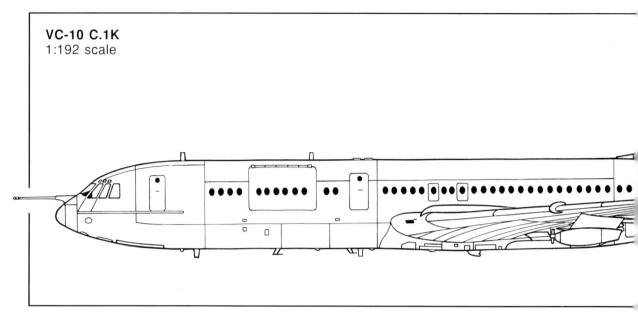

Airport facility. Work on the first aircraft commenced in February 1991, and it was returned to Brize Norton in early 1993. In February 1992, a further contract was announced which covered the conversion of the remaining five VC-10 C.1 transports. These modifications have resulted in a designation change to C.1K, to denote the added tanker role. The conversion programme is expected to continue into 1995.

In its passenger-carrying role, the VC-10 C.1/.1K can accommodate 137 in a standard layout, although this can be increased to 146 if required. For freight transport, eight standard NATO pallets can be carried, up to a maximum

The RAF's VC-10 transports are being given an added tanker capability by fitting one of these HDUs under each wing.

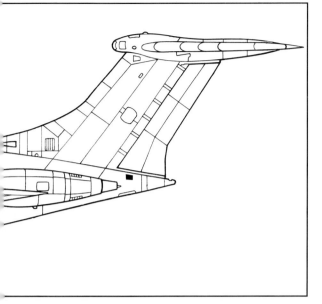

payload of 45,000 lb (20,412 kg). Alternatively, there is room to carry up to 66 stretcher cases. The interiors of the VC-10s have recently been refurbished, to give a brighter atmosphere. The elctrical wiring looms and systems have been replaced, and the airframes have been inspected for signs of fatigue. As such, these aircraft, having already given excellent service to the RAF, have a current life expectancy that extends to the year 2010.

Vickers (BAe) VC-10 K.2/.3/.4

Powerplant Four Rolls-Royce Conway 550B turbofan engines, each rated at 21,800 lb (97 kN); **Wing span** 146 ft 2 in (44.55 m); **Length (K.2, including AAR probe)** 166 ft 1 in (50.62 m), **(K.3, including AAR probe)** 179 ft 1 in (54.59 m); **Height** 39 ft 6 in (12.04 m); **Max take-off weight (K.2)** 323,000 lb (146,510 kg), **(K.3)** 335,000 lb (151,956 kg); **Max cruising speed** 568 mph (914 km/h); **Range** 3,900 miles (6,275 km). **Operating Unit** No 101 Squadron.

Long-term plans in the 1970s to increase and upgrade the RAF's tanker assets were developed through to 1978, and in April of that year a design study for the conversion of VC-10 civil airliners to the AAR role was awarded to BAe. The positive conclusions revealed by this study led to an order being placed with BAe in July 1978 for the conversion of nine VC-10s into tankers. This involved the modification of five ex-British Airways (BA) standard VC-10s built in the early 1960s and four ex-East African Airways Super

VC-10s constructed in the late 1960s. One feature of this work was that the resultant tankers should be compatible with the RAF's existing fleet of VC-10 C.1 transports, for ease of maintenance and operations. The RAF designated the standard VC-10 conversions as K.2s, with the K.3 designation being allotted to the converted Super VC-10s.

All nine aircraft were modified as three-point tankers, with an HDU pod under each wing and a further HDU under the rear fuselage, the latter being level with the front of the rear-mounted engine nacelles. The underfuselage HDU can deliver fuel at a rate of 500 gal (2,270 l) per minute, via a 70-ft (21 m)-long hose. The underwing HDUs can extend a hose 48 ft (14.6 m) in length, through which fuel can be dispensed at a rate of 350 gal (1,590 l) per minute; these underwing HDUs can be detached if required. Floodlights are installed in various positions under the wings and rear fuselage for illumination to assist in night-time refuelling operations, and a CCTV system is fitted to enable the crew to monitor activities behind each drogue's position. An AAR probe to enable fuel to be received by the tanker is fitted to the nose.

Internally, a small section of the original airliner cabin is retained at the front of the main fuselage, to accommodate groundcrews and other passengers, with a capacity for up to 18 passengers in three rows of seats. However, the main part of the cabin was converted to house five cylindrical fuel tanks to increase the aircraft's fuel capacity for the AAR role. These tanks are of double-skinned construction, with an inner flexible bag, and each has a capacity of 700 gal (3,182 l). They are mounted in substantial supporting frames, and are interconnected with the VC-10's existing fuel system. The controls for the IFR equipment are located at the flight engineer's station, on the starboard side of the cockpit, as is the CCTV monitor, displaying activity to the rear of the aircraft. The forward underfloor cargo compartment was retained for use during long-range deployments.

The VC-10 K.2/.3 conversion programme was undertaken at BAe's Filton facility, near Bristol, with the first K.2 taking to the air on 22 June 1982. Following pre-service trials, initial deliveries of the new variant were made in July 1983 to RAF Brize Norton, the aircraft constituting the equipment of the reformed No 101 Squadron. The first of the K.3s made its maiden flight in July 1984, and was delivered to Brize Norton the following February. All nine aircraft had been delivered to No 101 Squadron by 1986.

A further contract was placed with BAe in 1990 for the conversion of yet more VC-10s to the tanker role. This order comprised five ex-BA Super VC-10s, which had been stored with other

VC-10 C.1K
1:192 scale

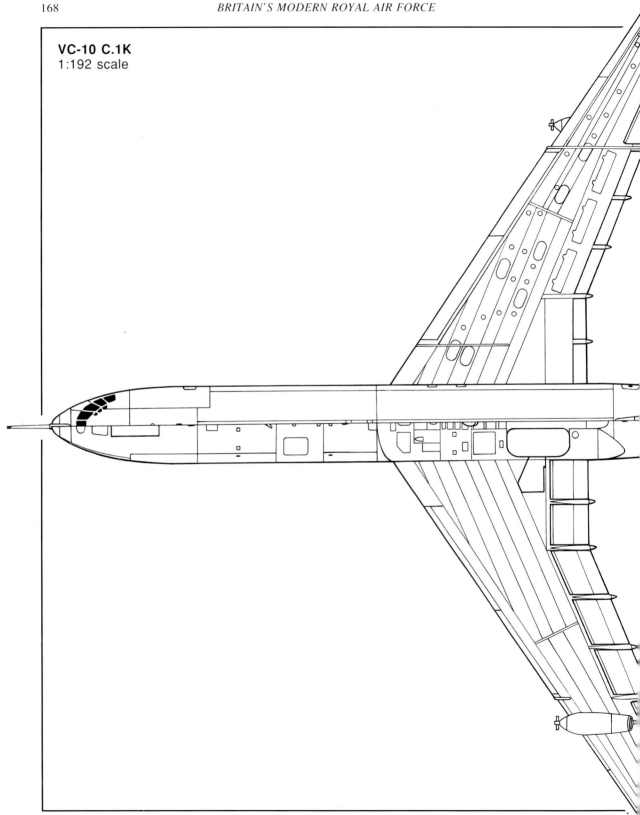

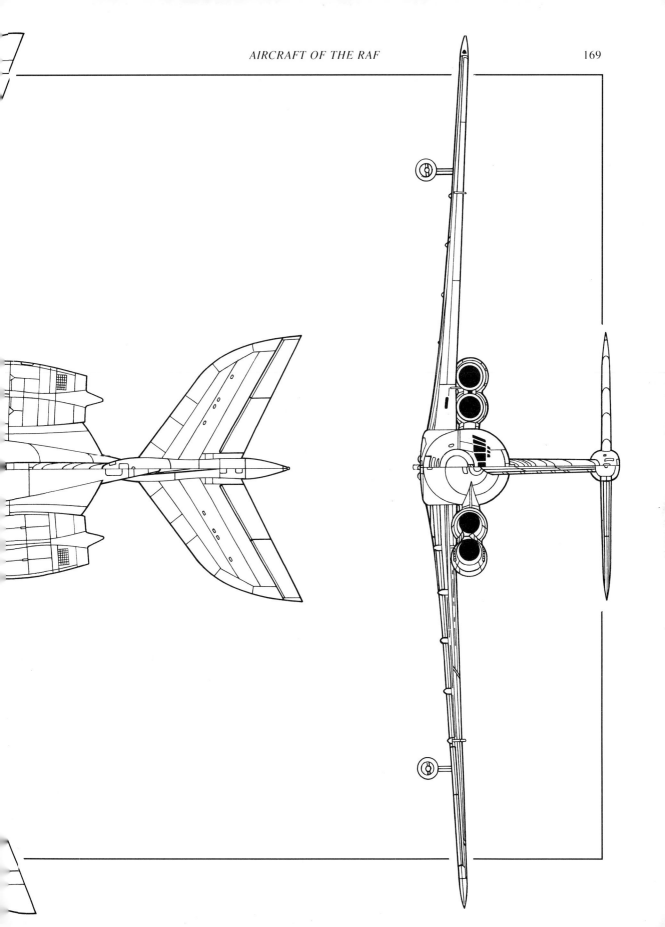

similar machines at RAF Abingdon for several years. The five aircraft were restored to flying condition and flown to BAe's Filton facility for modification. Designated as VC-10 K.4s, the aircraft have been modified to a similar standard as the K.2/.3s, with the exception that no extra fuel tanks have been installed in the fuselage. The five aircraft concerned are due to be delivered during 1994, probably to No 101 Squadron.

Lockheed L-1011 TriStar K.1/KC.1/C.2/.2A

Powerplant Three Rolls-Royce RB.211-524B turbofans, each rated at 50,000 lb st (222.41 kN); **Wing span** 164 ft 4 in (50.09 m); **Length** 164 ft 3 in (50.06 m); **Height** 55 ft 4 in (16.87 m); **Max take-off weight** 540,000 lb (244,950 kg); **Max speed** 600 mph (965 km/h); **Service ceiling** 43,000 ft (13,135 m); **Range (fully-loaded)** 6,025 miles (9,696 km). **Operating Unit** No 216 Squadron.

The Falklands conflict of 1982 revealed the short-fall in tanker capacity and capability then facing the RAF. The vast distances involved, even allowing for the useful staging point of RAF Wideawake, on Ascension Island, meant that the existing force of Handley Page Victor tankers had eaten rapidly into their remaining airframe hours. There was also the prospect that British Forces would be required to garrison the Falkland Islands for many years to come, and thus would require considerable resources for resupply tasks. So there was a dual need for an increase in both tanker and transport capacity over long ranges.

By a coincidence, a recession in trade and a slump in air travel meant that British Airways (BA) had surplus capacity in its fleet of airliners, with the added problem that the prospects for selling these machines on the second-hand market were very poor. Thus, a decision was announced in December 1982 whereby the RAF would purchase six surplus TriStar 500 three-engined, wide-bodied airliners from BA, and that these would be converted to fulfil a dual tanker/transport role.

Conversion of the aircraft was to be a considerable undertaking, but in order for the RAF to benefit from its new equipment immediately, two of the TriStars were operated on passenger services from mid-1983, with the aircraft being operated by BA flight-deck and cabin crews. Throughout that year, BA training captains undertook conversion tuition for RAF flight crews, and by February 1984 the first transport mission with an all-RAF flight-deck crew was undertaken. Later that year, three more TriStars were purchased from Pan American World Airways, and No 216 Squadron was reformed at RAF Brize Norton to operate the type.

In early 1983, Marshalls of Cambridge (Engineering) Ltd was contracted to carry out the conversion programme. The aim of using a large aircraft such as the TriStar was to retain the large passenger/cargo capacity on the main deck, with additional fuel tanks for the AAR role being fitted in the underfloor cargo holds. A twin HDU was installed under the rear fuselage, although only one drogue can be deployed at any one time. The reason for a twin-hose installation was to allow a stand-by facility in the event of a malfunction, which could have serious consequences with just a single HDU on long, over-water sorties. An AAR probe was fitted above the flight-deck, offset to starboard. The aircraft's existing fuel system was modified to enable it to be integrated with the new fuel tanks and refuelling points, so that the full load of fuel is available for all requirements. Suitable controls for fuel management were added to the flight engineer's position in the cockpit. AAR operations can be observed and monitored by the TriStar's crew via a CCTV system.

The task of modifying a civil airliner into a military tanker/transport was a major undertaking, involving the whole airframe, and this has resulted in a significant increase in all-up weight. In the event, only six ex-BA aircraft were converted to the tanker role; the three ex-Pan Am aircraft are primarily used as passenger transports.

The first TriStar was converted to operate in a dual tanker/transport configuration, with the designation of K.1, and this took to the air for the

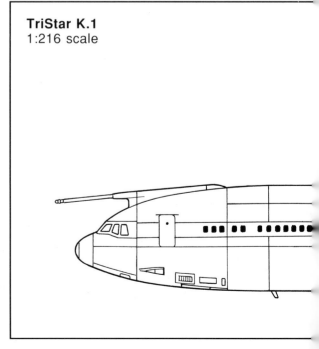

TriStar K.1
1:216 scale

The KC.1 variant of the TriStar is fitted with this large door to facilitate the loading of cargo and palletized loads.

first time, following conversion, in July 1985, prior to going to the A&AEE at Boscombe Down for service trials two months later. The second converted aircraft, also a K.1, was delivered direct to No 216 Squadron in March 1986. These two aircraft are used as tanker/transports, with a limited freight-carrying capacity.

A further four aircraft, all ex-BA, received an additional modification in the form of a large, upwards-opening door on the port side of the forward fuselage. This door is 11 ft 8 in (3.56 m) x 8 ft 6 in (2.59 m) in size, and the four aircraft thus configured have a strengthened floor and a cargo-handling system to cater for palletized loads. The main cabin in these TriStars can be configured with more than 20 diferent layouts, to cater for

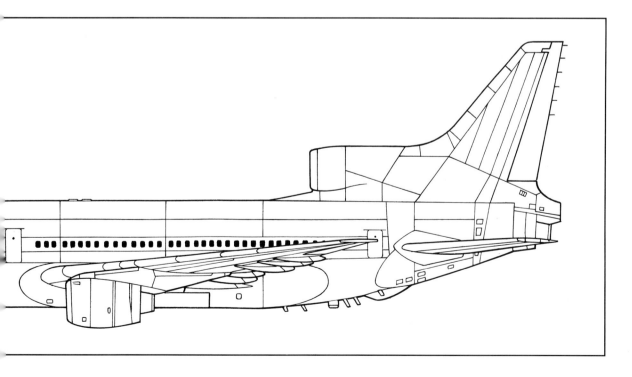

various combinations of passenger, cargo and aeromedical loads. As a passenger transport, seats for over 260 can be fitted on pallets. For freight-carrying, the TriStar can accommodate 20 pallets, some three times the number that can be carried by a Hercules C.3P. In this form the quartet are designated as TriStar KC.1s, with tanking, freight- and passenger-carrying capabilitites. The KC.1s have had their AAR probes removed, as their need to receive additional fuel has diminished, and in order to improve aerodynamc airflow. However, these probes can be refitted in a few hours, if required.

Two of the ex-Pan Am TriStars entered service with the RAF soon after purchase, continuing in their designed role of high-capacity passenger transport, and these aircraft have seen extensive use on the long flights to and from the Falkland Islands. They have not received the AAR modifications, or the increased freight-carrying capability, and in this form they are designated as TriStar C.2s. The third ex-Pan Am aircraft was retained by Marshalls of Cambridge for many years, and was finally delivered to the RAF in early 1993. It has updated avionics and other modifications, which has resulted in yet another designation, namely C.2A. Like the two C.2s, it is used as a passenger transport.

The flight-decks of the RAF's TriStars have been modified to suit military requirements, although the instrumentation in the two C.2s varies slightly from the other variants. The flight engineer's instrument panel has been extended on the K.1s and KC.1s to cater for this crewmember's tasks in the AAR role. Currently, the RAF is introducing a full blind auto-land capability, in order to widen the aircraft's operating flexibility. The heaviest aircraft type to have been operated by the RAF, introduction of the TriStar has provided the Service with a significant increase in capacity and the ability to move freight and passengers over long distances, with the added facility of AAR.

Lockheed Hercules C.1K/.1P/W.2/C.3P

Powerplant Four Alison T56A-15 turboprops, each rated at 4,508 eshp (3,326 kW); **Wing span** 132 ft 7 in (40.14 m); **Length (C.1K/.P)** 97 ft 9 in (29.79 m), **(C.3P)** 112 ft 9 in (34.37 m); **Height** 38 ft 3 in (11.66 m); **Max take-off weight (C.1P)** 155,000 lb (70,308 kg), **(C.3P)** 160,000 lb (72,576 kg); **Max cruising speed** 374 mph (602 km/h); **Max Range (C.1K/.1P)** 4,770 miles (7,675 km). **Operating Units C.1K:** Nos 24 & 30 Squadrons; No 1312 Flight; **C.1P/.3P:** Nos 24, 30, 47, 57(R) & 70 Squadrons; **W.2:** DRA.

The Lockheed Hercules is fast establishing itself as one of the most important aircraft types ever built. Its regular appearances on TV news reports, as it delivers aid to the more unfortunate regions of the world, means that it is well-known to the general public. It has now been in continuous production since the mid-1950s, and the 2,000th example was delivered in 1992.

Up until the mid-1960s, the RAF employed a variety of aircraft to fulfil its transport needs, but most had limited performance in terms of range and payload. There was an intention to build and operate a jet-powered STOL transport, the HS.601, but this fell victim to defence and spending cuts. An alternative had to be found, and eventually this led to an order for 66 Hercules, these being a version of the C-130H model then in production for the USAF and other air forces. The aircraft for the RAF were modified in many respects from the standard production version, with many items of equipment coming from British sources, including instruments, avionics and parts of the aircraft structure being specified. The RAF version was designated the C-130K in the USA.

The initial RAF crews to convert to the Hercules were trained in the USA, and in December 1966 the first aircraft for the RAF was delivered to Marshalls of Cambridge in a bare metal finish, for final painting and fitting-out. RAF Thorney Island in Hampshire was the first station to operate the Hercules, from the spring of 1967, when No 242 OCU commenced the task of training RAF crews for the new transport.

No 36 Squadron at RAF Colerne became the first front-line unit to receive the Hercules in mid-1967, while later that same year No 48 Squadron, based at Changi, Singapore, also converted onto the type. In 1968 three more units, Nos 24 (based at Colerne), 30 and 47 Squadrons, all began to operate the Hercules, the last two units being based at RAF Fairford in Gloucestershire. In 1970, No 70 Squadron received the Hercules at its base of RAF Akrotiri in Cyprus.

However, cuts in defence spending meant that the days of the RAF's overseas bases were numbered, and in 1971 the Hercules units started to consolidate at RAF Lyneham. Nos 30 and 47 Squadrons moved the short distance from Fairford, whilst No 48 Squadron made the longer journey from the Far East. Nos 36 and 48 Squadrons were disbanded in 1975, and No 70 Squadron returned home from Akrotiri the same year, with No 242 OCU transferring from Thorney Island to Lyneham early in 1976. The Hercules Major Servicing Unit also moved from Colerne to Lyneham in 1975. With these moves, the Lyneham Transport Wing (LTW) became the main Hercules operating unit, the aircraft being

Of the RAF's 60-strong fleet of Hercules, five aircraft are designated as C.1Ks, one of which is seen here on take-off. The bump under the rear fuselage houses the drogue unit, while the wing-tip pods contain ESM equipment.

'pooled' and used by the four squadrons and the OCU as and when required.

In 1969/70 severe problems arose within the Hercules fleet due to corrosion in some integral wing fuel tanks. This required emergency remedial treatment, with the most corroded tanks having to be replaced, thus necessitating major rebuilding work on the wings of some aircraft.

In 1972, the Meteorological Research Flight, part of the then Royal Aircraft Establishment at Farnborough, identified the need for an additional research aircraft, and the Hercules was selected for the task. Accordingly, one aircraft was withdrawn from service at Lyneham and extensively modified for its new role, the most obvious features being a large pod housing weather radar mounted atop the cockpit, and a 16-ft (4.88 m)-long nose-probe. The aircraft also received a new white and light grey colour scheme. With the new designation of Hercules W.2, this aircraft was delivered for its new role in 1973, and has since carried out numerous weather research tasks on a worldwide basis.

In the late 1970s a programme was initiated to 'stretch' 30 of the RAF's Hercules C.1s to the length of the civiliam L-100-30, which involved adding 15 ft (4.57 m) to the overall length. This was achieved by adding an 8 ft 4 in (2.54 m)-long section ahead of the main wing, as well as a 6 ft 8 in (2.03 m)-long section added just behind the wing. The first of these conversions was carried out by Lockheed at their Hercules manufacturing plant in Georgia, with the remaining 29 machines being modified by Marshalls of Cambridge. The resulting aircraft was redesignated the C.3, with the troop-carrying capacity raised from 92 to 128, whilst the cargo volume rose by 37 per cent.

In early 1982 the Falklands crisis called upon the full resources of the LTW, it being tasked with moving vast amounts of supplies to Ascension Island. However, to move supplies further south was beyond the range of the Hercules at that time. An urgent request was made to industry for the rapid design and installation of an AAR probe and associated fuel pipes to enable the Hercules to continue to the Falkland Islands for supply-dropping missions. The first such modification was completed in just two weeks, and AAR probe-equipped Hercules carried out sorties of many hours' duration, assisted by Victor tankers.

This modification was later fitted to the remainder of the RAF's fleet of Hercules. A further modification, again inspired by the Falklands conflict, was the installation of an HDU in the rear of the cargo hold, to enable the Hercules to act as an AAR tanker. Fuel capacity was increased by the installation of four fuel tanks in the main cargo hold; these tanks have a total capacity of 3,300 gal (15,000 l). After some initial problems were overcome, the system was cleared for operational use, and a total of six aircraft were converted, each being redesignated as a Hercules C.1K.

Further modifications have been carried out, including the reskinning and protecting of the aircrafts' undersides, due to damage sustained whilst operating from unprepared airfields, such as those encountered during the numerous humanitarian flights undertaken by the RAF following natural disasters, or in areas hit by famine. In addition, a

Hercules C.3P
1:192 scale

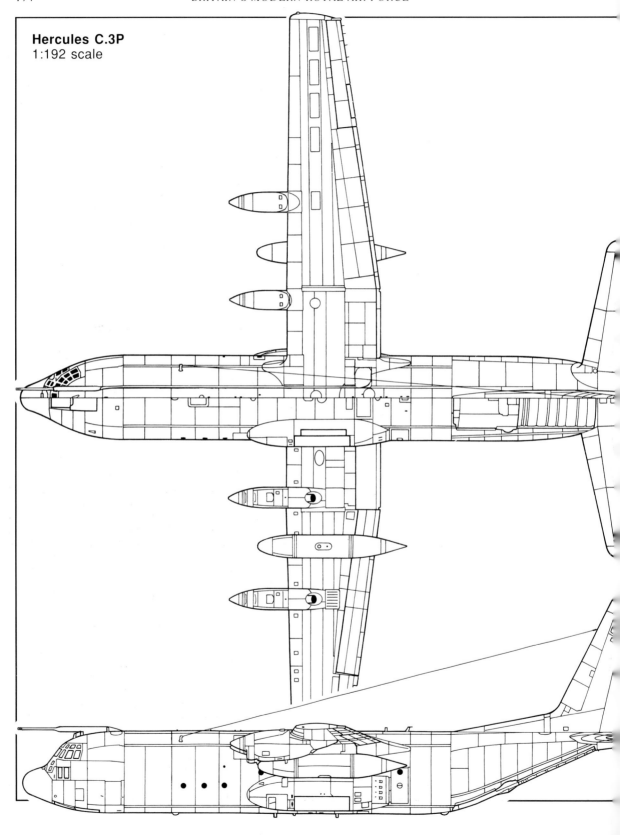

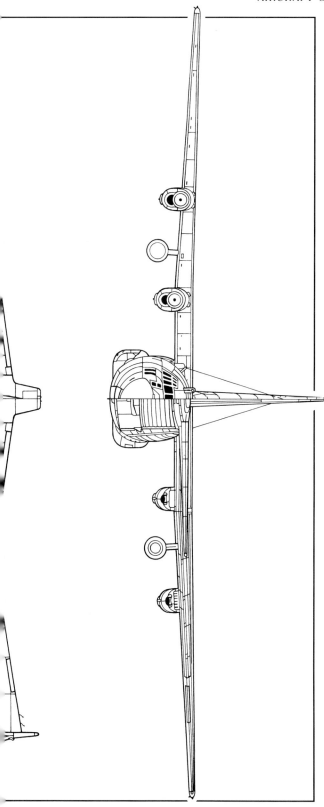

number of RAF Hercules have been fitted with slender wing-tip pods, which house ECM/ESM equipment.

In March 1990, the Hercules fleet celebrated 1,000,000 flying hours of service with the RAF. Soon the LTW's resources would once again be tested to the full, as the build-up to the Gulf War of early 1991 got underway during the second half of 1990. Since then, the RAF's Hercules have continued to be heavily utilized, with mercy aid missions being operated to Somalia and Bosnia, and support flights connecting RAF and UN operations in many other parts of the world.

In 1992 the Hercules celebrated its 25th anniversary with the RAF, and one aircraft was specially marked with the insignia of all the RAF units to have operated the type. At the time of writing, studies are being undertaken to find a replacement for the RAF's Hercules in the tactical transport role.

Hawker Siddeley (BAe) 125 CC.2/.3

(Data applies to CC.3) **Powerplant** Two Garrett AiResearch TFE731-3-1H turbofans, each rated at 3,700 lb st (16.46 kN); **Wing span** 47 ft 0 in (14.32 m); **Length** 50 ft 8 in (15.46 m); **Height** 17 ft 7 in (5.37 m); **Max take-off weight** 25,500 lb (11,565 kg); **Max cruising speed** 495 mph (796 km/h); **Range** 2,785 miles (4,482 km); **Service ceiling** 41,000 ft (12,500 m). **Operating Unit** No 32 Squadron.

The RAF have purchased various models of the BAe 125 executive transport over the years, hence the variety of type designations. The first batch comprised four aircraft that were the equivalent of the civil Model 400B, these being designated as CC.1s, with delivereies taking place in the spring of 1971. Two further CC.1s were acquired in the autumn of 1972, but these were returned to what was then Hawker Siddeley when two Model 600Bs, designated as CC.2s, were delivered in April 1973.

During the early 1980s, further examples of this successful aircraft were obtained by the RAF. Six Model 700Bs were acquired, all receiving the CC.3 designation in RAF service. These aircraft are powered by quieter, cleaner and more fuel-efficient Garrett turbofan engines, and the earlier CC.1/.2s were subsequently fitted with engines of this type, replacing the existing Viper turbojets.

The BAe 125 fleet is used to transport government ministers, senior officers, and VIPs at high speed to and from destinations throughout Europe and occasionally further afield, and are furnished to a high standard of comfort. Only one unit has operated the aircraft, this being No 32 Squadron, based at RAF Northolt. Alas, the current political and security-conscious climate has meant that the aircraft have had to be fitted with various self-defence devices to counter possible threats from terrorist organizations.

In the early 1990s, the CC.2/.3s were modified to enable them to undertake aeromedical flights, with the capacity to carry stretcher cases and incubator units. On 31 March 1994, the four BAe 125 CC.1s were withdrawn from service.

British Aerospace 146 CC.2

Powerplant Four Avco Lycoming ALF502R turbofans, each rated at 6,970 lb st (31.0 kN); **Wing span** 86 ft 5 in (26.34 m); **Length** 85 ft 11 in (26.19 m); **Height** 28 ft 3 in (8.61 m); **Max take-off weight** 84,000 lb (38,102 kg); **Max operating speed** 345 mph (555 km/h); **Range (max fuel)** 1,900 miles (3,080 km). **Operating Unit** The Queen's Flight.

The history of the BAe 146 transport can be traced back to 1973, when the then Hawker Siddeley Company announced its plans to produce a quiet four-engined, turbofan-powered aircraft for medium-range transport tasks. However, problems with government funding support brought the programme to a halt, although the company (and later BAe) continued design and research aspects of the project. The aircraft was reborn in mid-1978, with various parts being manufactured by sub-contractors in the USA and Sweden. The first prototype, a Series 100 aircraft, flew for the first time in September 1981, and the BAe 146 entered commercial service in May 1983. Since then, the type has enjoyed a reasonable amount of commercial success, with exports to airlines in many parts of the world.

By the early 1980s, it was apparent that the Hawker Siddeley Andover CC.2s in service with The Queen's Flight since the mid-1960s would need to be replaced. Thus, in 1983, two BAe 146-100 commercial transports were obtained for evaluation purposes, to study the type's suitability for use with this prestigious unit.

The first two examples obtained by the MoD, which were designated as CC.1s, did not serve with The Queen's Flight, but were flown by a specially-formed unit known as the 146 Evaluation Flight. This unit was based at RAF Brize Norton, and formed part of No 241 OCU. Following a two-year trial period, during which the unit thoroughly evaluated the type for use in the VIP role, the aircraft were disposed of on the civil market, and the 146 Evaluation Flight was disbanded. That this evaluation had been successful was borne out by an order for two BAe 146-100s for actual use by The Queen's Flight, with

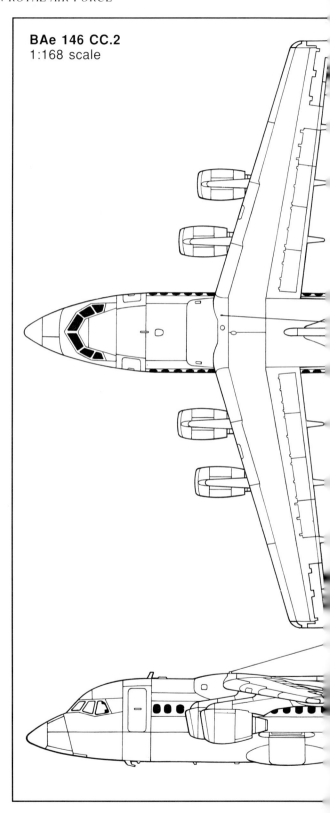

BAe 146 CC.2
1:168 scale

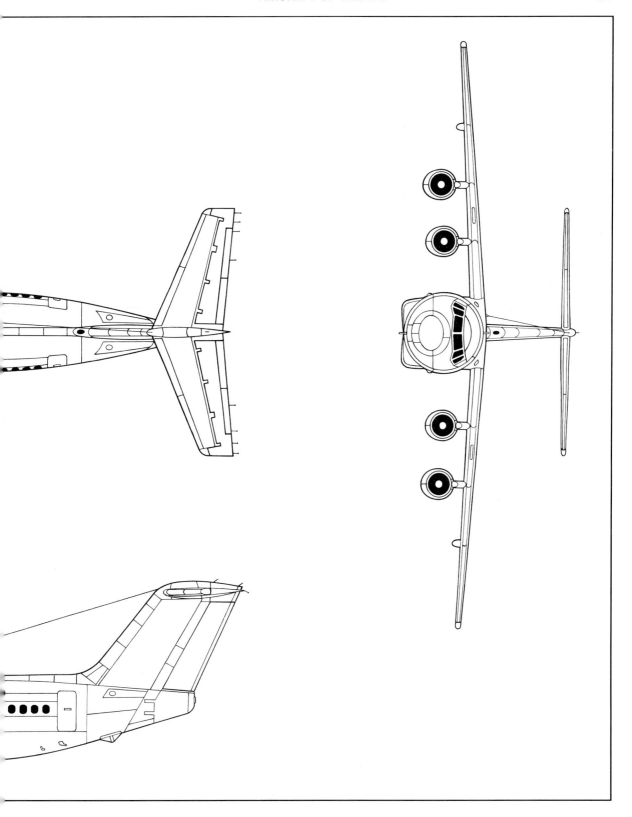

With everything down, one of the three BAe 146 CC.2s in service with The Queen's Flight makes its final approach prior to landing. (Bob Munro)

both aircraft receiving the designation of CC.2. The first of these was handed over in April 1986, the second following two months later. A third machine was ordered in October 1990, and was delivered to The Queen's Flight in December 1990. All three aircraft are currently based at RAF Benson.

Obviously, the interiors of these aircraft are unlike those found in the normal commercial versions. There is capacity for about 20 passengers in VIP conditions. The interiors can be arranged in three sections, one of which is for Her Majesty The Queen, with wardrobe and toilet facilities. There is also a communications and work area, and a further section with seating for support staff. The aircraft are fitted with a comprehensive array of communications equipment and navigational aids, and are capable of operating into and out of airfields with limited facilitites and in poor weather conditions.

TRAINERS

Hawker Siddeley (BAe) Hawk T.1/.1A

Powerplant One Rolls-Royce/Turbomeca Adour 151 non-afterburning turbofan engine, rated at 5,200 lb st (23.13 kN); **Wing span** 30 ft 10 in (9.39 m); **Length** 38 ft 11 in (11.86 m); **Height** 13 ft 1 in (3.99 m): **Max take-off weight** 17,085 lb (7,750 kg); **Max speed** 647 mph (1,041 km/h); **Range** 1,957 miles (3,150 km); **Service ceiling** 48,000 ft (14,630 m). **Operating Units** No 100 Squadron; Nos 4, 6 & 7 FTSs (Nos 19(R), 74(R), 92(R) & 208(R) Squadrons); CFS; RAF St Athan Station Flight.

In the 1960s, studies were carried out to define the future training requirements of the RAF, with

Hawk T.1
1:72 scale

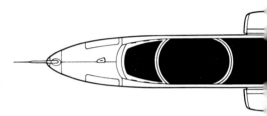

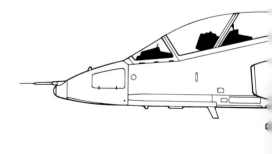

one aspect concerning advanced trainers to replace the aircraft then in service. These were the Folland Gnat and the two-seat versions of the Hawker Hunter, which were used for training in advanced flying techniques, as well as tactical weapons delivery. At one stage, it was envisaged that the RAF's requirements would be met by a supersonic trainer, with added weapons delivery capability. However the emphasis on roles was reversed, and the latter requirement was to be met by orders for the SEPECAT Jaguar.

This still left the requirement for an advanced trainer unfilled, and this was redefined as an aircraft with a high subsonic performance, combined with the ability to carry out tactical weapons delivery training. The Hawker Siddeley Company proposed an advanced two-seat trainer design, known as the HS.1182, to meet these tasks, and to replace both the Gnat and Hunter. In October 1971, this design was chosen in preference to other proposals, and an order was placed in March 1972 for 176 machines, which had now become known as the Hawk T.1. This programme was unique, in that there was no prototype, with testing being undertaken on one pre-producton machine and the first five production Hawk T.1s off the assembly line. These were later refurbished for service with the RAF.

The pre-production aircraft took to the air on 21 August 1974, with the first and second production Hawks flying during the spring of 1975. Testing and development of the new trainer went smoothly and initial deliveries to the RAF were made in late 1976, these being to No 4 FTS at RAF Valley. Further Hawks were supplied to Valley for use by the CFS detachment. From early 1978, Hawks were delivered to No 1 TWU at RAF Brawdy, and No 2 TWU at RAF Chivenor

started to receive the new trainer during 1980. The Hawk T.1s of the RAF became well-known to the general public when the famous 'Red Arrows' formation aerobatic team re-equipped from Gnats in 1980, and their specially-painted aircraft are seen at some 100 events in the summer months each year.

The Hawk's airframe is of conventional design, with a low wing of moderate sweep and an aerofoil section which enables the aircraft to go transonic in a dive. The two-seat tandem cockpit is fitted with Martin-Baker zero-zero rocket-assisted ejection seats, the rear seat being raised to provide a good forward view for the instructor. Ease of servicing and maintenance were also features that were incorporated into the design.

In order to attract export contracts, the Hawk was designed from the outset to have a weapons-carrying capability, with two pylons under each wing (although RAF aircraft are only fitted with the inner pylons) and another stores station under the fuselage centreline. The normal fit on RAF Hawks involved in weapons training is a 30 mm Aden cannon and ammunition pod on the centreline station, with practice bomb carriers carried beneath the wings.

Apart from their mainly red special paint scheme, the Hawks used by the 'Red Arrows' (a mix of T.1s and T.1As) differ in a few respects from other Hawks of the RAF. A small pod is fitted under the fuselage, in the position normally occupied by the 30 mm cannon, and this contains diesel fuel and colour dyes. Operated by switches on the control column, these fluids are pressure-fed via pipework into the jet exhaust at the rear of the Hawk, the heat from which creates the coloured smoke that so enhances the team's displays. Another modification involves changes to

The famous 'tiger' markings of No 74 Squadron adorn this Hawk T.1A. No 74 is one of two Reserve squadrons in No 4 FTS at RAF Valley.

the fuel system and the engine, to make them more suitable for aerobatic display manoeuvres.

In 1983 the Hawk was selected to undertake a secondary air defence role, providing local short-range cover, and to be flown by weapons instructors in the event of an emergency. This resulted in 88 Hawks being modified to carry two AIM-9L Sidewinder AAMs each, one on each underwing pylon, with a gunsight being fitted in the front cockpit. With these modifications the aircraft concerned were redesignated as Hawk T.1As, and the last was redelivered to the RAF in mid-1986. As the Hawk does not possess a radar, it was envisaged that they would operate in conjunction with other, more sophisticated, interceptors, acting as a mixed force. Alternatively, the Hawk T.1As would undertake local air defence, operating as a standing patrol and engaging potential threats visually. There are also a few Hawks that carry the unofficial designation of 'T.1W'; these are fitted with the gunsight, but lack the full weapons- and missile-carrying capabilities of the T.1As.

The disposition of the RAF's fleet of Hawks underwent many changes in the early 1990s. They replaced the ageing Canberras of No 100 Squadron in 1991; No 1 TWU closed in 1992, with its aircraft being distributed amongst other units; and there were many transfers of T.1/.1As between Valley and Chivenor. In 1993 Hawks were added to the variety of types operated by No 6 FTS at Finningley, as part-replacements for the ageing Jet Provosts.

There is no planned or obvious successor in sight for the RAF's Hawks, and thus the type will remain in service for many years to come.

Shorts Tucano T.1

Powerplant One Garrett TPE331-12B turboprop, rated at 1,100 shp (820 kW); **Wing span** 37 ft 0 in (11.28 m); **Length** 32 ft 4 in (9.86 m); **Height** 11 ft 2 in (3.40 m); **Max take-off weight** 6,470 lb (2,935 kg); **Max level speed** 320 mph (515 km/h); **Service ceiling** 34,000 ft (10,363 m); **Range** 1,082 miles (1,742 km). **Operating Units** Nos 1, 3 & 6 FTSs; CFS.

For many years the RAF has trained aircrew to operate at low-level, but this policy had a significant effect on the fatigue life of the Hunting Jet Provost, the RAF's basic jet training aircraft for more than 30 years. This aircraft pioneered the programme of all-through jet pilot training in the RAF, first entering service in 1955. At one stage, studies were undertaken into the modification and updating of the Jet Provost for further service into the 1990s, but the costs involved were considered to be excessive, meaning that a replacement aircraft would have to be obtained. Also, the Jet Provost was becoming less suitable to train aircrew for the front-line types they would eventually fly. The side-by-side seating, once considered to be innovative, was dissimilar to the tandem arrangement of current front-line aircraft, its performance was relatively sluggish, and its fuel consumption was high in these cost-conscious times.

Thus, in the early 1980s, the Air Board issued Air Staff Target 412 (AST 412), requesting submissions from industry for a Jet Provost replacement. Initially, it seemed probable that the new type would be another pure-jet aircraft. However, the advent of small, high-powered turboprop engines, with far lower fuel consumption and thereby operating costs, dictated that training aircraft types with this form of power would have to be seriously considered.

The RAF specified the ability to operate two sorties of one-hour duration each, between refuelling, with sufficient fuel reserves to allow for diversions. The aircraft structure would have to be able to withstand aerobatic stresses up to +6/−3g, with a projected airframe life of 12,000 flying hours over 20 years. The cockpit canopy had to provide good visibility for both student and instructor, and be able to withstand a bird-strike at 240 kts. Ejection seats suitable for operation at ground level were also requested.

Over 20 submissions were made to the MoD, seeking the prestigious order for a Jet Provost replacement aircraft. From these, four main contenders emerged, these being the British NDN Firecracker, the Australian A-20 (which was still in the design stage and had not yet been built), the Swiss Pilatus PC-9, and the Brazilian Embraer 312 Tucano. The last two types became the favourites, but neither fully met the stringent requirements of AST 412.

The Belfast-based aircraft manufacturer Shorts, who were promoting the Tucano, then offered an extensively modified version of the Brazilian machine, and they were rewarded with an order for 130 aircraft, placed in 1986.

Shorts carried out a major redesign of the Tucano, and the machines for the RAF differ by some 80 per cent from the original Brazilian design. The most significant changes were the replacement of the original Pratt & Whitney turboprop with a Garrett turboprop, strengthening of the airframe to double its life to the required 12,000 flying hours, replacement of the cockpit canopies, and the addition of an airbrake under the fuselage. Equipment from British sources was also fitted, including TACAN, VOR and ILS avionics.

The first production Tucano T.1 for the RAF made its maiden flight on 30 December 1986, and

Tucano T.1
1:72 scale

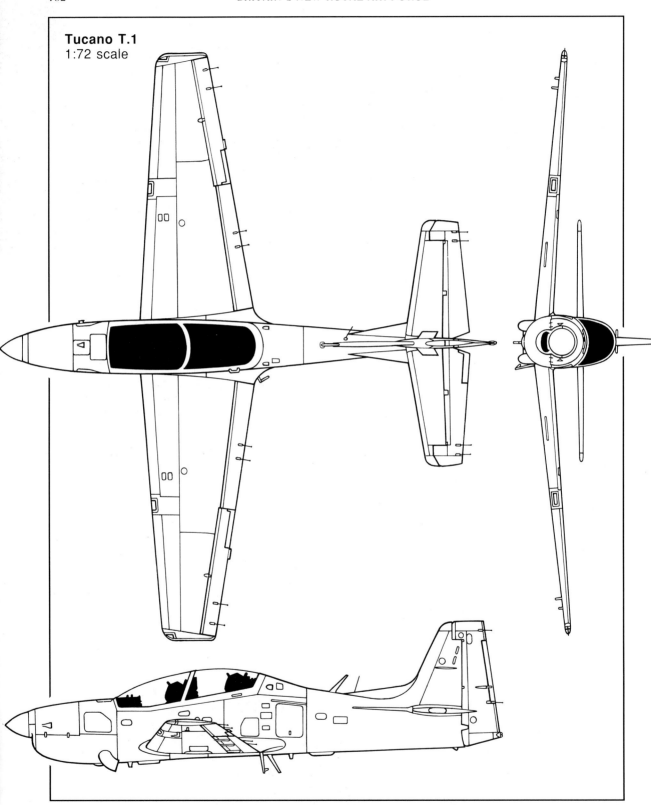

The Central Flying School operates this Tucano T.1 trainer from RAF Scampton. Supporting equipment stands ready for the aircraft's next sortie.

was delivered to the A&AEE at Boscombe Down for pre-service trials. The first deliveries of Tucano T.1s were made to the CFS at RAF Scampton in September 1988, followed by No 7 FTS at RAF Church Fenton, and No 3 FTS at RAF Cranwell. With the run-down in aircrew training requirements as a result of the 'Options for Change' defence review, No 7 FTS closed in mid-1992, with some of their aircraft transferring to RAF Finningley for use by the Air Navigation School. The last FTS to use the Jet Provost, No 1 at RAF Linton-on-Ouse, started to receive Tucanos in late 1992, and has now built up to its full establishment of some 50 aircraft. The last Tucano T.1 for the RAF was delivered in early 1993.

Although slower in level flight than its predecessor, the Tucano T.1 has a better rate of climb, far longer endurance, and offers a major reduction in operating costs of fuel and maintenance in comparison with the Jet Provost. It is now well-established in service with the RAF, and will no doubt be a familiar sight around the training bases for the next 20 years.

Hawker Siddeley (BAe) Dominie T.1

Powerplant Two Bristol Siddeley Viper 300 turbojets, each rated at 3,120 lb st (13.88 kN); **Wing span** 47 ft 0 in (14.33 m); **Length** 47 ft 5 in (14.45 m); **Height** 16 ft 6 in (5.03 m); **Max take-off weight** 21,200 lb (9,615 kg); **Max cruising speed** 493 mph (793 km/h); **Range** 1,700 miles (2,736 km); **Service ceiling** 40,000 ft (12,000 m). **Operating Unit** No 6 FTS.

The BAe 125 twin-engined executive jet, first built by Hawker Siddeley, has now been in production for over 30 years. The RAF's connection with the type dates from September 1962, when

Navigator training is the domain of No 6 FTS's Dominie T.1s, each of which has two workstations in the fuselage for trainee navigators. (Bob Munro)

20 modified Hawker Siddeley 125 Series 2 aircraft were ordered to fulfil the role of navigator trainers. The first of these made its maiden flight in December 1964, and initial deliveries to the RAF commenced in the autumn of 1965, the type entering service at RAF Stradishall with No 1 Air Navigation School. The RAF aircraft, known as Dominie T.1s, differ from the civil models in having a large fairing attached under the fuselage, forward of the wing, which contains radar equipment used in the navigator training role.

Internally, the Dominie T.1 is fitted-out with workstations to enable two students to train and gain expertise in navigational procedures. Each workstation comprises a rearward-facing seat and a console, which provides a realstic environment for the students. Each console has a working surface for charts, combined with space for the stowage of charts, instruments and manuals. The aircraft is fitted with a periscope sextant, and an extensive range of navigational and communications equipment. Apart from the two students, the Dominie T.1 can carry one or two pilots, a navigator instructor, and one other crewmember.

A number of Dominie T.1s had been withdrawn from service by the early 1990s, but a contract has been placed to provide improved navigational training equipment and updated avionics on 11 of the surviving aircraft, and these modified machines are expected to re-enter service from mid-1995 onwards.

Scottish Aviation (BAe) Jetstream T.1

Powerplant Two Turbomeca Astazou XVI turboprops, each rated at 996 eshp (743 kW); **Wing span** 52 ft 0 in (15.85 m); **Length** 47 ft 2 in (14.37 m); **Height** 17 ft 6 in (5.32 m); **Max take-off weight** 12,550 lb (5,692 kg); **Max speed** 278 mph (448 km/h); **Range** 1,380 miles (2,224 km/h); **Service ceiling** 26,000 ft (7,928m); **Operating Unit** No 45(R) Squadron.

The Jetstream was an attempt by the Handley Page Company to break into the light business and utility transport aircraft market, but before the full potential of the design could be realized, the company went into liquidation. Eventually, Scottish Aviation Limited (and later, BAe) took over development and production, and subsequent versions have enjoyed considerable sales success, particularly in the USA and other export markets.

The RAF's involvement with the Jetstream can be traced back to the early 1970s, when an order was placed for 26 machines, designated as T.1s and intended as replacements for the Vickers Varsities then in service. The first Jetstream T.1 was delivered in June 1973 to No 5 FTS at RAF

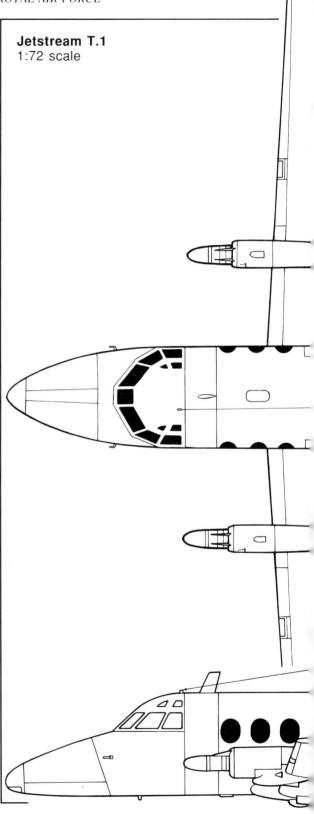

Jetstream T.1
1:72 scale

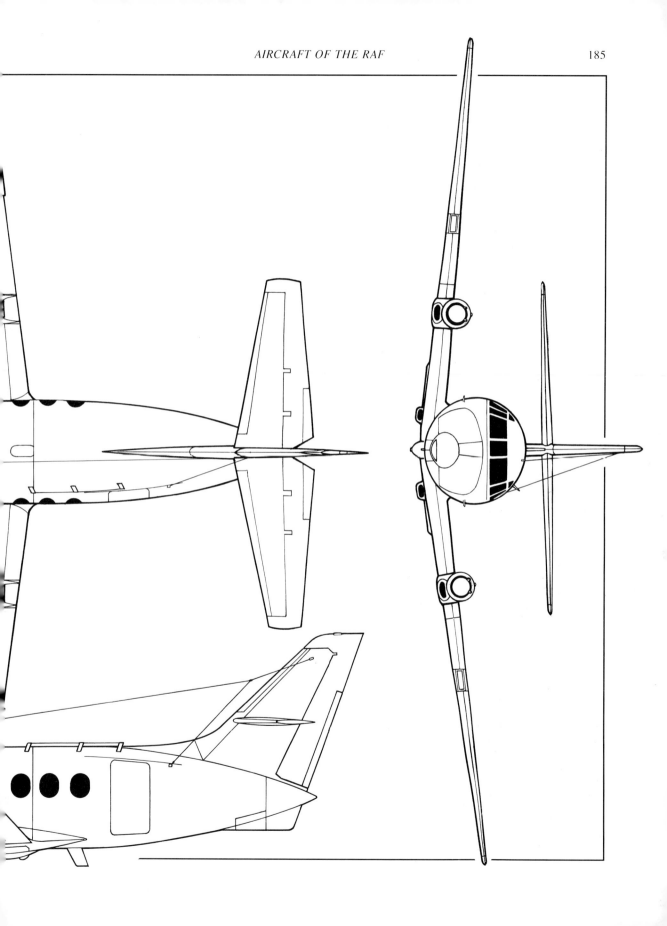

Canberra T.17A
1:72 scale

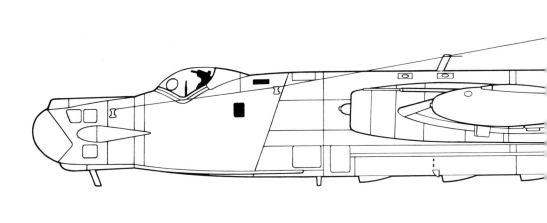

Oakington in Cambridgeshire. Here, as with the Varsity before, advanced training for pilots in multi-engined flying was carried out.

However, drastic cuts in defence spending in the mid-1970s particularly affected transport units, and the requirement for aircrew for multi-engined types was consequently severely reduced. This resulted in the entire Jetstream T.1 fleet being withdrawn from service and placed in storage for a number of years. Eventually, 14 aircraft were transferred to the Royal Navy; these acquired nose-mounted radar and were redesignated as T.2s.

In 1976, the remaining T.1s were restored to RAF service with the newly-formed Multi-

The unlovely but distinctive nose profile of the Canberra T.17 electronic warfare trainer.

Engined Training Squadron (METS), based at RAF Leeming. The METS moved to RAF Finningley in April 1979, to form part of No 6 FTS. In 1992, the unit was retitled No 45 (Reserve) Squadron, and the Jetstream T.1s began to acquire this squadron's markings.

The RAF's Jetstreams are used for Group Two pilot training only, with just a few seats in the fuselage, although they could be used as light transports if required.

English Electric (BAe) Canberra T.17/.17A

Powerplant Two Rolls-Royce Avon 101 turbojets, each rated at 6,500 lb st (2,948 kg); **Wing span** 64 ft 0 in (19.51 m): **Length** 65 ft 6 in (19.96 m); **Height** 15 ft 7 in (4.80 m); **Max take-off** weight 42,500 lb (19,278 kg); **Max speed** 570 mph (917 km/h). **Operating Unit** No 360 Squadron.

Over 900 Canberras, of some 20 different models, were produced in the UK, together with more than 450 in the USA and Australia. Numerous RAF squadrons operated the many variants of the type, but No 360 Squadron, currently based at RAF Wyton, is the only unit to have operated the Canberra T.17/.17A variants. These are used for EW and ECM training. The T.17 started life as a Canberra B.2 bomber variant, and over 400 of this early version were produced, entering service with No 101 Squadron at RAF Binbrook in 1951. In the mid-1960s, about 25 B.2s were converted to become T.17s, with an extensively modified

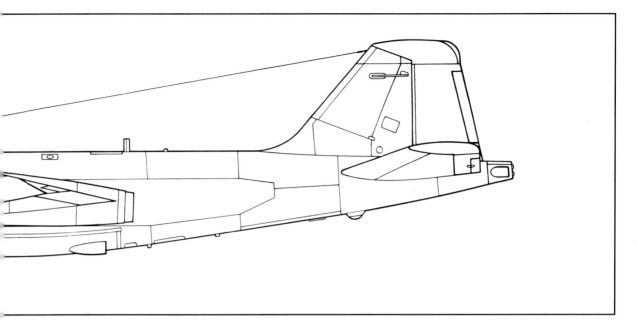

nose profile and other alterations.

The bulbous nose, with four small external blisters, contains the various aerials, antennae and transmitters that enable the T.17/.17As to carry out their training tasks. Additional aerials are fitted to the fuselage and tail, while the T.17A displays even more external aerials to cater for its enhanced avionics suite. The T.17A variant dates from the mid-1980s, when six T.17s were fitted with improved equipment to bring the ECM training task into line with the technology then available. Both variants carry a crew of three: pilot, navigator and electronic warfare operator.

With the imminent changes to EW and ECM training within the RAF, in which it is envisaged that the task will be contracted out to civilian operators, the days of the Canberra T.17/.17As are numbered, and they may well have all been withdrawn from service by the end of 1994.

Scottish Aviation (BAe) Bulldog T.1

Powerplant One Lycoming IO-360-A1B6 four-cylinder piston engine, rated at 200 hp (149 kW); **Wing span** 33 ft 0 in (10.06 m); **Length** 23 ft 3 in (7.09 m); **Height** 7 ft 6 in (2.28 m); **Max take-off weight** 2,350 lb (1,065 kg); **Max speed (at sea level)** 150 mph (240 km/h); **Service ceiling** 17,000 ft (5,180 m); **Range** 628 miles (1,010 km). **Operating Units** No 6 FTS; CFS; RAF College Air Squadron; UASs.

The attractive Bulldog two-seat basic training aircraft was originally conceived by Sussex-based Beagle Aircraft, who flew the first prototype in May 1969. When that company succumbed to financial problems, it seemed likely that the Bulldog would die too. However the project passed to Scottish Aviation Limited (later part of BAe), who set up a production line at their Prestwick plant. A second prototype, assembled in Scotland, took to the air in February 1971, and the type went on to win a number of export orders, principally to the Swedish Air Force.

The RAF was looking for a replacement for the de Havilland Chipmunks then equipping its

Standard equipment of the University Air Squadrons is the Bulldog T.1, which has now seen over 20 years of service. This example belongs to the London UAS at RAF Benson.

UASs, and the Bulldog was selected with an order for 132 machines. The first of these was delivered to the A&AEE at Boscombe Down in February 1973 for pre-service trials, following which the Bulldog T.1 entered service with the CFS at RAF Little Rissington, and No 2 FTS at RAF Church Fenton. The RAF received the last of its Bulldogs in early 1976.

The bulk of the order was delivered to the various UASs located around the country, where they provide basic flying training for undergraduates. Bulldogs were, until 1993, also used by the Royal Navy Elementary Flying Training Squadron (part of the RAF's No 1 FTS), based at RAF Topcliffe; this task has now been taken over by a private contractor operating Slingsby Fireflies.

Of all-metal construction, the Bulldog T.1 features side-by-side seating, with dual controls, and is fully aerobatic. There is space behind the front seats for a third occupant, or 220 lb (100 kg) of baggage.

---

de Havilland Chipmunk T.10

Powerplant One de Havilland Gipsy Major 8 piston engine, rated at 145 hp (108 kW); **Wing span** 34 ft 4 in (10.46 m); **Length** 25 ft 8 in (7.82 m); **Height** 7 ft 1 in (2.16 m); **Max take-off weight** 2,100 lb (953 kg); **Max speed** 138 mph (222 km/h); **Range** 280 miles (451 km); **Service ceiling** 16,000 ft (4,877 m). **Operating Units** AEFs; RAF Gatow Station Flight.

Apart from a few historical preserved aircraft, and a handful of machines in use at various test estab-

lishments, the Chipmunk T.10 is now the oldest type in active service with the RAF, and is unique in having a 'taildragger' undercarriage, with a rear tailwheel. Originally designed in Canada as the DHC.1, the Chipmunk was primarily built in the UK, with over 1,000 being produced, many of which were exported.

In all, 735 Chipmunks were ordered for the RAF, in six batches, with the first deliveries taking place in late 1949 and continuing for four years. Many Chipmunks were transferred to the Army Air Corps and the Royal Navy, and in recent years several have been sold to civilian owners, often retaining their former military markings.

For many years the Chipmunk was the mainstay of the UASs, providing basic flying training for students at various locations around the country, prior to them joining the RAF. However, it was displaced by the Bulldog T.1 in the mid-1970s.

Up until mid-1993, the largest single unit operating the Chipmunk T.10 was the Elementary Flying Training Squadron (EFTS) at RAF Swinderby, tasked with pilot screening. However, this training task was turned over to a civilian company with more modern aircraft during 1993, and the EFTS was disbanded.

Currently, some 50 Chipmunk T.10s remain in service with the RAF and are operated by 12 AEFs. As their title suggests, their role is to provide air experience flights, primarily for members of the ATC.

Being conceived in the late 1940s, the Chipmunk is a 'basic' aircraft in every way, with limited instrumentation. The fuselage, tail unit and the leading-edges of the wings are metal-

The simple lines of the Chipmunk T.10 tandem-seat trainer. This example serves with No 6 AEF, based at RAF Benson.

skinned; the remainder of the wings and all of the control surfaces are fabric-covered. It is a demanding aircraft to fly well, and is thus ably suited to demonstrate airmanship to cadets, some of whom may possibly be future pilots with the RAF.

HELICOPTERS

Boeing Vertol (Boeing Helicopters) Chinook HC.1/.2

Powerplant (HC.1) Two Avco Lycoming T55-L-11E turboshafts, each rated at 3,750 eshp (2,796 kW); **Rotor diameter** 60 ft 0 in (18.29 m); **Length (rotors turning)** 99 ft 0 in (30.18 m), **(fuselage)** 51 ft 0 in (15.55 m); **Height (top of rear rotor head)** 18 ft 8 in (5.69 m); **Max take-off weight** 50,000 lb (22,680 kg); **Max speed (clean)** 183 mph (295 km/h); **Service ceiling** 10,500 ft (3,200 m). **Operating Units** Nos 7, 18, 27(R) & 78 Squadrons.

In response to a requirement issued by the US Army, design and development of the Chinook helicopter began as far back as 1956, with the first prototype making its maiden flight in 1961. Since then, vast numbers of several models have been produced for the US Army, with exports to many other countries around the world, mainly for military use but also for civilian operators carrying out oil-rig support flights.

There were plans to introduce the Chinook into RAF service in the late 1960s, and an order was placed with Boeing-Vertol as far back as 1967 for 15 machines. These would have been the equivalent of the CH-47A model, then in service with the US Army, and were intended as replacements for the Bristol Belvedere. However, this contract fell victim to cuts in defence spending at that time.

The spending cuts may have been a blessing in disguise, for when the Chinook was finally obtained by the RAF, it was to the standard of the more capable CH-47C model, but with updated features similar to those of the CH-147 model in use with the Canadian Armed Forces, together with items of British equipment. The order, placed in 1978, was for 33 Chinook HC.1s, and the first of these took to the air in March 1980, with initial deliveries commencing the following year.

These deliveries were to RAF Odiham, where conversion training on the new type commenced

This Chinook HC.1 of No 18 Squadron, RAF Laarbruch, is shown on a field exercise in Germany, hence the mud splashed up on to the fuselage. Note the lowered rear loading ramp.

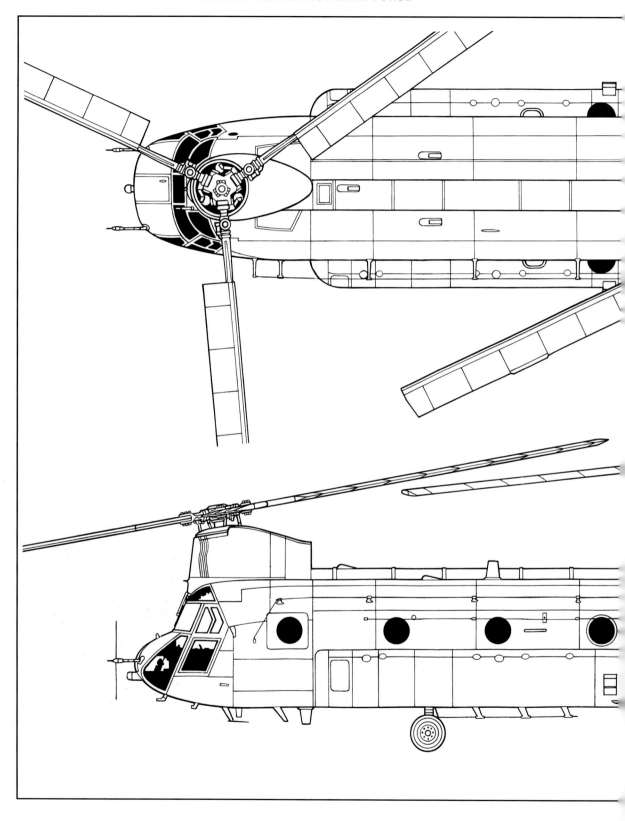

Chinook HC.1
1:72 scale

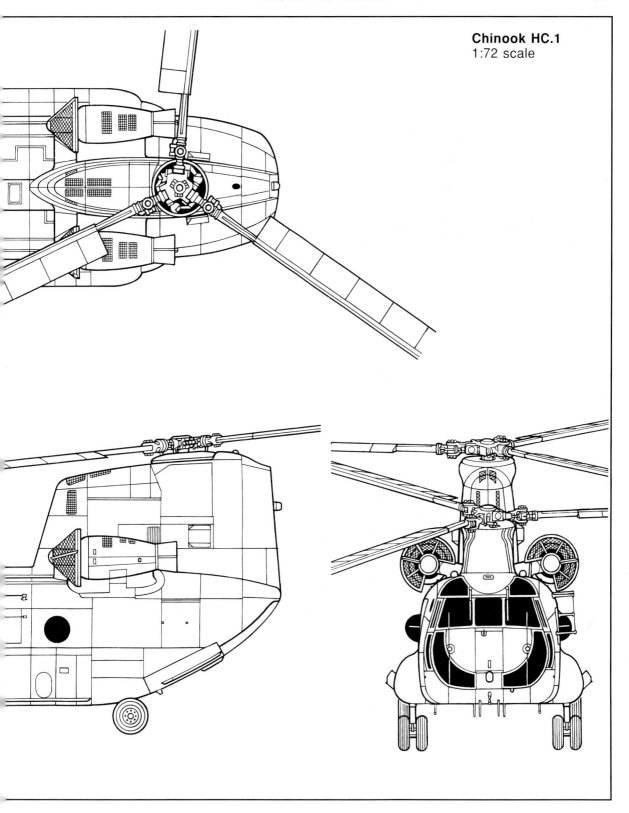

Interior of a Chinook HC.1; note the basic seating along the sides.

in May 1981. The first RAF Chinook-equipped squadron, No 18, reformed in February 1982, and should have returned to RAF Gutersloh in West Germany, its former base when equipped with Westland Wessex helicopters. However, the Falklands conflict intervened, and No 18 Squadron was extensively involved in support of British Forces. A second Chinook unit, No 7 Squadron, was reformed in September 1982, to be based at Odiham, whilst No 18 Squadron at last returned to West Germany in the spring of 1983. A few Chinook HC.1s continued to be based in the Falkland Islands after the conflict, and No 1310 Flight was created in August 1983 to operate the type from the islands; this unit was later to become part of the reformed No 78 Squadron.

In the early 1980s, programmes were initiated to improve the RAF's Chinooks, with the fitting of glass-fibre rotor blades, a single-point pressure refuelling system, and the addition of RWRs. As a result of the loss of three Chinooks in the South Atlantic, three replacement aircraft, together with five additional machines, were ordered, and the first of these arrived in the UK in mid-1984. These later machines were fitted with the uprated T55-L-712 turboshaft engines.

The Chinook is fitted with three hooks under the fuselage, for the carriage of external loads; these points have a combined capacity of 25,000 lb (11,340 kg). Internally, the aircraft can accommodate loads of up to 20,000 lb (9,072 kg), including small vehicles, which are loaded via the ramp at the rear of the fuselage. The Chinook can accommodate 54 fully-equipped troops, or, alternatively, 24 stretcher cases.

In November 1990, a contract was placed with the Boeing Helicopter Division for the conversion of 33 RAF Chinook HC.1s to HC.2 standard. This work involves replacing the Chinook's power-plants, instrumentation, dynamic components, and other systems with new items. A self-defence suite comprising indicators to warn of approaching missiles is being fitted, along with infra-red jammers and chaff and flare dispensers, and fittings to mount machine guns have also been added. A further enhancement will be the fitting of a new, long-range fuel system. The contract also covers logistical support, training, and technical publications.

The current Chinook HC.1s are being shipped to and from the USA by sea, and thus use of the type by the RAF, particularly by No 27 (Reserve) Squadron at Odiham, will be curtailed whilst the conversion programme is carried out. The first

Chinook HC.2 was rolled out at Boeing Helicopters' Philadelphia plant in January 1993, and then shipped to the UK for a trials and evaluation programme with the A&AEE at Boscombe Down. In fact, this first converted machine was the same aircraft that survived the sinking of its transporting ship, the MV *Atlantic Conveyor*, during the Falklands conflict, and which then continued to give yeoman service in support of British Forces tasked with recapturing the Falklands.

Further Chinook HC.2s have been redelivered to the RAF, and the conversion programme calls for the final aircraft to be shipped back to the UK in mid-1995. Three all-new HC.2s were ordered from Boeing Helicopters in 1993, and these are due to be delivered from mid-1995.

Aerospatiale/Westland Puma HC.1

Powerplant Two Turbomeca Turmo III C4 tuboshafts, each rated at 1,320 eshp (984 kW); **Rotor diameter** 49 ft 3 in (15.0 m); **Fuselage length** 46 ft 2 in (14.06 m); **Height** 16 ft 10 in (5.13 m); **Max take-off weight** 14,110 lb (6,400 kg); **Max speed** 174 mph (280 km/h); **Service ceiling** 15,100 ft (4,600 m); **Range** 390 miles (630 km). **Operating Units** Nos 18, 27(R), 33 & 230 Squadrons; No 1563 Flight.

The development of small turbine engines, with good power-to-weight performance, transformed the payload-range capabilities of helicopters when compared with earlier piston-engined designs. The origins of the Puma go back to the early 1960s, when the French Army issued a requirement for a medium-sized troop-carrying helicopter. The French Sud-Aviation Company had vast experience in helicopter design and manufacture, with types ranging from the small Alouette series to the large Super Frelon, and called upon this expertise to design what was designated the SA.330.

Thus the Puma was conceived, with the prototype making its first flight on 15 April 1965. Testing and development work continued for three years, with the use of a second prototype and six pre-production machines. Deliveries to the French Army and Air Force commenced in 1969. In January 1970, Sud-Aviation was merged with other French aircraft manufacturing companies to form the Aerospatiale concern.

In 1967, the RAF had a requirement for a medium-sized tactical transport helicopter, and the Puma was selected to fulfil this need, replacing the Westland Whirlwinds then in service. They were also required to supplement the Wessex transport helicopters that equipped a number of RAF squadrons. The Puma was the largest of the three types involved in the Anglo-French helicopter agreement (the others being the Lynx and the Gazelle), with joint production being undertaken by Sud-Aviation/Aerospatiale in France and Westland Helicopters in the UK to meet the needs of each nation's Services.

An order for 40 Pumas for the RAF was placed with Westland Helicopters and a production line was set up at Hayes, near London's Heathrow Airport. The RAF version carried the designation of SA.330E, and a French-built machine was delivered to the company's plant in late 1968 to act as a pattern aircraft. With the British service designation of HC.1, the first production aircraft were delivered in January 1971 for trials work at Boscombe Down. No 33 Squadron, based at RAF Odiham, reformed in June of the same year to operate the new type, and the following October saw No 230 Squadron commence its use of the type. Conversion to type was carried out by No 240 OCU (recently retitled as No 27 (Reserve) Squadron), also based at Odiham.

Following the loss of a few Pumas in accidents, the production line was reopened in 1979 at the Westland plant for the manufacture of eight replacement aircraft, the first of which took to the air in May 1980.

The Puma HC.1 has a capacious cabin which can accommodate 16 fully-equipped troops, or 20 passengers, or up to six stretcher cases in the casualty evacuation role. The flight crew varies between two and three, depending on the task. Loads of up to 5,511 lb (2,500 kg) can be carried internally, whilst bulkier items, such as the 105 mm Light Gun, up to a weight limit of 7,055 lb (3,200 kg), can be carried in the underslung position below the fuselage. Ease of servicing was a feature of the original design, and the engine cowlings open outwards to form work platforms to enable servicing personnel to gain access to the powerplants and rotor head equipment.

As a result of the 'Options for Change' defence review, No 230 Squadron, along with some of its Pumas, was transferred to Northern Ireland in 1992. The remaining Pumas at RAF Gutersloh in Germany were absorbed into No 18 Squadron, to operate alongside that unit's Chinooks. The squadron moved to RAF Laarbruch in early 1993.

The Puma HC.1 has now seen over 20 years of service with the RAF, and is expected to continue in the tactical support helicopter role for the forseeable future, with no obvious successor in sight. Various modifications have been incorporated over the years, such as the addition of engine intake filters and the fitting of new main rotor blades of composite materials.

Puma HC.1
1:72 scale

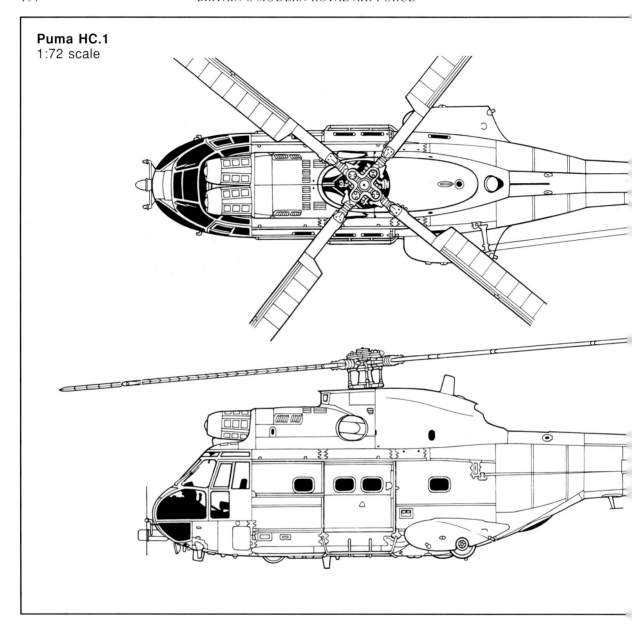

Westland Sea King HAR.3/.3A

Powerplant Two Rolls-Royce Gnome H.1400-1T turboshafts, each rated at 1,660 eshp (1,238 kW); **Rotor diameter** 62 ft 0 in (18.90 m); **Length (overall, rotor turning)** 72 ft 8 in (22.15 m), **(fuselage)** 55 ft 10 in (17.02 m); **Height (top of rotor head)** 15 ft 11 in (4.85 m); **Max take-off weight** 21,000 lb (9,525 kg); **Max speed** 170 mph (274 km/h); **Range** 764 miles (1,230 km). **Operating Units** Nos 78 & 202 Squadrons; SKTU

The Sea King is a Sikorsky design from the USA, for which Westland Helicopters obtained a licence to develop and produce the type. The Royal Navy have used various models of this helicopter for many years, mainly in the anti-submarine warfare role, and the type has won a number of export orders. The original order for the RAF, placed in 1975, was for 15 machines, to be fitted out for the SAR role, with the designation of HAR.3. The first of these made its maiden flight in September 1977, and the SKTU, based alongside the Royal Navy's Sea Kings at RNAS Culdrose, began to operate the type later that

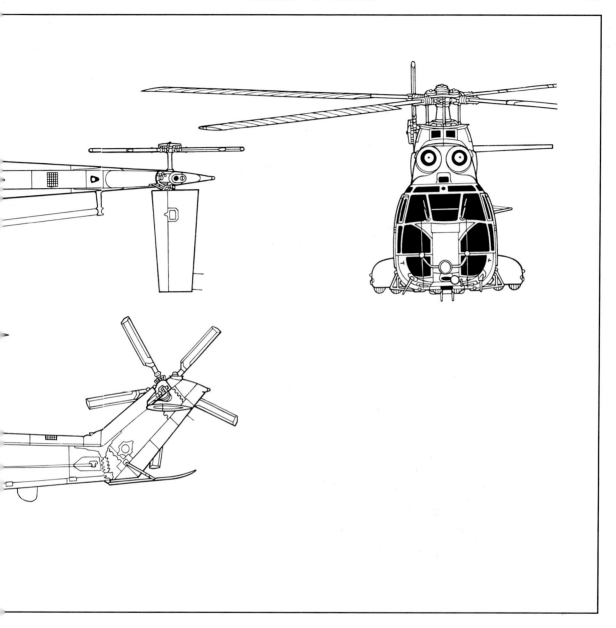

year. No 202 Squadron followed suit in September 1978, when 'D' Flight replaced its Westland Whirlwinds at RAF Lossiemouth. Further flights within No 202 Squadron converted to the type in the late 1970s.

The RAF's Sea King HAR.3s are fitted with various advanced avionics aids, the main element of which is the Tactical Air Navigation System computer, which displays data defining the aircraft's current position, together with information relative to a programmed waypoint, such as bearing, distance to and from, and time to travel. Data on interception points of known target tracks is also available. Another major aid is the Automatic Flight Control System, which will keep the aircraft in an automatic hover position, with control available to the winch operator from a position by the cabin door. The winch cable has a length of 245 ft (74.4 m). The aircraft has the capacity to carry up to 19 passengers, or six stretcher cases.

Four additional HAR.3s have since been obtained, to meet the extra tasks required of the Sea Kings deployed to the Falkland Islands. These machines, now operated by No 78 Squadron, had their bright SAR yellow colour scheme replaced by an overall coat of dark sea

The RAF's principal SAR helicopter is the Sea King HAR.3, in service with the detached flights of No 202 Squadron.

grey. Also, RWRs and enhanced communications equipment have been fitted.

Six Sea King HAR.3As were ordered for the RAF in 1993, as replacements for Wessex helicopters still used in the SAR role; these new aircraft are expected to be delivered from late 1995. The HAR.3A differs from the HAR.3 in the standard of its internal fit. It is possible that the existing HAR.3s may be brought up to HAR.3A standard in due course. In connection with the new variant, the RAF is also due to receive a Sea King cockpit dynamic simulator and a rear-crew trainer in 1996.

Westland Wessex HC.2/HCC.4/HC.5C

Powerplant Two coupled Rolls-Royce Bristol Gnome 110/111 turboshafts, each rated at 1,350 eshp (1,007 kW); **Rotor diameter** 56 ft 0 in (17.07 m); **Fuselage length** 48 ft 5 in (14.70 m); **Height** 16 ft 2 in (4.93 m); **Max take-off weight** 13,500 lb (6,124 kg); **Max speed** 132 mph (213 km/h); **Range** 478 miles (769 km/h); **Service ceiling** 12,000 ft (3,658 m). **Operating Units HC.2** Nos 22, 28, 60 & 72 Squadrons; SARTU; No 2 FTS; **HCC.4** The Queen's Flight; **HC.5C** No 84 Squadron.

In common with some other helicopter types built by Westland Helicopters, the Wessex has its ori-

gins in the USA, in this case as the piston-engined Sikorsky S-58. Westland obtained a production licence for the type, and proceeded to modify the aircraft extensively to suit British Service requirements, the most significant change being the conversion to turbine engines. The initial Westland version for the Royal Navy had a single turboshaft engine, but the variant for the RAF introduced the coupled twin-Gnome powerplant, and this variant first flew in early 1962.

The initial RAF order for the Wessex was for 30 aircraft, under the designation of HC.2, and deliveries commenced in early 1963. No 18 Squadron began operations with the type from RAF Odiham in February 1964. A further 41 machines were subsequently ordered, in four batches, and deliveries were completed in 1968. Various RAF units have operated the Wessex HC.2 from many locations around the world for more than 30 years.

Two Wessex, with VIP interiors and a distinctive red and blue livery, were obtained for The Queen's Flight, with the designation of HCC.4, and these first flew in 1969. Both continue to operate with The Queen's Flight from RAF Benson. Also, a small number of the HC.5C variant were obtained from the Royal Navy, these currently being used by No 84 Squadron, based at RAF Akrotiri in Cyprus.

In 1976 the Wessex HC.2 started to replace the Westland Whirlwind in the SAR role, the aircraft being operated by No 22 Squadron through its

The robust Wessex HC.2 continues to serve in the SAR role in small numbers, although it will have been replaced by all-new Sea King HAR.3As by 1996. (Bob Munro)

detached flights at RAF Chivenor, Leuchars, Valley and Coltishall. It is also used by the SAR Training Unit, based at RAF Valley. The SAR Wessex is fitted with a winch having a 300 ft (91.40 m) cable, together with a Decca Navigator, radio compass, radio altimeter and a transponder as navigational aids.

Although it has been in service for more than 30 years, the Wessex is still regarded as a powerful and robust machine. It is being replaced in the SAR role by Sea Kings, but it should continue with support and training tasks for a few years yet.

Aerospatiale/Westland Gazelle HT.3/HCC.4

Powerplant One Turbomeca Astazou IIIN turboshaft, rated at 592 eshp (440 kW); **Rotor diameter** 34 ft 6 in (10.50 m); **Fuselage length** 31 ft 3 in (9.52 m); **Height** 10 ft 3 in (3.15 m); **Max take-off weight** 3,747 lb (1,700 kg); **Max speed** 165 mph (265 km/h); **Range** 403 miles (650 km); **Service ceiling** 16,400 ft (5,000 m). **Operating Units HT.3** Nos 7 & 32 Squadrons; No 2 FTS; **HCC.4** No 32 Squadron.

The concept of the Gazelle helicopter can be traced back to the early 1960s, when the French company of Sud-Aviation commenced design studies for a suitable replacement for the best-selling Alouette. Various innovations were to be incorporated in the new design, including fibreglass main rotor blades, a rigid-rotor system, and a shrouded tail rotor. However, when the prototype SA.340 Gazelle took to the air in April 1967, it was fitted with conventional main and tail rotors. The second prototype flew one year later, and was completed to the design concept. The 'fenestron' shrouded tail rotor allows a higher proportion of engine power to be transmitted to the main rotor, but problems with this feature caused delays in the programme. Further problems were encountered with the proposed rigid main rotor, and this was replaced by a semi-articulated system, which resulted in a change of designation to SA.341. Despite these early problems, the Gazelle has proved to be a success, with over 1,300 sold worldwide to civil and military operators.

The Gazelle was the smallest of the three helicopter designs involved in a joint Anglo-French production programme, the other two being the French Puma and the British Lynx. As with the Puma, final assembly of Gazelles ordered for the British Services was undertaken by Westland Helicopters, firstly at Yeovil and later at its Weston-super-Mare plant, with over 280 being built in the UK.

The initial order for Gazelles for the British Services was for 60 aircraft, 10 of which were for the RAF, who designated them as HT.3 trainers. Deliveries commenced in July 1973, to RAF

The stylish lines and distinctive fenestron tail rotor of the Gazelle HT.3 helicopter trainer, in service with No 2 FTS at RAF Shawbury.

Ternhill in Shropshire, as replacements for Sioux helicopters then in service with the CFS. Further orders were placed, and the RAF also obtained a number of Gazelle HT.2s from the Royal Navy, these being converted to HT.3 standard. Currently, 23 Gazelle HT.3s are in use at RAF Shawbury, these being shared between No 2 FTS and the helicopter element of the CFS.

The Gazelle HT.3 has dual controls for the front two side-by-side seats, with room for three passengers behind. Three HT.3s were reconfigured internally for operation as VIP transports, to be used by No 32 Squadron at RAF Northolt. An additional Gazelle with a VIP interior, designated as an HCC.4, was also acquired by the squadron, for use in the VIP communications role.

CHAPTER NINE

Airborne Missiles, Ordnance and Defensive Equipment

THIS CHAPTER PROVIDES known specifications and information for some of the various types of guided weapons, ordnance, defensive countermeasures equipment, and other items that may be carried on front-line aircraft of the RAF. It should not be regarded as a complete guide to such items currently in use by the RAF.

AIRBORNE GUIDED MISSILES

British Aerospace ALARM

Powerplant Solid propellant rocket motor; **Length** 14 ft 1 in (4.3 m); **Body diameter** 8.82 in (224 mm); **Weight** 584 lb (265 kg).

ALARM stands for Air-Launched Anti-Radar Missile, and it is produced by the Dynamics Division of British Aerospace (BAe). As its title indicates, ALARM is designed to attack hostile radar installations, such as air defence and SAM systems and can be fired from the carrier aircraft at long range and low-level. The missile's attack sequence can be pre-programmed into its built-in computer prior to the take-off of the carrier aircraft, such information including the mode of operation, together with the type and priorities of targets. Alternatively, the aircraft can programme ALARM from its own avionics, if compatible, up to the time of launching.

ALARM has various modes of operation, all independent from the launch aircraft. These include the Direct Mode, in which the missile is fired towards its target at medium range, giving a minimal flight time. A further mode involves the missile being launched at low-level, followed by a zoom-climb to high altitude, at which point the

Two BAe ALARM missile drill rounds, seen here fitted under the fuselage of a Tornado GR.1 of No 9 Squadron.

This ASRAAM air-to-air missile drill round has been fitted to the outer pylon of a Harrier GR.7 of the SAOEU. (BAe Dynamics)

missile deploys a parachute. ALARM can then loiter for several minutes as it drifts down, seeking out hostile radar transmissions that may be intermittent. Once a suitable radar emission has been located, the missile's sensors lock-on to it, and the parachute is jettisoned. The missile then descends with increasing speed towards the target. In all modes, the carrier aircraft can turn away safely after launching. Alternatively, these missiles can be fired in salvos against multiple targets in a known area.

Development work was still being carried out on ALARM in 1990 when the crisis in the Gulf area broke out. The missile was rushed into service with the RAF, and more than 100 examples were fired during the conflict by Tornados. Further quantities of this missile were ordered for the RAF in 1992.

British Aerospace ASRAAM

Powerplant Rocket motor; **Length** 9 ft 6 in (2.9 m); **Body diameter** 6.5 in (166 mm); **Weight** 192 lb (87 kg).

ASRAAM stands for Advanced Short-Range Air-to-Air Missile, and it is under development by BAe Dynamics Division, following an order from the British Government in early 1992. It is intended as a replacement for the AIM-9L Sidewinder AAM and is due to enter service in the late 1990s, equipping Harrier GR.7s, amongst other types.

The missile's target seeker will be an imaging infra-red unit, currently being developed by the Hughes Company in the USA, while the rocket motor will be produced by the Royal Ordnance Division of BAe. Other sections of this weapon, such as the warhead, are being supplied by

Messerschmitt-Bolkow-Blohm in Germany. Designed as a 'fire and forget' weapon, ASRAAM is intended to be fired at targets at right angles to the line of launch, and against sophisticated ECM.

AIM-9L Sidewinder

Length 9 ft 6 in (2.87 m); **Body diameter** 5 in (127 mm); **Weight** 191 lb (86.6 kg); **Weight of warhead** 20.8 lb (9.4 kg); **Range** 10 miles (16 km); **Speed** Mach 2+.

The origins of the Sidewinder AAM go back to the 1950s, and it was developed at the US Naval Weapons Centre in California. Several tens of thousands have been produced by a number of civilian contractors, including Ford and Raytheon in the USA, and Bodenseewerk Geratetechnik GmbH in Germany, which is the prime contractor to meet the requirements of European air arms. Numerous variants and model updates have been produced over the years, and the version currently in front-line service with the RAF carries the US designation of AIM-9L.

The Sidewinder is designed for close range air-to-air combat, with an infra-red heat-seeking target detection, guidance and proximity fuse system. Flight path corrections are accomplished by the use of double-delta-shaped fins fitted behind the missile head. The Sidewinder is fitted principally to the Tornado F.3 and Hawk T.1A for use in the air defence role, but it can also be carried for self-defence purposes by the Harrier GR.7, Jaguar GR.1A, Tornado GR.1, and Nimrod MR.2P.

For training purposes, many of these aircraft types can be seen carrying Sidewinder acquisition rounds. These comprise the body of the missile

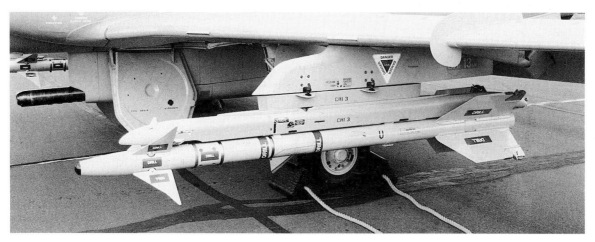

Many thousands of Sidewinder AAMs have been produced. The AIM-9L version, seen here in drill round form, can be fitted to a number of front-line RAF aircraft. It is shown here fitted to a Hawk T.1A, for local air defence.

with full sensor equipment, but lack the fins, warhead and rocket motor. These training rounds can simulate the signals that the pilot would receive from an actual missile during the target search, lock-on, and attack phases.

British Aerospace Sky Flash

Powerplant Rocket motor; **Length** 12 ft 2 in (3.7 m); **Body diameter** 8 in (0.2 m); **Weight** 425 lb (192.8 kg); **Range** 31 miles (50 km); **Speed** Mach 4.

The BAe Sky Flash, a radar-guided medium-range AAM, is now the principal air defence weapon employed by the RAF, and is a development of the earlier American AIM-7 Sparrow AAM. Amongst a number of improvements, Sky Flash has a greater range and a more advanced monopulse semi-active homing system. The fusing system was also enhanced and the missile is capable of operating in various situations at both high and low altitude in the face of adverse ECM. The missile can be fired from the carrier aircraft at supersonic speeds, with a warm-up time of just a few seconds.

McDonnell Douglas AGM-84 Harpoon

Powerplant One Teledyne Continental J402 turbojet, rated at 680 lb (3.02 kN) thrust; **Length** 12 ft 7 in (3.84 m); **Body diameter** 1 ft 1.5 in (0.34 m); **Weight** 1,160 lb (526.2 kg); **Weight of warhead** 488 lb (221.4 kg); **Range** 120 miles (193 km); **Speed** 645 mph (1,038 km/h).

The Harpoon was first developed in the USA in the late 1960s, and is an air-launched, all-weather, long-range cruise missile for use against surface vessels. Power comes from a small turbojet, which although providing less thrust than a rocket motor, gives the Harpoon a far longer range. Cruise guidance to the target area is controlled by an inertial system combined with a radio altimeter, with the target being acquired by the on-board active radar system for the terminal attack phase. Devices are fitted to provide resistance against ECM.

British Aerospace Sea Eagle

Powerplant One Microturbo TRI-60 turbojet, rated at 787 lb (3.50 kN) thrust; **Length** 13 ft 7 in (4.1 m); **Body diameter** 1 ft 4 in (0.4 m); **Weight** 1,325 lb (601 kg); **Weight of warhead** 507 lb (230 kg); **Range** 80 miles (130 km); **Speed** 685 mph (1,102 km/h).

First entering service during the early 1980s, the Sea Eagle is a long-range anti-ship missile based on the Anglo-French Martel system. The missile is guided to the target area by an inertial system pre-programmed with the necessary data prior to launch. It then flies at very low level to avoid detection, aided by a built-in radio-altimeter. The final phase of the flight is guided by a built-in active radar-homing device, to ensure an accurate final impact by the heavy warhead. Sea Eagle has been designed with the capability to analyze and discriminate between a number of targets in the same area, and to continue its attack path through sophisticated ECM and decoy systems.

OTHER WEAPONS

WE177

This is the designation given to the UK's free-fall nuclear bomb, for possible use in the sub-strategic strike role. There have been proposals to replace the WE177 with an air-launched nuclear weapon with a stand-off capability, but monetary constraints and the fundamental changes in the international situation have resulted in the decision not to fund a replacement.

Hunting JP233

Container length 21 ft 6 in (6.55 m); **Weight (complete system)** 5,148 lb (2,335 kg); **Weight (SG357)** 57.3 lb (26 kg); **Weight (HB876)** 5.5 lb (2.5 kg).

The JP233 Low-Level Airfield Attack System was developed in the UK in the early 1980s, with Hunting Engineering as the prime contractor, assisted by several other companies. It was conceived as an airfield attack weapon, incorporating features designed to destroy runways and other areas, and measures to delay repairs to the damage thus caused. This large weapon pod is carried by the Tornado GR.1, two of the containers being fitted side-by-side on the outer stores positions under the fuselage. The JP233, as used by the RAF, consists of a container in two sections, each of which accommodates several smaller weapons which can be delivered simultaneously for airfield or area attack.

One of the weapons is the SG357 cratering bomb, designed to inflict serious damage to runways and other aircraft operating areas. Following ejection from the rear section of the carrying pod, the SG357 is stabilized by fins at the rear of the weapon, and its fall is retarded by a small parachute. Upon impact, the primary shaped warhead charge penetrates the surface being attacked, thus allowing the secondary charge to detonate below the surface. This creates not only a crater, but distortion in the surrounding area, particularly on concrete slabs.

In order to hamper the repair of damage caused by the SG357, the JP233 system also deploys the HB876 area-denial mine, which presents a hazard to equipment and personnel deployed on restoration work. These mines are carried in the front section of the carrying pod, and once ejected, the HB876 is retarded and stabilized to its correct descending attitude by the use of a small parachute, which is jettisoned on impact. The mine is then turned into an upright position by means of spring-steel legs, which places the warhead charge uppermost. Various fuses can be used to detonate on contact or at random time delays. Once the main pod has dispensed its contents of small bombs and mines, it is then also jettisoned.

Although designed for attack against airfields, the JP233 weapons can also be used against other area targets, such as transportation junctions. The JP233 system was used extensively by the RAF on attacks against Iraqi airfields in the early stages of the Gulf War in 1991. It can be fitted on underwing pylons, but only in smaller pods that contain either the SG357 bomb or the HB876 mine.

The JP233 area denial weapon consists of two types of bomb, carried in these large, two-section pods. Two of these pods are shown here in drill round form, fitted beneath a No 9 Squadron Tornado GR.1.

Hunting BL755

Length 8 ft 0.5 in (2.451 m); **Body diameter** 1 ft 4.5 in (419 mm); **Weight** 582 lb (264 kg).

This cluster bomb was conceived to counter large concentrations of armoured or other vehicles, by saturating the target area with a shower of small bomblets ejected from the carrying pod. It can be deployed at low-level and high speed, and several can be carried on types such as the Tornado GR.1, Harrier GR.7 and Jaguar GR.1A.

Once the bomb-shaped pod is released from the carrying aircraft, its primary striker is activated by the nose-mounted 'windmill'. This striker in turn fires the primary cartridge after a preselected time interval, and the internal gas pressure thus produced ejects the outer skins of the bomb body. The main gas cartridge then ejects the bombload of 147 bomblets, which are arranged in seven bays, each containing 21 weapons, this ejection sequence being designed to evenly spread the bomblets over the target area. As it falls, each bomblet is retarded by a small parachute; earlier versions employed a spread of steel strips to stabilize its fall. The bomblet is armed as it falls, and detonates on impact, with its shaped warhead having the ability to penetrate armour plate up to 10 in (254 mm) thick.

CBU-87 (CEM)

This cluster bomb is similar in concept and operation to the BL755, described above. It is built in the USA, and was obtained for use in the Gulf War, during which it was deployed for strikes by the Jaguar force. CEM stands for 'combined effects munitions', with the bomblets being effective against vehicles and personnel.

Texas Instruments Paveway II

This laser-guided weapon consists of a 1,000 lb (454 kg) general-purpose bomb, fitted with the US-designed CPU-123/B Paveway II laser marked-target seeker and guidance system on the nose, and a folding-wing assembly on the tail. The nose unit consists of a sensor to detect the target that has been marked by the laser, and a processor that transmits guidance signals to the small fins on the nose unit.

The Paveway II was used extensively by the RAF in the 1991 Gulf War, in conjunction with Buccaneer S.2Bs carrying the Pave Spike laser target designator pod, and Tornado GR.1s fitted with the TIALD pod.

Bristol Aerospace CRV-7

Length (excluding warhead) 3 ft 5 in (1.04 m); **Body diameter** 2.75 in (70 mm); **Speed (approx)** 3,000 mph (4,830 km/h); **Range (approx)** 7,000 yds (6,400 m).

Produced in Canada, this unguided air-to-surface rocket was introduced into RAF service during the Gulf War, where it was fitted to LAU-5003 pods, each containing 19 rounds, and carried by Jaguars. It can be fitted with a variety of warheads.

Thomson Brandt/SNEB

Body diameter 2.68 in (68 mm).

This unguided rocket has been in service for several years, and continues to be used, mainly by the Harrier-equipped squadrons. It is fitted into the Matra pod, which can carry up to 18 rounds. From this pod the rockets can be fired as single rounds, in a ripple effect, or all 18 can be fired together in a complete salvo.

Marconi Stingray

Stingray is an advanced lightweight anti-submarine torpedo intended for use from aircraft, helicopters and surface vessels. It has been designed to counter the projected submarine threat until well past the year 2000. It first entered service with the RAF in 1983, and is also deployed by the Royal Navy and overseas air arms.

Carrier Bomb, Light Stores (CBLS)

Various forms of this pod-like carrier are used by such aircraft types as the Tornado, Harrier, Jaguar and Hawk for the carriage of practice bombs employed on training sorties. Two main types of practice bomb are used for training by the RAF, with the smaller 7 lb (3 kg) device being used to simulate a 1,000 lb (454 kg) retarded bomb, whilst the 30 lb (14 kg) practice bomb represents a 'slick' bomb also of 1,000 lb (454 kg). Up to four of each type of practice bomb can be carried in a single CBLS, although these are not usually of mixed weights.

AIRBORNE ORDNANCE

Mauser BK27

Calibre 1.063 in (27 mm); **Overall length** 7 ft 6.5 in (2.3 m); **Weight** 220.5 lb (100 kg); **Rate of fire** 1,000 or 1,700 rounds/min.

Development of this weapon commenced in the mid-1970s, as a new generation of cannon to be fitted in the Tornado. The specification called for a high muzzle velocity, together with demanding criteria for accuracy, reliability and performance with a wide range of ammunition. Fuses were required to be effective at various angles of impact.

There are several types of ammunition that can be used with the BK27. For air-to-ground strafing, three types of round can be used: armour-piercing, armour-piercing high explosive, and a version of this second type with built-in self-destruct. Air combat requirements are met by two types of ammunition: high explosive and high explosive self-destruct. Ammunition used for training falls into three categories: target practice, target practice with a break-up capability, and inert drill rounds, the last being utilized for ground training.

Aden 30 mm

Calibre 1.18 in (30 mm); **Overall length** 5 ft 3 in (1.59 m); **Total weight** 192 lb (87 kg); **Rate of fire** 1,200 or 1,400 rounds/min.

Developed by the Royal Small Arms Factory in the late 1940s, the origins of this cannon go back even further, as it was based on the German Mauser MK213 cannon of the Second World War.

The 30 mm Aden can be used for both air combat and ground attack. It is gas-operated, with a revolver feed system, although some applications of this weapon employ pneumatic cocking and electrical firing. The revolver has five chambers. Three main types of ammunition can be used: high explosive, armour-piercing, and practice. In RAF service this gun is fitted to the Jaguar, and can be carried by the Hawk in an underfuselage pod.

Aden 25 mm

Calibre 0.98 in (25 mm); **Overall length** 7 ft 6 in (2.29 m); **Weight (twin pods)** 948 lb (430 kg); **Rate of fire** 1,650 to 1,850 rounds/min.

The Aden 25 mm cannon was developed for use by the second generation of Harrier aircraft for the RAF. The design consists of two assemblies, one being the barrel section with a blast suppressor, the other comprising the revolver-type gun, with the whole contained in a cradle unit. The weapon employs pneumatic cocking and the belt-fed ammunition, with disintegrating links, is fired by percussion.

The well-proven principles used in the 30 mm Aden cannon have been continued in the 25 mm

The Hawk carries the Aden 30 mm cannon in this pod fitted under the fuselage centreline.

model. The revolver is gas-operated, which in turn delivers energy for feeding and firing the next round, together with ejecting the belt link and the spent case. The gun was designed to use NATO-standard 25 mm ammunition. The Harrier GR.7 is designed to carry two pods under the fuselage, with a total ammunition capacity of 200 rounds.

OTHER EXTERNAL STORES

Thermal Imaging Airborne Laser Designator (TIALD)

For more than 20 years, studies have been carried out to gather information on the effective combination of electro-optical sensors. This includes the use of television, low-light TV, thermal imagers, laser rangefinders and designators and marked target seekers, and is part of the continuing programme to improve the effectiveness of so-called 'smart' bombs and weapons, with the aim of accurately hitting and destroying targets using the least possible number of weapons launched. 'Smart' bombs can be released outside the range of defensive weapons systems, thus reducing the risks to the attacking aircraft.

The basic principle involves the target being illuminated (or designated) with the narrow beam of a laser. This laser can be aimed from the attacking aircraft, a supporting aircraft, or supporting ground forces. These designating systems are used in conjunction with weapons such as the Paveway II laser-guided bomb.

Following various early trials, the MoD issued a requirement in the mid-1980s for a laser targeting pod to be fitted to the Tornado GR.1 aircraft of the RAF. This led to an order being placed in 1988 with GEC-Ferranti for the production of Thermal Imaging Airborne Laser Designator (TIALD) pods.

TIALD is a lightweight pod that contains electro-optical equipment for the guidance of laser-guided weapons onto their targets at all times of day and night. The principal sensor is Thermal Imaging (TI), which provides an infra-red image of the target, and this is complemented by a TV sensor. The choice of which sensor to use can be made from the cockpit of the carrying aircraft during the approach to the target, depending on the conditions at the time. Images of the target scene can be displayed in real time, or simultaneously recorded. The TI telescope has two settings: a wide field-of-view which would be employed to acquire the target, or a narrow field-of-view which would be used for target recognition. The TV sensor has a narrow lens, aligned to the TI.

The Thermal Imaging Airborne Laser Designator – TIALD – has seen operational use in Iraq, fitted to the Tornado GR.1. (GEC-Ferranti)

The sensors on the TIALD pod are capable of being connected to the carrying aircraft's navigational computer, to assist in target acquisition, and this information can be updated manually. The target, once acquired, can be tracked automatically, and the image is presented with the horizon in a level attitude. The TIALD pod can also be used for reconnaissance, with images being obtained from both sensors at various operating levels.

The TIALD system is of a modular design, being composed of a number of line-replaceable units, any of which can be replaced whilst the pod is attached to the carrying aircraft. The system has been designed to be compatible with existing cockpit controls and displays.

At the time of the Iraqi invasion of Kuwait in August 1990, the development programme of the TIALD system was proceeding satisfactorily, but it was not due to enter service for some months. In late 1990 contracts were awarded to accelerate development and production of the pod, with the aim of providing the RAF with an operational laser target designator system. This was to be capable of use by day and night should the Gulf crisis develop into full-scale war.

Several organizations participated in the TIALD Accelerated Programme, including GEC-Ferranti, the Royal Aircraft Establishment at Farnborough, and the Central Trials and Tactics Organization (part of Strike Command) at the Aeroplane and Armament Experimental Establishment at Boscombe Down. The RAF provided a number of Tornado GR.1s and crews to assist in the programme. A major task to be undertaken was the rewriting of the software in the Tornado's on-board computer. The first TIALD pods were deployed to the Gulf region in early February 1991, exactly 50 days after the accelerated development programme commenced.

The TIALD-equipped Tornados were deployed to Tabuk, in western Saudi Arabia, and following a few days of in-theatre training, the system was declared operational on 9 February 1991, with the first mission being flown against an Iraqi Air Force base the following day. Thereafter, only LGBs were released on raids undertaken by the RAF Tornados from Tabuk. Two TIALD pods were used in the Gulf War, flown on five Tornado GR.1s that had been modified for their use. These pods were development models, and as they lacked the TV sensors, only the TI sensors were used on the raids against Iraq.

In August 1992, the RAF once again deployed Tornado GR.1s to the Gulf area, under Operation 'Jural', to enforce the no-fly sanctions against Iraq in the area to the south of the 32nd Parallel. The TIALD pod system was also deployed, but these carried the full dual-sensor capability, which was fully utilized when the RAF again mounted raids against targets within Iraq in mid-January 1993, almost exactly two years after the main Gulf War.

Development of the TIALD system is continuing, with such refinements as an electronic zoom

The large Westinghouse AN/ALQ-101 ECM pod, fitted here to a Jaguar GR.1A of No 6 Squadron, has seen service for several years.

A Tornado GR.1 of No 14 Squadron with a Bofors BOZ-107 chaff and flare dispensing pod fitted to the starboard outer underwing pylon.

facility on the sensor lenses, combining the sensor images and data-linking of information being examined whilst airborne.

Philips/Matra PHIMAT

Length 11 ft 10 in (3.6 m); **Body diameter** 7.09 in (180 mm); **Weight** 231.5 lb (105 kg).

This slender pod, of French origin, is a chaff dispenser, carried by such aircraft as the Jaguar and the Harrier. Chaff consists of fine strips of foil which are deployed to confuse hostile radars, in a similar fashion to the 'Window' used in the Second World War.

Westinghouse AN/ALQ-101

Length 12 ft 10 in (3.9 m).

Manufactured in the USA, this large ECM pod has been in service for many years, and is usually carried on the port outer underwing pylon on the Jaguar. Its main function is the deception and jamming of hostile electronic emissions and communications.

Marconi Skyshadow

This ECM pod is primarily used by the Tornado GR.1/.1A force, and is carried on the port outer underwing pylon. It is an active and passive EW device, with capabilities to receive, transmit and process information. It is designed to counter multiple EW threats and can deceive or jam surveillance, missile system or airborne radars.

Bofors BOZ-107

Length 13 ft 2 in (4.0 m); **Body diameter** 1 ft 3 in (380 mm); **Weight** 716 lb (325 kg).

Forming part of the carrying aircraft's defensive suite, the BOZ-107 chaff dispenser pod is usually to be found fitted on the starboard outer underwing pylon of the Tornado GR.1/.1A, but can also be seen mounted on the underwing pylons of the Nimrod MR.2P. Developed in Sweden, this large pod is capable of dispensing chaff to confuse hostile radar transmissions, and can also deploy flares to counter and decoy infra-red seekers on missiles fired at the carrying aircraft. Its advanced systems are microprocessor-controlled, and it has an internal memory which is reprogrammable.

CHAPTER TEN

Specialist Vehicles
of the RAF

AS MAY BE expected, an organization such as the RAF, with its wide range of activities and tasks, needs to utilize many types of vehicles to support and assist in these operations. These vehicles can, in broad terms, be divided into two classes. One of these covers general-purpose vehicles that are used both on and off RAF stations for the carriage of personnel, spares, tools, freight and equipment. These vehicles include various makes and models of small, medium and large cars, vans, trucks, lorries, buses and coach-

es. Most of these are commercially produced vehicles, purchased in batches under competitive tender from a wide range of suppliers, both in the UK and, increasingly, from throughout the European Community.

The other main class of vehicles used by the RAF are specialist items primarily for support of aircraft and their operational roles and tasks. Some of these vehicles are specifically built for the RAF, whilst others are essentially commercial products modified or adapted for their required

Truck, Airfield Crash Rescue (TACR), Mks 2/2A

Truck, Fire-Fighting, Mk 9

task. These specialist vehicles can cover such requirements as fire/crash/rescue, aircraft fuellers, aircraft tugs, cranes, aircraft de-icers and cargo loaders, and a representative selection are illustrated and described in this chapter. There are many variations in these models and classes of special-purpose vehicles, along with other similar types that are not included, so this chapter should not be regarded as a complete guide to such vehicles currently operated by the RAF.

Truck, Airfield Crash Rescue (TACR), Mks 2/2A

Length 17 ft 3 in (5.25 m); **Width** 5 ft 10 in (1.78 m); **Height (overall)** 7 ft 7 in (2.32 m); **Weight (laden)** 9,009 lb (4,090 kg); **Weight (unladen)** 3,745 lb (1,700 kg); **Chassis** Extended Range Rover; **Bodywork** Carmichael; **Engine** Rover V8, 3,528 cc, petrol, 127 bhp.

Known in the Fire Service as the TACR 2, this is a rapid intervention vehicle for use in aircraft crash rescue and fire-fighting. It carries 200 gal (909 l) of water, and a crew of up to four. It has a limited off-road capability, and is used at most RAF flying stations, with over 100 currently in service.

Truck, Fire-Fighting, Mk 9

Length 28 ft 7 in (8.73 m); **Width** 8 ft 2 in (2.48 m); **Height** 11 ft 4 in (3.45 m); **Chassis** Thorneycroft 6x6; **Bodywork** Dennis.

Approximately 90 of these general-purpose fire/crash/rescue vehicles are in service with the RAF, and they can be seen at most flying stations. Each can carry some 1,200 gal (5,455 l) of water, together with foam. This robust design dates from the early 1970s, and is thus nearing the end of its useful life.

Truck, Fire-Fighting, Mk 10 Series

Length 27 ft 10 in (8.48 m); **Width** 8 ft 4 in (2.54 m); **Height** 10 ft 8 in (3.24 m); **Weight** 35,650 lb (16,185 kg); **Chassis** Scammell Nubian 4x4; **Engine (at rear)** Cummins V903 diesel, 300 hp.

This is a primary dual-purpose airfield foam tender, the cab of which can accommodate four, including the driver who is seated centrally. This vehicle's internal tanks have the capacity to carry 600 gal (2,730 l) of water and 80 gal (363 l) of foam. The contents of these tanks can be com-

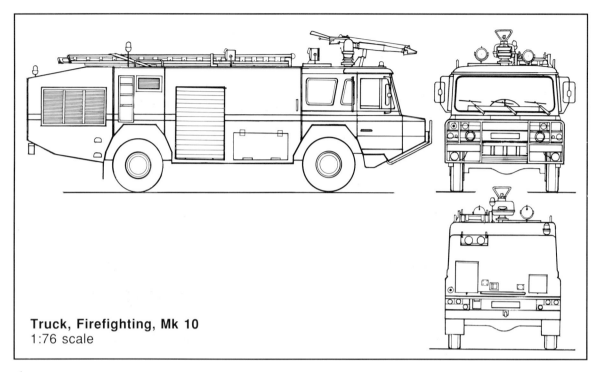

Truck, Firefighting, Mk 10
1:76 scale

bined and discharged under pressure from one of four delivery points, these being: roof-mounted monitor, two sidelines and a First Aid Hosereel. Water from an external source can also be delivered through any of these delivery points. Some 35 are in service with the RAF.

Truck, Fire-Fighting, Mk 11

Length 34 ft 7 in (10.56 m); **Width** 8 ft 2 in (2.50 m); **Height:** 10 ft 9 in (3.28 m); **Weight (laden)** 62,709 lb (28,470 kg); **Chassis** Scammell Nubian 6x6; **Bodywork** Gloster-Saro; **Engine (at rear)** Cummins V8, turbocharged, 500 bhp.

A special-purpose high-performance military design, primarily used for aircraft crash rescue and firefighting, with appropriate equipment. It also has a secondary role of firefighting and rescue throughout RAF stations. The front end is designed to smash through airfield perimeter crash-gates, and the vehicle has on off-road capability. It can carry 1,250 gal (5,683 l) of water and 150 gal (682 l) of foam, plus a crew of four, fully-equipped with breathing apparatus. The Mk 11A variant is capable of high access reach in connection with TriStar operations. Some 16 Mk 11/11As are deployed to main transport bases, such as Lyneham, Brize Norton, Ascension, Mount Pleasant, etc.

Truck, Fire-Fighting, Mk 11

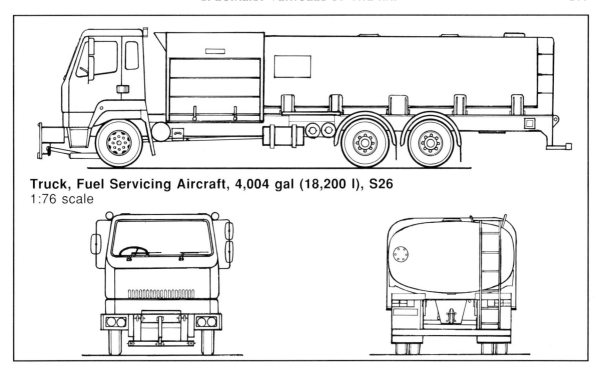

Truck, Fuel Servicing Aircraft, 4,004 gal (18,200 l), S26
1:76 scale

Truck, Fuel Servicing Aircraft, 4,004 gal (18,200 l), S26

Length 36 ft 0 in (10.97 m); **Width** 8 ft 2 in (2.50 m); **Height** 10 ft 4 in (3.15 m), with booms; **Weight (laden)** 62,907 lb (28,560 kg); **Weight (unladen)** 29,185 lb (13,250 kg); **Chassis** Leyland-Daf S26; **Bodywork** NEI-Thompson; **Engine** Rolls-Royce Eagle, six-cylinder, 12.17 l diesel.

This vehicle is one of the latest in a range of sim-ilarly configured fuel tankers that have been delivered in recent years. They are located at all major RAF stations for pressure refuelling and defuelling of all types of aviation fuel to and from aircraft. In addition to pressure delivery (the more usual method), some of these vehicles are fitted with open lines (supported by booms) and hand-held nozzles. It has a tanker capacity of 4,004 gal (18,200 l), and can tow (and act as a pump for) a trailer which is capable of carrying 4,399 gal (20,000 l) of fuel. The use of trailers is usually to be found at airfields that regularly operate large

Truck, Fuel Servicing Aircraft, 4,004 gal (18,200 l), S26

Truck, Fuel Servicing Aircraft, 3,000 gal (13,638 l), Bison

aircraft types. Blades can be fitted to the front bracket for snow-clearing operations.

It can also act as a snowplough with a blade fitted to the front.

Truck, Fuel Servicing Aircraft, 3,000 gal (13,638 l), Bison

Length 33 ft 3 in (10.13 m); **Width** 8 ft 2 in (2.48 m); **Height** 9 ft 1 in (2.78 m); **Weight (unladen)** 27,379 lb (12,430 kg); **Chassis** Leyland Bison; **Bodywork** Gloster-Saro; **Engine** Leyland, six-cylinder, 8.2 l.

This large aircraft refuelling/defuelling tanker has been in service for several years, with about 100 examples deployed at major airfields. Its fuel capacity is 3,000 gal (13,638 l), and it can tow a trailer with a further 4,500 gal (20,457 l) of fuel.

Truck, Fuel Servicing Aircraft, 1,000 gal (4,546 l), Bedford

Length 22 ft 0 in (6.70 m); **Width** 7 ft 6 in (2.29 m); **Height** 9 ft 1 in (2.78 m); **Weight (laden)** 20,812 lb (9,449 kg); **Weight (unladen)** 12,504 lb (5,677 kg); **Chassis** Bedford 4x2; **Bodywork** Zwicky; **Engine** Bedford, six-cylinder, 5.4 l.

Used mainly at training bases with smaller aircraft, such as the Tucano, this tanker can fuel or defuel all types of aviation fuel via pressure transfer, or through open lines supported by the

Truck, Fuel Servicing Aircraft, 1,000 gal (4,546 l), Bedford

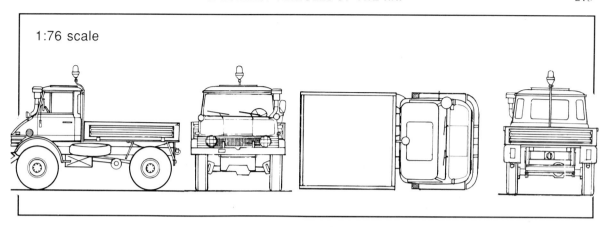

1:76 scale

Tractor, Wheeled Industrial Winterized Aircraft, Support

swivelling booms. It has a capacity of 1,000 gal (4,546 l).

Tractor, Wheeled Industrial Winterized Aircraft, Support

Length 13 ft 5 in (4.10 m); **Width** 6 ft 7 in (2.00 m); **Height** 7 ft 9 in (2.36 m); **Weight (laden)** 15,419 lb (7,000 kg); **Weight (unladen)** 7,709 lb (3,500 kg); **Chassis** Unimog; **Bodywork** Unimog; **Engine** Mercedes, four-cylinder, 3,780 cc.

Mainly used in support of tactical aircraft, such as the Harrier or Jaguar, this tug can move both air-craft and other associated items. The version depicted is 'winterized', with window blinds and engine heaters. Over 60 'non-winterized' exam-ples are also used, mainly in Germany.

Tractor, Wheeled Industrial Aircraft Towing Light, Massey

Length 12 ft 4 in (3.76 m); **Width** 8 ft 0 in (2.44 m); **Height** 8 ft 0 in (2.44 m); **Weight** 7,907 lb (3,590 kg); **Chassis** Massey Ferguson; **Bodywork** Massey Ferguson; **Engine** Perkins, six-cylinder, 8.2 l diesel, 47 bhp at 2,250 rpm.

This is the standard light tractor for towing small-er aircraft, and most of the 75 examples in service are to be found at stations with training aircraft and helicopters. It can move aircraft weighing up to 65,000 lb (29,510 kg) and is based on the stan-dard MF agricultural tractor, but with the addition

Tractor, Wheeled Industrial Aircraft Towing Light, Massey

*Tractor, Wheeled Aircraft Towing Heavy,
Cummins*

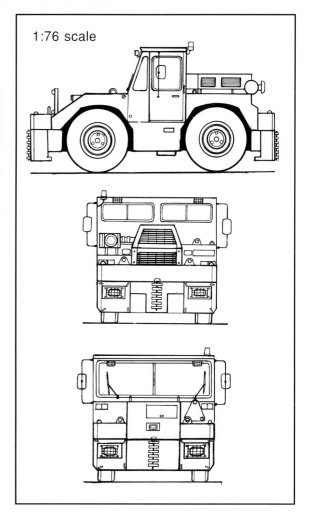

1:76 scale

of a 4/5 person cab, plus aircraft towing points
front and rear.

Tractor, Wheeled Aircraft Towing Heavy, Cummins

Length 16 ft 7 in (5.05 m); **Width** 8 ft 2 in
(2.50 m); **Height** 8 ft 4 in (2.55 m); **Weight
(with ballast)** 68,282 lb (31,000 kg); **Weight
(without ballast)** 25,608 lb (11,626 kg);
Chassis Douglas Tugmaster; **Bodywork** ML
Douglas; **Engine** Cummins 5.9 l, 177 bhp.

These recently delivered aircraft tugs have a two-
or four-wheel steering capability. The ballast can
be removed in order that the tug may be transported by air.

Tractor, Wheeled Aircraft-Towing Heavy, Reliance Mercury

Length 30 ft 2 in (9.20 m); **Width** 8 ft 9 in
(2.67 m); **Height** 5 ft 2 in (1.58 m); **Weight**
79,053 lb (35,890 kg); **Chassis** Reliance
Mercury; **Engine** Cummins V8 diesel, 14.8 l,
265 bhp.

The low profile of this aircraft tug enables it go
under the nose of very large aircraft such as the
TriStar. The engine is centrally mounted, and the
driver can manoeuvre the vehicle while seated, or
standing through a hatch in the roof of the cab.
There is a further standing position for driving at
the rear.

Tractor, Wheeled Aircraft Towing Heavy, Reliance Mercury

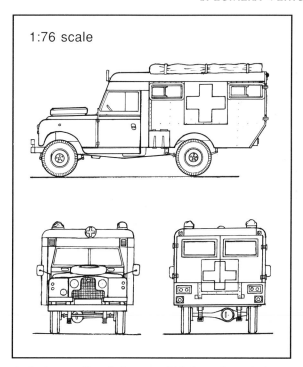

1:76 scale

Ambulance, Crash Rescue, 2/4 Stretcher, 4x4, Land Rover

Primarily used for the rescue of air crash victims, with an off-road capability.

Snow Removal Unit, 4x4, Rolba

Length 18 ft 0 in (5.49 m); **Width** 6 ft 2 in (1.88 m); **Height** 9 ft 3 in (2.82 m); **Weight** 11,101 lb (5,040 kg); **Chassis** Rolba (Switzerland); **Bodywork** Rolba; **Engine** Deutz air-cooled diesel, developing 101 bhp at 2,500 rpm.

This device comes into its own when snow has accumulated to a depth beyond the capabilities of snowploughs. The rotating blades at the front feed the snow to the rotors that then throw it sideways. It is used mainly to clear aircraft operating areas, and the 34 in service are positioned at airfields that operate continuously, or are at risk from heavy snowfalls due to their location.

Ambulance, Crash Rescue, 2/4 Stretcher, 4x4, Land Rover

Length 15 ft 9 in (4.74 m); **Width** 6 ft 4 in (1.88 m); **Height** 7 ft 6 in (1.99 m); **Weight** 4,559 lb (2,070 kg); **Chassis** Land Rover; **Engine** four-cylinder, 2,500 cc diesel.

Sweeper, Rotary Self-Propelled, 4x2, Lacre Bedford

Length 23 ft 5 in (7.15 m); **Width** 8 ft 2 in (2.50 m); **Height** 10 ft 6 in (3.20 m); **Weight** 18,788 lb (8,530 kg); **Chassis** Bedford; **Bodywork** Lacre; **Engine** Perkins, 6,354 cc.

The prime purpose of this sweeper is to ensure that all aircraft operating areas are kept free of any loose debris or small objects. Foreign Object Damage (FOD) is a serious hazard to jet engines, and dangerous repercussions are possible if items are ingested into the air intakes of aircraft power-plants. At worst, FOD can cause extensive damage leading to costly repairs. These vehicles are

Snow Removal Unit, 4x4, Rolba

Sweeper, Rotary Self-Propelled, 4x2, Lacre Bedford

also fitted with magnets to pick up ferrous metal objects that may have fallen off other equipment, vehicles or machinery. The 26 examples of this sweeper are deployed at most RAF flying stations.

Crane, Truck-Mounted, 5- to 10-ton, Fully-Slewing, 4x4, Smiths

Length (jib stowed) 28 ft 8 in (8.74 m); **Width** 8 ft 2 in (2.50 m); **Height (jib stowed)** 11 ft 1 in (3.38 m); **Weight (complete)** 43,987 lb (19,970 kg); **Chassis** Smiths; **Bodywork** Smiths; **Engine** Perkins, six-cylinder, 167 bhp at 2,800 rpm; **Lifting capacity (on wheels)** 6.6 tons (6,706 kg) at 10 ft (3.05 m) radius, 1.1 tons (1,118 kg) at 30 ft (9.15 m) radius; **Lifting capacity (on jacks, on level ground)** 10.3 tons (10,465 kg) at 10 ft (3.05 m) radius, 1.8 tons (1,829 kg) at 30 ft (9.15 m) radius.

A general-purpose crane used for the lifting of engines, aircraft components, and other equipment. It can be used on both prepared or unprepared surfaces, and about 50 are in service.

Crane, Wheel-Mounted, 7-tonne, Fully-Slewing, Coles

Length (jib stowed) 21 ft 6 in (6.55 m); **Width** 8 ft 0 in (2.44 m); **Height** 9 ft 3 in (2.82 m); **Weight** 29,934 lb (13,590 kg); **Chassis** Coles Crane; **Bodywork** Coles Crane; **Engine** Perkins, six-cylinder, 6.35 l diesel; **Lifting capacity** 8 tons (8,130 kg) at 8 ft (2.45 m) radius, 1.6 tons (1,620 kg) at 22 ft (6.71 m) radius.

A general-purpose crane for use on prepared and unprepared surfaces, with 14 in service at various RAF stations.

Aircraft De-icing Equipment, Truck-Mounted, 10-tonne, 4x2, Bedford

Length 27 ft 10 in (8.50 m); **Width** 7 ft 10 in (2.40 m); **Height (boom stowed)** 11 ft 10 in (3.60 m); **Weight (unladen)** 35,815 lb (16,260 kg); **Chassis** Bedford TL; **Engine** Bedford, 8.2 l.

Crane, Truck-Mounted, 5- to 10-ton, Fully-Slewing, 4x4, Smiths

Crane, Wheel-Mounted, 7-tonne, Fully-Slewing, Coles

Aircraft De-icing Equipment, Truck-Mounted, 10-tonne, 4x2, Bedford

Truck, Cargo, Aircraft Loading, 4x4, Atlas

All large RAF aircraft are parked outside (except when under maintenance or overhaul) in all weathers, and thus the formation of frost and ice on flying surfaces can present a serious hazard to flying operations. This vehicle is used for aircraft de-icing, which is carried out just before the aircraft is required. It can carry 1,250 gal (5,682 l) of water/glycol de-icing fluid, and the boom can elevate to 45 ft (13.7 m). The fluid can be sprayed in hot (the usual method) or cold forms.

Truck, Cargo, Aircraft Loading, 4x4, Atlas

Length 26 ft 3 in (8.00 m); **Width (cab extended)** 12 ft 6 in (3.80 m); **Height (elevated)** 16 ft (4.88 m); **Chassis** Aircraft Maintenance Support Services; **Bodywork** Aircraft Maintenance Support Services; **Engine** Cummins diesel.

This aircraft loader is one-person operated and self-propelled. The cab can be extended out to provide a clear loading area, or can be slid inwards for transporting. The loader is air-transportable within a Hercules, and is designed for tactical deployment to airheads. It is capable of loading aircraft up to TriStar deck level, and has a powered pallet conveyer system. The deck of the loader can be adjusted both sideways and fore and aft to cater for any variations between the levels of the aircraft's cargo deck and the adjacent ground surface. Loaders of this type are still being delivered to the RAF.

Index

AAFCE (Allied Air Forces Central Europe) 24
AAITC (Airman Aircrew Initial Training Course) 75-6
Aeroplane & Armament Evaluation Establishment 134, 171, 183, 188, 193, 206
ACCGS (Air Cadet Central Gliding School) 130
ACCHAN (Allied Command Channel) 9
ACE (Allied Command Europe) 9
ACMI (Air Combat Manoeuvring Instrumentation) 25
Aden cannon (25mm, 30mm) 144, 150, 180, 204-5
ADOC (Air Defence Operations Centre) 30
AEELS (Air Electronics, Engineer and Loadmaster School) 75-8
AFNORTH (Allied Forces Northern Europe) 9, 24
AFNORTHWEST (Allied Forces Northwest Europe) 9
Airborne Brigade 20, 47, 49
Air Cadets 128-32
AIRCENT (Allied Air Forces Central Europe) 24
Airmobile Brigade 20
AIRNORTHWEST (Allied Air Forces Northwest Europe) 9
Air Support Command 9
Air-to-Air Refuelling 44-7, 49, 51, 54
Air Traffic Control 58, 83
Air Training Corps, see Air Cadets
ALARM (Air-Launched Anti-Radar Missile) 25, 93, 199-200
Allied Command Europe Mobile Force 22
AN/ALQ-101, Westinghouse 206-7
Andover C.1/CC.2 24, 52-3
ANS (Air Navigation School) 74-5, 183
AOCinCSTC (Air Officer Commanding-in-Chief Strike Command) 9
APC (Armament Practice Camp) 41
ASRAAM (Advanced Short-Range Air-to-Air Missile) 141, 200
AT (Air Transport) 47
ATAF (Allied Tactical Air Force) 24
AV-8A/B, see Harrier GR.5/.7

BA (British Airways) 45
Bands, see RAF Music Services
BBMF (Battle of Britain Memorial Flight) 33-4
Blindfire (radar) 116
Bloodhound SAM 118
BL755 203
BMEWS (Ballistic Missile Early Warning System) 31
Bomber Command 9
Bosnia 46, 48
BOZ-107, Bofors 207
British Aerospace
    125 CC.1/.2/.3 53, 97, 133, 175-6
    146 CC.1/.2 52, 176-8
British Air Force of Occupation 23
Buccaneer S.2A/B 36-7, 67, 138, 140
Bulldog T.1 62, 64-5, 71-4, 98, 187-8

C-130K, see Hercules
Canberra
    PR.9 40, 96, 162-5
    T.17/.17A 42, 99, 186-7
CATCS (Central Air Traffic Control School) 83
CBLS (Carrier Bomb Light Stores) 150, 203
CBU-87 150, 203
Central Flying School 43, 71-4, 98, 178, 181, 183, 187-8
CH-47C/D, see Chinook HC.1/.2
Chinook HC.1/.2 20-1, 24-5, 54, 71, 99, 104, 134, 189-93
Chipmunk T.10 25, 34, 65, 99, 188-9
Clear (Alaska) 31
Coastal Command 9
Comet 2, 4, 43
CRC (Control and Reporting Centre) 31
CRP (Control and Reporting Point) 31
CRV-7 150, 203
CSDE (Central Servicing Development Establishment) 101-2

CTTO (Central Tactics and Trials Organization) 22, 55-6, 206
CTTS (Civilian Technical Training School) 82-3
CVRT (Combat Vehicle Reconnaissance Tracked) 106-7

Dakota 34
Defence Fire Services Central Training Establishment 43
Defence Research Agency 34, 134, 172
Department of Initial Officer Training 62-3
Devon C.2 34
Dominie T.1 74-5, 101, 183-4
DSGT (Department of Specialist Ground Training) 78

E-3, *see* Sentry AEW.1
ENJJPT (European and NATO Joint Jet Pilot Training) 66-7
EOD (Explosive Ordnance Disposal) 106-7
Equipment Supply Depots 103-4
Eurofighter 2000 13, 18, 102, 151

F.3OEU (Tornado F.3 Operational Evaluation Unit) 55-6
Fighter Command 9
Firefly, Slingsby 65, 188
FOB (Forward Operating Base) 10
Foxhunter (radar) 151, 154

Gazelle HT.3/HCC.4 21, 53, 67, 70-1, 74, 100, 197-8
GIA (Ground Instructional Airframe) 76-7
GT (Ground Training) 13, 16-18, 28, 50, 68, 70-1
Gulf War 11, 46, 51-2, 57, 135, 140, 147

Harpoon (AGM-84) 201
Harrier GR.1/.3 53, 140
Harrier T.4/GR.5/.5A/.7/T.10 13-15, 24, 55, 67, 90-1, 94, 115, 134, 140-7, 200
HAS (Hardened Aircraft Shelter) 30, 109
Hawk T.1/.1A 27, 41, 67, 74, 91, 98, 101, 133, 178-81, 200-1, 204
Hercules
    C.1K/.1P/.3P 48-51, 54, 57, 59, 77, 97, 112, 133-4, 172-5
    W.2 173
Hunter (all variants) 37, 78-9, 81-2
Hurricane IIc 34

IAM (Institute of Aviation Medicine) 56
Improved UK Air Defence Ground Environment 30-2, 154
Islander CC.2 53

Jaguar GR.1A/T.2A 10-13, 67, 78, 94, 111, 146-51, 200, 206
JEFTS (Joint Elementary Flying Training School) 65
Jet Provost (all Marks) 65
Jetstream T.1 67, 69, 98, 101, 184-6
Jindivik 57
Joint Air Transport Establishment 58-9

Joint Services School of Photography 81
JP233 138, 202
JTIDS (Joint Tactical Information Distribution System) 32

Lancaster B.1 34
Logistics Command 40, 90-2, 101-7

Maintenance Command 60
Maintenance Units
    No 7 104
    No 11 105
    No 14 103
    No 16 103-4
    No 30 104-5
    No 217 105
    No 431 25
Mauser 27mm cannon 16, 19, 135, 138, 154, 203-4
Meteorological Research Flight 173
Metropolitan Communications Squadron 52
MHU (Maritime Headquarters Unit) 125
MSC (Major Subordinate Command) 9
Multi-Engine Training Squadron 69, 186

NAEWF (NATO Airborne Early Warning Force) 33, 155
NATO (North Atlantic Treaty Organization) 9-10, 13, 24, 30-1, 33
Night-Vision Goggles 22, 39, 49, 51, 138, 143
Nimrod
    AEW.3 76-7, 162
    MR.2P/R.1P 34-6, 42-3, 54, 77, 96, 127, 133, 158-62, 200

Officers and Aircrew Selection Centre 61-2
Operational Conversion Units, *see* RAF OCUs

Parachute Training School, No 1 47-8
Paveway II 203
Personnel and Training Command 60-89, 114, 124
Phantom FG.1/FGR.2 24, 27-8, 54, 67, 91, 147, 155
PHIMAT 147, 207
PMRAFNS (Princess Mary's Air Force Nursing Service) 83-4
PRU (Photographic Reconnaissance Unit), No 1, *see* No 39 (1 PRU) Squadron
Puma HC.1 21-2, 24, 53, 71, 193-5

QCS (Queen's Colour Squadron) 114-16
QRA (Quick Reaction Alert) 27, 56
Queen's Flight, The 52, 176, 178, 196

RAE (Royal Aircraft/Aerospace Establishment) 34, 204
Royal Air Force
    Airmen's Command School 81
    Aerial Erector School 106
    Careers Information Office 60, 80
    College 61, 78, 84
        Air Squadron 62, 187

Flights
    No 1312 49, 54, 172
    No 1417 53
    No 1435 54, 151, 155
    No 1563 22, 53, 193
Flying Training Schools
    No 1 65-7, 72, 181, 183, 188
    No 2 70-1, 100, 188, 196-8
    No 3 65-7, 72, 97, 181, 183
    No 4 67-9, 73, 178, 180
    No 6 69-70, 74-5, 178, 181, 183, 186-7
    No 7 67-9, 73, 178, 183
Germany 23
Groups
    No 1 10-23, 114
    No 2 23-6, 114-15
    No 11 26-34, 114-15
    No 18 34-43
    No 38 27, 43-54
Movements School 57-8
Music Services 84-5
OCUs
    No 226 12, 147
    No 229 28, 154
    No 233 14, 144
    No 236 35, 162
    No 240 22, 37, 193
    No 241 47, 176
    No 242 50, 172
Personnel Management Centre 60, 71, 124
Regiment 79, 84-5, 113-23
Reserve Units 124-7
School of
    Catering 79
    Education 79
    Fighter Control 33
    Physical Training 79, 81
    Recruit Training 80
    Technical Training
        No 1 81
        No 2 81
        No 4 82
    Winter Survival 26
Squadrons, list of 85-7
    No 1 13-14, 140-1, 144-5
    No 2 15-16, 25, 134, 139, 147
    No 3 14, 24, 94, 140, 144
    No 4 14, 24, 94, 140, 144
    No 5 27, 113, 151, 155
    No 6 10-12, 94, 111, 146-7, 206
    No 7 20-1, 99, 189, 192, 197
    No 8 31-3, 95, 155, 158
    No 9 25, 93, 134, 138, 199, 202
    No 10 45, 163
    No 11 27, 95, 109, 151, 155
    No 12 36-7, 134, 140
    No 13 15-16, 93, 134, 139
    No 14 25-6, 134, 138, 147, 207
    No 15(R) 18-20, 25, 134, 138
    No 16(R) 12-13, 25, 138, 146-7, 151

    No 17 25, 134, 138, 147
    No 18 24-5, 189, 192-3, 196
    No 19(R) 24, 67, 178
    No 20(R) 14-15, 25, 140, 145-7
    No 22 37-9, 196
    No 23 27, 155
    No 24 48-9, 54, 172
    No 25 27, 151, 155
    No 27(R) 15, 20, 22, 36-7, 138, 140, 189, 192-3
    No 28 39, 54, 196
    No 29 27, 95, 151, 154-5
    No 30 48-9, 54, 172
    No 31 25, 93, 134, 138, 147
    No 32 52-3, 97, 100, 175, 197-8
    No 33 20-2, 193
    No 36 172
    No 39 (1 PRU) 40-1, 96, 162-3
    No 41 10-11, 94, 146-7
    No 42(R) 35-6, 96, 159, 162
    No 43 27, 151, 155
    No 45(R) 18, 69-70, 98, 138, 184, 186
    No 47 48-50
    No 48 172
    No 51 36, 42-3, 159, 162
    No 54 10-11, 146-7
    No 55(R) 47
    No 56(R) 28-30, 151
    No 57(R) 50-1, 172
    No 60 22-3, 52, 172
    No 63 67
    No 65 28, 154
    No 70 48-9, 172
    No 72 23, 196
    No 74(R) 67, 178
    No 78 39, 54, 189, 192, 194-5
    No 84 39, 53-4, 196
    No 92(R) 24, 67-8, 178
    No 100 41, 98, 178, 181
    No 101 45-6, 96, 167, 170
    No 111 26-7, 151, 155
    No 115 53
    No 120 35, 96, 159, 162
    No 151 67
    No 201 35, 96, 159, 162
    No 202 38-9, 100, 194-6
    No 206 35, 96, 159, 162
    No 208(R) 36-7, 178
    No 216 43-5, 170-1
    No 230 23-4, 193
    No 234(R) 67
    No 360 41-3, 99, 186
    No 617 15, 36, 71, 134, 138, 140
Staff College 79
Stations/operating locations
    map of 88-9
    Aberporth 56
    Abingdon 47, 90-1, 101, 131, 170
    Alconbury 107
    Aldergrove 23, 64, 114, 129
    Aldershot 79

Akrotiri 41, 43, 53-4, 84, 115
Arbroath 132
Ascension Island 43, 45, 51, 54
Ash 31
Bad Kohlgrub 26
Barkston Heath 62, 66
Belize 22, 45, 49, 53, 115
Benbecula 31
Benson 10, 22-3, 52-3, 64, 129, 178, 187-8, 196
Bentley Priory 26-7
Biggin Hill 61
Boscombe Down 55, 64, 183, 188, 193, 206
Boulmer 31, 33, 38-9, 79
Bournemouth (Hurn) 129
Bracknell 79
Brampton 60, 90, 102, 126
Brawdy 38, 67
Brize Norton 43-8, 51, 57-8, 79, 83-4, 90, 96, 115, 125-6, 163, 167, 170, 176
Bruggen 25-6, 93, 114, 138, 147
Buchan 30
Cambridge (Teversham) 64, 97, 129
Cardington 105
Carlisle 103
Catterick 79, 84, 114, 126, 132
Chilmark 105
Chivenor 13, 38, 67-9, 132, 180-1, 197
Church Fenton 66, 183, 188
Colerne 64, 105, 129
Coltishall 10-12, 37, 111, 147, 151, 197
Coningsby 27-30, 33-4, 55, 95, 109, 154-5
Cosford 64, 79, 81, 132
Cottesmore 16-18, 92, 138
Cranwell 56, 61-3, 65-6, 75, 78-9, 81, 84, 97, 183
Culdrose 39, 194
Decimomannu 25, 194
Defford 105
Digby 106
Edinburgh (Turnhouse) 64, 125, 128-9
Ely 84
Exeter 129
Fairford 107
Falkland Islands 49, 51, 54, 58, 115-17
Farnborough 56
Finningley 38-9, 41, 64, 69-70, 74-8, 98, 129, 181, 183, 186
Fylingdales 31
Gatow 25
Gioia del Colle 11, 28
Glasgow 64
Goose Bay 54-5
Gutersloh 24, 146, 192-3
Halton 78-81, 84, 132
Harrogate 90
Headley Court 84
Henlow 79, 105, 128, 132
Hereford 78, 81
High Wycombe 9, 31, 43, 55, 126-7
Hong Kong 49, 51, 54
Honington 15, 79, 114-15, 117, 126, 138-9

Hullavington 125, 132
Incirlik 13, 25
Innsworth 60, 71, 124
Kemble 90
Kenley 132
Kinloss 34-6, 40, 41, 96, 127, 132, 162
Kirknewton 132
Laarbruch 15, 24-5, 94, 114-15, 138-9, 147, 189, 193
Lakenheath 107
Leconfield 38
Leeming 27, 39, 48, 64, 95, 114, 129, 155, 186
Leuchars 27, 37, 40, 64, 114, 155, 197
Linton-on-Ouse 65-6, 128, 132, 183
Little Rissington 132, 188
Llanbedr 56-7
Locking 82, 84, 128
Lossiemouth 12-13, 18-20, 36, 38, 41, 114, 126, 140, 147, 151
Lyneham 48-51, 59, 84, 97, 125-6, 172
Manston 38, 43, 129, 132
Marham 15, 36, 40, 47, 50, 114, 126, 138-9, 162
Mildenhall 107
Mona 68
Mount Pleasant, *see* Falkland Islands
Neatishead 30
Newton 64, 79, 81, 128-9
Nocton Hall 84
Nordhorn 26
North Luffenham 50, 72, 74, 106
Northolt 52-3, 97, 100, 128, 176, 198
Northwood 35, 125
Oakhanger 105
Odiham 20-2, 37, 55, 71, 99, 189, 192-3, 196
Pembrey (range) 68-9
Pitreavie 37
Portreath 31
Predannack 132
Quedgeley 104
Rheindahlen 23-4, 26
St Athan 39, 64, 69, 81, 90-2, 101, 111, 126, 128, 132
St Mawgan 35, 38-9, 50, 125-6, 162
Samlesbury 132
Saxa Vord 31
Scampton 66, 71-3, 81-2, 98, 126, 183
Sealand 82-3, 104-5, 128, 132
Sek Kong, *see* Hong Kong
Shawbury 39, 70-1, 73-4, 79, 83, 100-1, 129, 198
Stafford 39, 103
Stanbridge 90, 103
Swansea 132
Swanton Morley 90, 101-2, 131
Swinderby 65, 80, 188
Syerston 130, 132
Ternhill 132, 198
Teversham, *see* Cambridge
Thorney Island 172
Topcliffe 65, 188
Turnhouse, *see* Edinburgh

Upavon 10, 71, 132
Uxbridge 84-5, 114
Valley 13, 26, 38-9, 56-7, 67-9, 71, 73, 180-1, 197
Waddington 31-3, 56, 95, 127, 158
Wattisham 28, 38
Wegberg 26, 84
West Malling 132
West Raynham 114-15
Weston-on-the-Green 48
Wethersfield 132
Wideawake, *see* Ascension Island
Wildenrath 24
Wittering 13-14, 106, 144-6
Woodvale 64, 129
Wroughton 83
Wyton 36, 40-3, 56, 79, 90, 102, 127, 162, 186
Station Flights
  Gatow 25, 188
  Northolt 53
  St Athan 101, 178
RAFVR (Royal Air Force Volunteer Reserve) 127
Rapid Reaction Force 10
Rapier SAM (all variants) 28, 53-4, 113-20
RAuxAF (Royal Auxiliary Air Force) 125
RAuxAF Regt (Royal Auxiliary Air Force Regiment) 125-7
RCC (Rescue Coordination Centre) 37, 54
'Red Arrows', The 73, 180
Red Flag (exercise) 49, 54
RIC (Reconnaissance Intelligence Centre) 16
RLG (Relief Landing Ground) 66, 68
ROC (Royal Observer Corps) 33
RP (Reporting Point) 31
RS (Radio School), No 1 83

SACEUR (Supreme Allied Commander Europe) 9
SAR (Seach and Rescue) 34-9, 53-4, 77
SAS (Special Air Service) 47
Scimitar (armoured vehile) 106-7
Sea Eagle 36, 140, 201
Sea King HAR.3/.3A 37-8, 54, 100, 194-6
Second Tactical Air Force 23
Sentry AEW.1 31-3, 41, 46, 77, 95, 134, 154-8, 162
SH (Support Helicopters) 20-3
Shackleton AEW.2 34, 155, 158
SHTTF (Support Helicopter Tactics and Trials Flight) 22-3
SHORAD (Short-Range Air Defence) 113-17
Sidewinder, AIM-9 19, 28, 56, 138, 141, 147, 150, 154, 181, 200-1
Signals 105-6
Signals Command 9
Sky Flash 56, 154, 201
Skynet (satellites) 105
Skyshadow, Marconi 207
Slingsby Firefly 65, 188
Small-arms weapons 120-3
SNEB 203
SOC (Sector Operations Centre) 30-1

Spartan (armoured vehicle) 106-7
Special Forces 50
Spitfire 34
Squadrons, *see* RAF Squadrons
STCAAME (Strike Command Air-to-Air Missile Establishment) 26, 56-7
Stiletto 57
Stingray 203
STO (Survive to Operate) 58, 114, 117
Strike/Attack Operational Evaluation Unit 55, 140, 145, 200
Strike Command 9-59, 114-15
STS (Sentry Training Squadron) 32-3
Support Command 60, 85, 90, 107
Support Helicopter Standards and Evaluation Unit 22

Tactical Weapons Unit 67, 180-1
TCW (Tactical Communications Wing) 58
TG (Trade Group) 81
Thule (Greenland) 31
TIALD (Thermal Imaging Airborne Laser Designator) 25, 92, 205-7
TMTS (Trade Management Training School) 81-2
TOCU (Tornado Operational Conversion Unit) 16-18
Tornado
  F.2/.3 26-31, 41, 46, 48, 54-6, 67, 74, 90, 95, 113, 133, 151-5, 200
  GR.1/.1A/.1B/.4 15-20, 25-6, 36-7, 39, 55, 67, 69, 74, 91-3 133-40, 147, 151, 199-200, 202, 205-7
Tornado In-Service Software Maintenance Team 18
Tornado Maintenance School 18
Tornado Standardization Unit 20
Training Command 60
Transport Command 9
TriStar (all Marks) 43-4, 51, 54, 77, 170-2
TSW (Tactical Supply Wing) 103-4
TTTE (Tri-National Tornado Training Establishment) 16-18, 92, 134, 138
Tucano T.1 65-6, 69, 71-4, 97, 181-3
TWCU (Tornado Weapons Conversion Unit) 18-20, 138

United Kingdom Air Defence Region 9, 27, 30-1, 35
United Kingdom Air Forces 9
United Kingdom Mobile Air Movements Squadron 51-2
University Air Squadrons 62, 64-5, 187
USAFE (United States Air Forces in Europe) 24
  bases 107, 115

VC-10 (all Marks) 45-7, 54, 57, 77, 90, 96, 133, 163, 166-70
Vehicles, specialist 208-19
Victor K.2 47, 50
Vigilant T.1 130-2
Viking T.1 130-2
Volunteer Gliding Schools 130-2

WE177 138, 202
Wessex (all Marks) 37-8, 52-4, 67, 71, 100, 196-7